**University of Hertfordshire**

College Lane, Hatfield, Herts. AL10 9AB

Learning and Information Services

For renewal of Standard and One Week Loans,
please visit the web site **http://www.voyager.herts.ac.uk**

This item must be returned or the loan renewed by the due date.
The University reserves the right to recall items from loan at any time.
A fine will be charged for the late return of items.

The Social Psychology of Experience

Studies in Remembering and Forgetting

David Middleton
and
Steven D. Brown

SAGE Publications
London ● Thousand Oaks ● New Delhi

First published 2005

SAGE Publications Ltd
1 Oliver's Yard
55 City Road
London EC1Y 1SP

SAGE Publications Inc.
2455 Teller Road
Thousand Oaks, California 91320

SAGE Publications India Pvt Ltd
B-42, Panchsheel Enclave
Post Box 4109
New Delhi 110 017

British Library Cataloguing in Publication data

A catalogue record for this book is available
from the British Library

ISBN 0 8039 7756 5
ISBN 0 8039 7757 3 (pbk)

Library of Congress Control Number: 2004099522

Typeset by C&M Digitals (P) Ltd., Chennai, India
Printed and bound in Great Britain by Athenaeum Press, Gateshead

Contents

Preface

In our modern understanding of memory there is an overwhelming tension between preservation and loss. Memory itself often seems to hang by a thread, to be balanced on the cusp between recovery and dissolution. In contrast, we address robust practices of remembering and forgetting at home and work, in public and commercial organisations, involving language and text-based communication, objects and place. Our aim is to overcome the spatial bias at work in both psychological and sociological studies of memory. To achieve this we argue that it is necessary to reconsider some of the basic conceptual tools of memory research and the manner in which they have imposed themselves on the way we relate to the past. Our overall aim is to provide a basis for social psychological enquiry where experience matters.

We ground the matters of remembering and forgetting in the classic works of Frederick Bartlett (on psychological schema as 'socially organised settings'), Maurice Halbwachs (on the sociology of 'collective frameworks' in memory) and Henri Bergson (on the philosophical discussion of 'durations' in experience). We illustrate the significance of their ideas for our arguments concerned with examples drawn from a range of situations where remembering and forgetting are matters of concern. We extend the argument beyond spatial metaphors concerning the passage of time and the consequences this has for the content of experience as finite. We argue that the actualization of experience in spatial terms is never complete and always maintains a relationship to continuous and indivisible experience, what Bergson termed 'the virtual'. This moves us away from experience as lived in some linear unfolding of time where memory is taken as the vehicle for linking past, present and future, whether individual or collective.

However, we still place memory at the centre of lived experience – not as the storehouse of that experience, but, instead, as a relational process at the intersection of different durations of living. As we endure in time, our rhythm of living is slowed or quickened in relation to the durations of others. To approach remembering and forgetting in this way is to deliberately blur the boundaries between the individual and the collective, between what is held in common and what is most intensely personal. If remembering and forgetting are to matter for a psychology of experience, we conclude that we must view selfhood not as a 'thing', but as a movement that is continuously refracted back through the stabilities it creates. In other words, we seek to demonstrate selfhood as the shifting intersection of experiences of which our present consciousness is only the leading edge. This also leads us to a view of remembering and forgetting as interdependent ways of actualising and virtualising experience rather than its presence or absence. We aim to arrive back at an account of a psychology of experience that encompasses the issues raised in contemporary discussions of social memory while accommodating experience that is not tied to spatialised views of time. We therefore offer an approach to the psychology of experience that is neither individually nor socially determined and where the dynamics of remembering and forgetting do not limit experience.

This work represents the intersection of our shared and individual interests in memory. We both have academic backgrounds in psychology – one in developmental and sociocultural psychology, the other in social psychology and social theory. We also share interests in the analysis of communicative action and the discursive turn in psychological studies. Our preference is for gathering data from within contexts of human practice. In other words, from within settings where the stake and interests of those involved is self-evidently theirs rather than an arbitrary or simulated concern of the psychologist. However, neither of us would claim that this work is thoroughly ethnographically informed, although we do hope that it will be of interest to those who pursue detailed anthropologies, geographies and sociologies of remembering and forgetting. While we have forsaken the tools of the psychological laboratory, we have aimed to make the work and ideas discussed here informative for those with interests in the experimental psychology of memory.

Acknowledgements

We owe an immense debt of gratitude to many people who have assisted us in completing this work for publication. Our publishers Sage Publications deserve special mention. Ziyad Marar and Michael Carmichael have been steadfast in their encouragement and support. Also our grateful thanks to Rachel Burrows for the production editing of the published volume.

Individually and jointly we have also benefited from exceptionally generous colleagues and supportive academic groups. Throughout the whole development and conduct of the reported studies the Loughborough University Discourse and Rhetoric Group has provided a wealth of academic and collegial assistance. Many people have passed through the Wednesday lunchtime meetings and we owe them thanks for their generosity in sharing with us their ideas, data and analytical insights. Charles Antaki, Malcolm Ashmore, Mick Billig, John Cromby, Derek Edwards, Alexa Hepburn, Jonathan Potter and many others have continuously engaged us in constructive and lively analytical debate. We are also appreciative of the assistance and support of other colleagues at Loughborough, including Charles Crook, Harriet Gross and Mark Lansdale.

The Human Sciences SCAR group has also been of invaluable assistance and we very much appreciate the discussion with Johanna Motzkau, Darren Ellis, Jeanette Rasmussen, Sally Sargeant, Ian Tucker and Jonathan Woodrow.

We have also been very fortunate in having access to other settings where social remembering and forgetting are of interest. Roger Säljö and Karin Aronsson generously assisted in facilitating contact with research and debate at Linköping University in Sweden. This resulted in access to a whole range of scholars with cognate interests associated with the Departments of Communication and Child Studies, including Viveka Adelsward, Jan Anward, Bodil Axelsson, Kerstin Bergqvist, Elisabet Cedersund, Jakob Cromdal, Kosta Econonou, Ann-Carita Evaldsson, Per Anders Forstorp, Michèle Grossen, Lars-Christer Hydén, Per Linnell, Claes Nilholm, Karin Osvaldsson, Ullabeth Sätterlund-Larsson, Anna Sparman, Michael Tholander, Cecilia Wajdensjö and many others. Ullabeth's friendship and enthusiastic interest in this work is sadly missed.

We are also most grateful to Karin Aronsson, Johanna Motzkau, Morten Nissen and Paula Reavey for taking the time to read and make helpful comments on earlier versions of the manuscript. We benefited greatly from their feedback and discussion.

Over the years, other scholars with interests in social memory and allied topics have encouraged and supported this work in many ways. Our thanks to Hans Christian Arnseth, Malcolm Ashmore, David Bakhurst, Adrian Bangerter, Joanna Bornat, Elisabeth Dos Santos Braga, Jens Brockmeier, Seth Chaiklin, Jennifer Cole, Michael Cole, Robert Cooper, David Curnock, Harry Daniels, Ron Day, Yjrö Engeström, Jan Derry, Ole Dreier, Anne Edwards, Sylvia Ghehardi, Faith Gibson, Sarah Green, Rom Harré, John Harris, Penny Harvey, Mariane Hedegaard, Christian Heath, William Hirst, Andrew Jefferson, Casper Jensen, Torben Jensen, Denise Jodelet, Kevin Hetherington, Robert Knight, the late Steen Larsson, John Law, Bruno Latour, Andy Leslie, Paul Luff, Kevin Mackenzie, Katie MacMillan, Manuel de la Mata, Pirjo Nikander, Tiago Moriera, Anne-Nelly Perret-Clermont, Phil Peters, Clothilde Pontecorvo, Alberto Rosa, Wolff-Michael Roth, Barry Schwartz, Michael Schudson, John Shotter, Ana Smolka, Paul Stenner, Antonio Strati, Lucy Suchman, Jeanine Suurmond, Peter Tulviste, Jaan Valsiner, Harald Welzer, Jim Wertsch, Steve Woolgar. Thanks also to Georgina Born for asking the question.

We are also very grateful for the enthusiastic collaboration of Miquel Domenech, Danny Lopez, Israel Rodriguez, Francisco Tirado, Sean Vernall, Ana Vitores, Jonathan Woodrow on a British Council-sponsored project on the 'Virtualisation of Social Institutions', which provided our initiation into Bergson. Thanks in particular to Israel for convincing us that Bergson and Halbwachs could be good bedfellows, and to Jon for demonstrating what a Bergsonian psychology could achieve.

All the studies detailed in this volume have resulted from collaborations with numerous other researchers. These include Kevin Buchanan, Charles Crook, Derek Edwards, Geoff Lightfoot, Helen Hewitt, Kyoko Murakami, Jonathan Woodrow. We thank them all for their intellectual and practical support in the conduct of this work.

A further test bed for the development and presentation of these ideas was within the teaching of the Human Sciences undergraduate course on social remembering at Loughborough University. We are particularly grateful to Sarah Aplin, Alison Ault, Philippa Hands and Lisa McGinty for work on family web sites. We also wish to thank the technical and administrative staff of the Department of Human Sciences at Loughborough University – David Eason and Peter Lockwood for their good humoured technical support and Mary Hewitt, Jane Purvey and John Rennocks for providing unflagging and patient administrative support of our teaching and other duties that really gave us so much more 'space' to work on this book.

We gratefully acknowledge permission to use the following material:

Finn Orvin (www.orvin.net/Home.html)
Julie and Kevin (www.juvin.com/julie/)
Andy Neale (www.neale.co.uk/)
McDeceno Maltezo (www.geocities.com/maltezo/home.html)
Rick Arndt (www.famteam.com/firesidechat.htm)
Shirley (http://members.tripod.com/bayouspirit/index.htm)

Independent Newspapers for reprinting copy from the front page published on 28 May 1998.

Cornelia Parker's 'Cold Dark Matter: An Exploded View' is reprinted by courtesy of the artist, the Frith Street Gallery and the Tate Modern, London.

Sumi Gupta Ariely for use of transcript data from Gupta, 1996.

Faith Gibson for use of video transcript data from Gibson, 1989.

Kyoko Murakami for the use of the photographic image of the Iruka Memorial Site.

Finally, none of our work would have been possible at all without the kindness and love of our families. Very special thanks and love to Ailbhe, Kittie, Jennie and Laura, and to Lorraine and Sue.

Transcript conventions

The following conventions are used in the presentation of conversational data. They are derived from those developed by Gail Jefferson for the purposes of conversation analysis (see Sacks, 1992). They are used as a way of presenting the talk as a social activity rather than, for example, as an expression of ideas, phonetics, or grammar (Edwards, 1997). We have kept their use to the minimum required for the purposes of the discussions presented here.

[yes]	short simultaneous talk of another speaker
soun-	cut off of preceding sound
start of [simultaneous talk [simultaneous talk	simultaneous talk
remember= it seems to me	'equals' marks the immediate 'latching' of successive talk with no interval
(&)	talk continues across the talk of another speaker
(…)	unclear
(….)	talk omitted form the transcript at this point
(memory)	sound like
((laughs))	additional comment
?	rising intonation
HELP	louder than preceding talk
>quieter<	quieter than preceding talk
(.)	micro pause
(1)	pause in seconds
Oi ko	(*italicised*) Japanese words
<u>do</u>	emphasis
par:k	elongation of prior sounds

ONE
Introducing remembering and forgetting in the social psychology of experience

Figure 1.1   Cornelia Parker's 'Cold Dark Matter: An Exploded View'

In 1991 the British artist Cornelia Parker arranged for a small garden shed to be blown up with high explosives in a field in Warwickshire. The 'garden shed' – a small outhouse structure commonly found outside many British homes – is rich in symbolism. It is traditionally the place where residents will store a curious selection of objects, including tools, broken electrical items, knick-knacks and other oddments that currently serve no great purpose but may 'one day' prove to be useful (see Thorburn, 2002, for further illustration). Parker had filled this particular shed with a heterogeneous range of objects, including household items such as cutlery, garden tools, an old briefcase, a hardback copy of Proust's *Remembrance of Things Past* and a small plastic model of a dinosaur. Prior to its destruction, the shed – including the objects – had been displayed as an installation piece in a London gallery. After the explosion, Parker collected the remaining pieces and placed them in the same gallery space, suspended on near invisible wires. A light bulb was hung in the middle of the fragments, creating a dramatic play of shadows on the gallery walls. A similar light bulb had previously illuminated the intact shed; the plastic explosive used to destroy the structure had been moulded into an identical shape and suspended in the same position. Parker named her installation 'Cold Dark Matter: An Exploded View'.

Viewing 'Cold Dark Matter' in its current home at the Tate Modern gallery in London, one is struck by the fragility of the piece. The objects appear to hang precariously in mid-air, at any moment threatening to collapse in a heap on one another. The fragmented wood of the shed exterior dominates and bears the marks of the explosion, as do a half-burnt satchel and innumerable bent spoons and forks. However, other objects appear intact and curiously untouched, looking for all the world like the contents of a lost luggage office.

The changes to the piece brought about by the explosion are then ambiguous. On the one hand, everything has changed – the shed has been literally destroyed and reduced to fragments, many objects damaged beyond all hope of recovery – but, on the other, many elements survive more or less in their entirety. The viewer is then required to make some sense of this juxtaposition beyond what appears to be preserved intact and what has been irrevocably altered or perhaps permanently lost.

Parker's work serves as a good metaphor for our modern understanding of memory. Here, too, the overwhelming tension is between preservation and loss, the reduction of the everyday flow of our lives to a series of fragments. Brief passing moments and images remain completely intact, unaltered, we feel, despite the passage of time, but the overall framework appears destined to disappear, to be worn away by ageing, the passage of time that levels all, or else by some sudden and fateful intervention.

We tend then to think of memory as a form of conflict, where the desire to retain the past as it was runs up against the inevitability of change or, worse still, a set of counter desires that seek to erase memory, to irrevocably have done with some aspect of the past. Here, Parker's work is fully resonant as memory itself often seems to hang by a thread, to be balanced on the cusp between recovery and dissolution.

To approach memory in this way is to deliberately blur the boundaries between the individual and the collective, between what is held in common and what is most intensely personal. If we do so, that is because in recent years there has been a shift in terms. 'Memory' has come to stand alongside 'history' in both popular and scholarly discourse. As Klein (2000) points out, this supplementing of the traditional vocabulary of historiography and historical consciousness often borders on outright replacement. We speak less of the power of historical processes and change and more of the fragile resistance of memory and its attempts to preserve what is no longer. Indeed, in the classic statement of this position, Pierre Nora (1989) mournfully states that 'we speak so much of memory because there is so little of it left'.

So little of what, though? What is the nature of this thing 'memory' that Nora claims is so threatened? Here we must work through a process of negative definition. Nora cannot be referring to the individual's powers and capacities to recall their own experiences. The memory that is disappearing is something that is shared between people. Yet, this sharing or common orientation to the past is different to 'history'. Typically viewed, history is singular. There is a privileged overview of the past that is granted to the historian by virtue of unrivalled access to documents, evidence and matters of record. Nora's point, which is by no means unfamiliar, is that, beneath the singularity of 'official' history, there is pluralism in our relationships to the past. That is, there is a variety of ways in which the past might be understood and made relevant in the present. This pluralism is threatened by historical discourse, giving rise to a contested field of interpretations that struggle to defend themselves and the forms of collectivity with which they become associated. It is this contestation that Nora calls 'memory'.

The roots of Nora's claims lie with the French sociologist Maurice Halbwachs. It is within his two texts – translated in to English as *The Collective Memory* (1950/1980) and *On Collective Memory* (1925/1992) – that we see a full account of memory as a social process, in which groups collectively participate in order to create frameworks for the preservation of their common identity. Halbwachs viewed memory as an intrinsically social process. Not only is the form remembering takes shaped by the collective, but the very content of any given memory is also, Halbwachs argued, a social product. We may then see that Halbwachs' texts mark a point at which the question of 'memory' becomes thoroughly entangled with other kinds of cognate issues, such as the preservation of tradition (Shils, 1981), the shaping of mind by culture (Cole, 1991; 1996) and the tension between historical consciousness and group identity (Tschuggnall & Welzer, 2002). Klein (2000) sees this entanglement as problematic and, ultimately, as leading to a situation where memory becomes treated in quasi-mystical terms. More moderate positions, such as James Wertsch (2002), also consider Halbwachs' apparent conflation of the cultural and the social with the individual and the personal to stand in need of some clarification.

That clarification might be provided, in part, by looking towards what Halbwachs is writing against – namely, the emergence of distinctive modern representation of the past, where tradition is superseded by rationalisation and a drive to systematise and standardise. Matsuda (1996) argues that this gives rise to a form of memory that is peculiar to modernity. One might say that its chief characteristic is its 'forensic' nature. Memory is seen as an activity that involves the bringing together of fragmentary pieces of information into a whole from which technical decisions can be made. Thus, Matsuda points to a range of cognate practices that emerge at the end of the nineteenth century – from the centralisation of criminal data and 'profiling' to the mapping of clinical findings on to the brain and the embedding of colonial histories in anthropological studies. However, arguably the most important practice is that of modern cinematography. Here, the past is literally captured as a series of fragments – the still images rapidly shot by the cinecamera – that are then rapidly reassembled to create the eerie illusion of a past come back to life.

Henri Bergson (1908/1991; 1911/1998), whose philosophical work spanned the turn of the nineteenth century, is perhaps the thinker who has done most to understand the nature of this 'illusion'. Bergson saw these kinds of practices – where the past is treated as a set of discrete images that are drawn together to create the impression of 'life' – as corrosive of a proper appreciation of not only memory, but also the very nature of time. For Bergson, time is not divisible in this way without substantial loss of what is particular to our human experience of existing as living, acting beings. Nevertheless, he was also able to diagnose precisely why such 'pulverised' views of time and memory had arisen. Modernity fosters and elaborates a form of thought – the 'cinematographical mechanism' – that is essentially spatial and orientated entirely towards the immediate demands of the present moment. It is this spatial thought that gives rise to both the forensic approach to memory (where memory consists of a spatially organised set of traces or data) and the overall rationalisation of social affairs that dominates modernity.

It is within this historical context that psychology takes hold of and claims expertise over the scientific study of 'memory'. As Danziger (2002) has shown, the experimental psychology of memory that developed in the late nineteenth century inherited a rich stock of metaphors for thinking about its subject matter. However, it chose from these spatial terms – mostly based on container metaphors – that are entirely of a piece with Bergson's 'cinematographical mechanism'. The result is that the subsequent psychology of memory that came to full fruition in early 1970s, following the 'cognitive revolution', not merely tends towards, but is in some cases entirely infused by, a spatial understanding of time. To take a recent example, Martin Conway's well-known work on autobiographical memory (see, for example, Conway, 1997; Conway & Pleydell-Pearce, 2000), has recently been the subject of an artistic interpretation by Shona Illingworth. One aspect of that work is a set of beautifully drawn sketches of Conway's formal theories. These sketches depict the key terms and relationships of Conway's modelling of autobiographical memory, which is transformed into a set of abstract forms and lines, along with handwritten labels and brief explication in spidery penmanship. The viewer is struck by the spatial form of the work – everything is given at once, distributed across the elegantly mounted series of drawings. One can see what autobiographical memory consists of in a glance (or two).

One might then argue that the psychology of memory is so profoundly shaped by the spatialised, rational impulse of modern thought that it is unable to allow its subject matter to exceed that framework. That point has been made at length in a number of critiques, which have focused in particular on the tendency to refer all processes involved in remembering back to the inner workings of the individual, more or less rational, psychological subject (see, for example, Casey, 1987; Shotter, 1990; Wittgenstein, 1953). Worse still, this is a 'subject' who is, in order to fulfil the technical demands of psychological experimentation, systematically cut off from the everyday social ecology in which remembering occurs (Neisser, 1976, 1982; Neisser & Winograd, 1988). These are telling critiques, which bear some repeating. However, at the same time, we should not ignore the push from within the psychology of memory to reach beyond its own conceptual limits. For example, Neisser's own work in recent years has attempted to contextualise a cognitive approach to information retrieval in a broader account of the environment as a system in which selfhood emerges (Neisser & Fivush, 1996). Similarly, Hirst and Manier (1996) have treated the information retrieval aspects of memory as one part of a communicative process between conversational partners. Finally, Conway (1997, 2003) himself has made clear a dissatisfaction with purely spatial accounts of memory.

The psychology of memory, then, is by no means untouched by the concerns arising from the broader social sciences, but how might it reach out to meet those concerns without subsuming them within its pre-existing 'spatialised' framework? It is our argument in this book that simply turning towards the social – while a necessary first step – does not solve the problem. For example, it is possible to make the case, following Halbwachs, that all occasions of remembering are essentially social matters. From this it follows that the collective rather than the individual is the most appropriate level of analysis. However, in making this gesture, we depart from one form of hypothesised spatial configuration – that of cognitive architecture – to that of another, such as, say, intergroup dynamics (see, for example, Bangerter, 2000, 2002). In so doing, we transpose all that was problematic about the former to the latter. Admittedly this 'higher-level' spatial configuration is initially somewhat easier to approach, as here memory can only be a public matter – something that is accomplished socially. However, then we encounter the equally intractable problem of understanding how members of a group commit themselves to or invest in this process. We end up back where we started, except with all of the terms inverted.

Our project is to work towards a social psychology of experience that overcomes the spatial bias at work in both experimental approaches and more sociologically orientated approaches to memory. What we seek is a way of addressing remembering and forgetting as social practices yet also as an intensely personal committing of oneself to the past as recalled. We argue that, in order to reach that understanding, it is necessary to reconsider some of the basic conceptual tools – the very 'grammar' – of memory research and the manner in which they have imposed themselves on how we relate to the past. As Ian Hacking (1995) argues, psychology, as the principal 'science of memory', has a profound effect on our personal abilities to understand ourselves. The categories of psychological research – 'storage', 'retrieval', 'processing' – shape the ways in which we think about remembering, such that we can find it difficult to think in any other way. We must find a way of overcoming this tendency.

We think that reintroducing the term 'experience' to mark the ambiguous and potentially indeterminate relationship we maintain with our own pasts is one way forward, but, already, we are in danger of running ahead of ourselves. As we will see later on, Bergson argues that, if we take the idea of change seriously, what becomes apparent is that not everything can be given at once. Indeed, the attempt to fully systematise – to lock down all the possible options in advance – is usually a doomed attempt to 'tame' change. In this book, by contrast, we want to avoid that error by thinking and working through the problems slowly. Our starting point is with collective approaches to memory, as outlined by the contributors to Middleton and Edwards' (1990a) edited volume *Collective Remembering*. Where we want to arrive, however, is back at an account of individual remembering that encompasses the issues raised in that volume and subsequent discussions of social memory (see, for example, Fentress & Wickham, 1992; Wertsch, 2002; Mistzal, 2003), while accommodating experience that is not tied to spatialised views of time. In order to get between these most unlikely points, we will have to pass through a series of problems and concerns, the importance of which will only become fully clear as we move between them. These we will have to 'fix up' as we go along.

The work of Maurice Halbwachs and of Henri Bergson is at the very core of this book. These two make for an unlikely couple. Halbwachs is typically seen as having committed the error of sociological reductionism, having envisaged something as strange as a 'group mind' (see, for example, Bartlett's 1932 early presentation of his work). Bergson, for his part, if he is recalled at all, is seen to have produced a philosophy of memory that is so subjective, so grounded in the particularities of personal experience, that it is inherently unworkable. Moreover, in the published work and in their crossed private lives, these two thinkers are held to be at odds. It is said that Halbwachs' entire career constitutes an attempt to reject Bergson, his former mentor (Douglas, 1980), while Bergson responded to the Durkheimian tradition of sociology that Halbwachs came to embody by writing of the biological origins of morality and religion. These two, then, appear to push in completely different directions.

At one level, this is why both are so vital to our project. No one has pushed further than Halbwachs in the 'socialising' of memory and no one has ever dared more than Bergson in a rethinking of what memory is for us, as individual living beings. As our argument unfolds, we will turn back and forth between these two thinkers, at times taking direction from one, then from the other. This does not mean that we will end up right back where we started. It is one of the basic principles of sailing that charting a straight course in turbulent waters requires the boat to be steered back and forth, to 'tack', rather than stick rigidly to the same direction. Halbwachs and Bergson allow us to tack through the difficulties of social remembering, yet, at the same time, we feel that the opposition between these two is somewhat overstated. We would even go far as to say that if one returns to their work, one finds that there a strong resonance, even to the extent that it might be said that their individual projects complement or even 'complete' one another. That contentious point will have to await the final chapters.

The structure of the book is as follows. In Chapter 2, we explore the 'social turn' in the study of remembering across the social sciences. We begin by discussing the classic work of Frederic Bartlett, where the conduct of remembering is situated within 'organised settings' (Bartlett's preferred definition of 'schemas'). We then turn to a number of approaches that follow in the wake of Bartlett's discursive agenda, such as Fentress and Wickam's historical studies, Jennifer Cole's ethnographic work, the communication and historical sociological programmes of Michael Schudson and Barry Schwartz, Paul Connerton's sociological re-evaluation of commemoration, the phenomenology of Edward Casey and the sociocultural work of James Wertsch. Our aim is to situate our own unfolding arguments in the context of the agendas set by these works, which span a variety of disciplines.

In the following two chapters, we introduce the two major figures to whom we refer throughout the book. Maurice Halbwachs is discussed at length in Chapter 3. By means of a close reading of his two major texts, we argue that Halbwachs' thought is not guilty of the charge of sociological reductionism. Rather, it is the case that Halbwachs' work maps out how a form of thought that is always and already social in character becomes embedded in a collective infrastructure. We describe at some length Halbwachs' notion of a 'collective framework' and how such frameworks 'territorialise' memory.

Chapter 4 introduces the thought of Henri Bergson – notably his attempt to defend a 'living' version of time – or 'duration' – against the reduction of time to space in which time is treated as a series of instants. Focusing in particular on his key work *Matter and Memory*, we describe how Bergson's location of memory within duration leads to a wholesale rejection of the common psychological doxa found within the cognitive–neurological paradigm in favour of an approach grounded in the 'unlimited' nature of experience.

The chapters that follow are then built on a discussion of research studies that we have conducted singly, together and in collaboration with a series of other researchers, including Derek Edwards, Kevin Buchanan, Charles Crook, David Curnock, Helen Hewitt, Geoff Lightfoot, Kyoko Murakami and Jonathan Woodrow. Each successive chapter features a series of empirical examples, around which we will elaborate our arguments.

Chapter 5 outlines our point of departure with a discursive approach to remembering and forgetting. Using conversational data recorded in families and conversational remembering in group settings (Edwards & Middleton, 1986a, 1988) and care groups for older people (Buchanan, 1993; Gibson, 1989), we display how treating practices of remembering as instances of communicative action allows us to understand how recollection is collectively accomplished in varied settings. In particular, we point to the use of memory to accomplish membership and the co-option of speakers into particular versions of events. However, we also point to the limitations of this approach – notably the sense that occasions of remembering can appear disconnected from one another, as though the past had to be rhetorically put together anew each time.

This point is pushed forward in Chapter 6, where we argue that issues of succession and change are threaded through practices of remembering. In this way, something of the past is always already 'inbuilt' in a given act of recollection. We show how participants in the variety of domestic and care situations discussed in Chapter 5 and workplaces are inevitably led towards the production of continuity in discursive action in order to manage live concerns with succession and change. This is typically handled by managing the boundaries between what can be presented as incidental and what as intentional, and between what is of relevance to the individual and to the collective.

Does this revised approach allow for us to understand how remembering becomes embedded in broader social and historical dynamics? Not quite. In Chapter 7, drawing on further data recorded in reminiscence groups by Kevin Buchanan (1993) and Faith Gibson (1989), in addition to work on remembering and reconciliation by Kyoko Murakami (2001a), we argue for a broader conception of the frameworks in which recollection is performed. Using Halbwachs' distinction between the 'discursive' and 'physiognomic' aspects of collective frameworks, we show that participants unfold 'zones of personal relations' in their recollection that serve to 'incorporate' other speakers. These zones of personal relations occupy an intermediate ground between personal memory and history. Most importantly, incorporation occurs not merely at the level of rhetoric, but by acting on the body. A link to Bergson's notion of 'habit memory' is then made.

Bergson then takes us forward to Chapter 8, where we discuss his notion of a 'pure past'. Using the famous example of Marcel's 'leap' into the past drawn from Proust, we display how objects provide a means for dividing up the past in the present. Objects then act to mediate practices of recollection. We demonstrate, with reference to both reminiscence data (Buchanan, 1993; Gibson, 1989) and life story work with profoundly learning disabled people, their families and carers (Hewitt, 1997), that this occurs in a variety of ways, from opening a 'network of translations' to acting to 'slow down' and mark out social relations. Indeed, so critical is the mediation of objects in this way that we need to think of social relationships as themselves interdependent with the organised setting in which they are performed and as entangled with mediating artefacts. Such a description of sociality is already to be found in Halbwachs' work, we argue.

In Chapter 9, we extend our discussion of object-mediated social relationships by exploring what happens when large-scale organised settings 'take charge' of remembering. Drawing on Bowker and Star's (1999) notion of infrastructures as interlocking arrangements of categories and standards, and using data concerning the organisational use of e-mail (Brown & Lightfoot, 2002; Brown, Middleton & Lightfoot, 2001) and studies of teamwork in neonatal intensive care (Middleton & Curnock, 1995), we discuss studies of organisations where remembering is obliged to pass through complex infrastructural arrangements involving the use of information communication technologies – in particular, the archival use of e-mail. We argue that, under such conditions, the work of disposal – of forgetting – takes on additional importance. Members then create spaces of liberty by managing their 'attachment' to the infrastructure by means of which they are obliged to remember.

Having tacked towards large-scale forms of social organisation, we take forward into Chapter 10 the problem of 'mass' as central to understanding remembering. Returning to Bergson, we contrast the common-sense account of remembering as synthesis and retrieval of experience with his account of the 'gnawing of the past into the present'. Here, what is at stake is how selfhood is constituted around a management of the 'burden' of the past. We show, via a discussion of family websites, how the past is tamed by a spatialisation of experience. However, this spatialisation is never complete and always maintains a relationship to continuous, indivisible forms of experience that Bergson calls 'virtual'. We argue that the relationship Bergson posits between 'virtualisation' and 'actualisation' allows us to understand the objectification of experience in relation to the inexhaustible character of our duration.

The relationship between 'virtualisation' and 'actualisation' and, in particular, the reflexive turning around on duration that Bergson identifies with the elaboration of selfhood serves as the basis for Chapter 11. Returning to the work of Kyoko Murakami (2001a) on remembering and reconciliation, we argue that the collective experience of singular durations is the point of contact between the personal and the collective. We show how chains of translation hold together singular, irreducible durations. However, by virtue of the mediation of 'blank' objects, a cutting out of experience is possible where the juxtaposition of durations enables a turning around on one's own 'unlimited' experience. At this point, the relationship between Bergson and Halbwachs becomes somewhat clearer.

The final chapter, Chapter 12, argues that a 'social psychology of experience' is the term for the evolving accounts of remembering, forgetting and selfhood that we have presented. This would constitute a way of doing psychology that was grounded in the tension between what Bergson calls the 'virtual' and the 'actual' or, more simply, between the demands for action, which are inevitably spatial in character, and our experience of ourselves as living, unlimited changing beings. This is precisely what, we argue, is typically excluded from the psychology of memory and yet is exactly what is demanded of psychology by social science.

TWO

Making experience matter: memory in the social sciences

Our concern in this book is to examine how we can approach the social psychology of experience in the study of the remembering and forgetting. This will involve approaching remembering and forgetting as public, social activities where individual experience is necessarily mediated by collective experience. Now we are by no means the first to have envisaged a social turn in the psychological study of memory. There have been numerous contributions by sociocultural researchers, such as Brockmeier (2002); Bruner and Feldman (1996); Cole (1996); Hirst and Manier (1996); and Wertsch (2002), along with ecologically orientated psychology, notably Neisser (1982), Neisser and Winograd (1988), Barclay (1994); social psychology such as Bangerter (2000, 2002); Wegner (1986) and Weldon (2001); Weldon and Bellinger (1997); and discourse analysis such as Norrick (2000). In addition, within psychology there is Bartlett's (1932) classic work on remembering, in which he aimed to put the study of memory on a properly social footing. We will discuss some of this work in more detail in a moment, but we should also note at this point that memory has been a fertile field for debate about the social basis of psychological functioning for as long as psychology has been established as a discipline.

William James (1890/1950), for instance, devotes considerable space in his *The Principles of Psychology* to discussing the basis whereby our consciousness becomes endowed with a form of continuity. For James, the question of memory is caught up in his distinctive and well-known account of human self-awareness as a 'stream of consciousness'. Memory is, then, to be approached in terms of the ability to connect together aspects of our experience as they appear in the ongoing flow of awareness. This implies some form of selectivity, we must exercise choice in relation to the nature of the connections to be made in order that our recollections can be best fitted to our current concerns and activities. Hence 'in the practical use of our intellect, forgetting is as important a function as recollecting' (James, 1950: 679).

We can turn back yet further than this to John Locke's (1690/1975) description of a 'forensic self' defined by memory, which some authors (for example, Douglas, 1992: Hacking, 1995) see as laying the foundations for the modern concept of selfhood. Locke argued – contrary to the dominant tradition of English idealism – that memory was every bit as powerful as perception, and that chains of memories and responsibilities linking the present into the depths of the past were the precondition of selfhood. Without such a 'forensic' link, the idea of justice or merely holding some person accountable for their past deeds has no meaning.

In this philosophical tradition inherited by psychology, there is, then, a series of deep conceptual links between persistence of the past into the present, the idea of selfhood, the possibility of judgement and social responsibility. What this all suggests is that 'memory' should not be regarded as a psychological function like any other. Rather, it is a key site where questions of personal identity and social order are negotiated. Witness, for example, the often fraught legal and scientific arguments fought around the issue of recovered memories (see Ashmore, MacMillan & Brown, 2004). What is at stake in these 'memory wars' ranges from particular concerns with justice for the abuse and trauma suffered by individuals to far broader concerns with the nature of the modern family, the status and standing of therapy, authentic versions of selfhood and so on (Pezdek & Banks, 1996).

In saying that we wish to approach memory as a social phenomenon, we are essentially 'knocking at an open door'. Public debate about the apparently flexible and contingent manner in which governments and official bodies construct past 'truths' rages in most Western nations (for instance, the debate at the time of writing about what was or was not known by the Bush and Blair administrations concerning the actual existence of weapons of mass destruction in Iraq during the preparations for war in 2003). At the same time, a routine engagement with commemorative activities, be they purely nostalgic (such as the recycling of popular culture from the 1970s and 1980s) or highly sensitive (Ronald Reagan's laying a wreath at they Bitburg cemetery where Nazi SS soldiers are buried during his presidential state visit to the then West Germany in 1985, for example) is part of the fabric of much daily life. In each case, the thoroughly social character of memory is a pure truism for a great many people, whether or not they are immediately touched by controversies such as the memory wars.

Barbara Misztal's 2003 book *Theories of Social Remembering* argues that what is required to understand this social landscape of everyday remembering is an approach that eschews both psychological and sociological reductionism. As with other sociological arguments (such as Schudson, 1992; Zerubavel, 1996, 1997), Misztal begins by attempting to clarify *who* is remembering *what* version of the past and to *which end*. The importance of such sociological concerns is its emphasis on the social organisation and mediation of individual memory. Although it is the individual who is seen as the agent of remembering, the nature of what is remembered is profoundly shaped by 'what has been shared with others', such that what is remembered is always a 'memory of an intersubjective past, of past time lived in relation to other people' (Misztal, 2003: 6). This shared intersubjective memory is forged, Misztal states, by means of social processes such as language, rituals and other commemorative practices and in relation to common memorial sites.

The insights provided by this intersubjective turn within sociological studies of memory are clear. They allow us to see that the work of remembering – and, hence, producing ourselves as people who have a past, a personal history – necessarily intersects with, and is shaped by, the groups and cultural forms we inhabit. However, at the same time, we need to grasp why it is that, despite the obvious influence of these social dimensions, for most of us the act of remembering still feels like a highly personal act. We feel that we 'own' our personal memories and speak them of our free will without undue influence from others. Ian Hacking (1995) argues that the modern experience of remembering takes this form because our self-understandings have been so profoundly shaped by psychology as a 'science of memory' that we find it difficult to grasp memory in any other way. This is to say that everyday practices of remembering have been recruited into psychologists' versions of what it means to remember and forget.

Doubtless it is the case that psychology in its myriad forms has acquired tremendous cultural authority over matters of self-knowledge, at least in North America and Europe (for a detailed account of this rise of the 'psy complex', see the work of Nikolas Rose, 1989, 1996). It is doubtless also the case that, as Danziger (2002) points out, this authority has led to a narrowing and constriction of the common stock of metaphors and cultural models by means of which memory has traditionally been understood. However, rather than simply dismiss psychology as being guilty of brute reductionism, we need instead to focus more clearly on this central paradox: why it is that an activity that is so thoroughly public and social feels so intensely private and personal. We need, in other words, to get a handle on the complex and often ambiguous forms of experience that are central to how remembering is performed.

In this chapter, we will begin this project by doing some groundwork. Here we look to a range of approaches to remembering that have been developed outside of contemporary psychology, in social anthropology, history and sociocultural theory. We will try to use these approaches as diagnostic tools to help shed light on our understanding of memory as a site where both the singularity and collectivity of experience intersect. Our broader aim is to reopen communication between social psychology and other social sciences. This will require that we identify what kinds of tools – that is, concepts, ideas or methodological elements – may usefully mediate between the approaches.

A conversation with Bartlett – social organisation of remembering in communicative action

A key starting point for us was the work of Frederick Bartlett. Although his work is frequently cited as a pivotal historical moment in the experimental study of memory, its influence extends well beyond the disciplinary concerns of psychology. Indeed, as Rosa (1996) argues, Bartlett's research career was forged in the use of psychological methods to pursue anthropological questions concerning the 'conventionalisation' of cultural materials – that is, how individuals and groups borrow, modify and adapt materials that are foreign or new to them. These ideas still generate contemporary interest in anthropological work on remembering and forgetting (Cole, 1998, 2001). However, the significance of Bartlett's focus on culture as the ongoing and highly particular production and reconstruction of meaning has not been fully exploited in contemporary social and cognitive psychology. As Kashima (2000: 384) notes, the tendency has been to treat culture as 'a repository of meaningful symbolic structures that structure people's experience' rather than a dynamic process of transmission and transformation.

Take, for example, Bartlett's celebrated and much quoted 1932 book, *Remembering: A study in experimental and social psychology*. This reports empirical studies and develops theoretical arguments concerning the dynamics of succession and change. Bartlett opens by questioning the reductionist strategy of aiming to isolate any form of simple mental faculty or processes occurring independently of each other. He rejects the Ebbinghaus (1885/1964) tradition of memory research. That tradition sought to eliminate the personal and idiosyncratic responses people might make to material that they are requested to memorise and recall under the controlled conditions of memory experiments. This is achieved by means of short and meaningless written material. Bartlett questions this strategy of paralysing the accompanying human responses. He doubts the general appropriateness of such a strategy that loses 'the special character' of human action – namely, the ability to render situations sensible for the purposes of current and future concerns. He argues that the improvised settings of experiments moulded in the Ebbinghaus image do not, as was supposed, allow us to see psychological capacities in their pure state by removing all extraneous social variables. Rather, they simply present a different kind of social context for the complex human organism to respond to.

Bartlett's description of psychological experimentation then emphasises that experiments are no less socially located than any other form of social setting (see Edwards & Middleton, 1986b). Indeed, his celebrated use of the serial reproduction technique was more than a simple documentation of the power of conventional symbols in dictating individual perception, as many introductory textbook summaries on psychology would imply. Rather, its aim was to try and capture, on the fly, the actual cultural process of 'conventionalization'. The remarkable feature of this concern with the practices of conventionalization is that it allows us to see not only that remembering is a constructive activity, where what is recalled is transformed in the act of communication, but also that such recollection involves selection and exclusion. In other words, what is not remembered, not passed on to another, is just as important as what is recalled and transmitted onwards.

Most contemporary citations of Bartlett's work, while not actually denying a place for these kinds of 'social' factors, tend to regard them as another set of independent variables that can be grafted on to procedures when appropriate (see, for example, Conway, 1992; Stephenson, Kniveton, & Wagner, 1991). However, to treat conventionalisation in this way is to create exactly the kind of dualism between the individual and the social settings in which they act that Bartlett strove to resist. A significant issue here is the way one of the key terms in *Remembering* – 'schema' – has come to be understood. In classic cognitive science texts (Neisser, 1967; Rumelhart, 1975; Schank, 1982), the term schema is defined as some form of knowledge structure stored in the brain or mind of the individual to assist in the interpretation of experience. Schemata allow for a quick pattern matching of perception against a summary of prior experience, such that rapid judgements can be made. This results in an overall reduction in expenditure of cognitive effort, but can increase the possibilities of error (as in the case of unwarranted stereotyping) if the schemata in use become too inclusive or rigid (see especially Neisser, 1967). Such a definition is, however, at odds with the use Bartlett makes of the word. He defines it instead as the ongoing dynamic adaptation between people and their physical and social environments. That is, as sociocultural arrangements that blur the boundaries between individuals and their social world. Bartlett's preferred definition (1932: 201) was then of schemas as 'organised settings':

> I strongly dislike the term 'schema'. It is at once too definite and too sketchy … it suggests some persistent but fragmentary, 'form of arrangement' and it does not indicate what is very essential to the whole notion, that the organised mass results of past changes of position and posture are actively *doing* something all the time; are so to speak carried along with us, complete, though developing, from moment to moment. It would probably be best to speak of 'active developing patterns'; but the word 'pattern' … has its own difficulties; and it like 'schema' suggests a greater articulation of detail than is normally found. I think probably the term 'organised setting' approximates most closely and clearly to the notion required.

It is striking, given the individualistic ways in which the notion of schema is typically used in cognitive and social psychology, just how highly critical Bartlett is of his own use of the term. However, if Bartlett has difficulty in arriving at the idea of an 'organised setting', it is because what he is pursuing is a complex and challenging account of psychological functioning. Very roughly, Bartlett states that our conscious awareness – or 'attitude' – stands in a dynamic relation, to the direction and range of concerns – or 'interests' – that characterise our ongoing relations with the social worlds we inhabit. As these relations are subject to continuous transformation, at least within certain parameters, it follows that our attitudes and interests are themselves evolving. An 'organised setting' is, then, a complex of cognition and emotion that is located within, and dependent on, the cultural and material particularities of the local environment. We cannot then separate out the mental from the social in any clear-cut manner. For instance, as Zangwill (1972: 126) notes, Bartlett's use of the term attitude does not easily resolve into clearly defined mental elements as it 'owes much to Betz's term *Einstellung*, which broadly signifies mental posture or set'. Likewise, the term 'feeling', which Bartlett explored in any earlier paper (1925) is an amalgam of affect and social judgement.

What Bartlett tries to capture is the essential integration of individual mentality and culture, of the interdependency of cognition, affect and cultural symbols. It is within this model of psychological functioning that Bartlett develops his account of remembering. For Bartlett, remembering is indicative of the kind of liberty that schemata, as organised settings, afford us. To exist within an organised setting is to have some of the burden of being forced to continuously adjust to the changing vicissitudes of the environment removed. Organised settings render the world stable, they free us from the 'chronological determinism' (Bartlett, 1932: 202) of the present moment, but, at the same time, they do not rigidly determine our thinking. Bartlett (1932: 208) argues that the 'special character' of human psychological functioning emerges as the human organism 'discovers how to turn round upon its own "schemata", or, in other words, it becomes conscious'. To be conscious is to have a reflexive awareness of the organised setting in which one's thoughts and actions are situated. From this it follows that schema are 'not merely something that works the organism, but something with which the organism can work' (Bartlett, 1932: 208).

It is this ability to turn around on schema that constitutes remembering as a constructive process of living development – in other words, as a kind of ongoing dialogue between our thinking and the cultural symbols that feature in a given organised setting. By remembering, we are then able to reconstruct and transform 'our daily modes of conduct'. This occurs via an interesting synthesis of sensory and symbolic issues – what can be termed as 'cross-modal remembering' (Edwards & Middleton, 1986b). The terms 'mode' and 'cross-modal' do not refer to the sense organs, but the forms of symbolisation or representation in which the materials that are the subject of attention are experienced and later re-presented or remembered. Bartlett clearly recognised the importance of studying how we put experience into words and the significance of conventional symbols in conscious activity. He also recognised the function of conversational discourse, where, for example, remembering occurs as people talk with one another. In such contexts, the purposes of communicative action very often take precedence over notions of reproductive accuracy (Bartlett, 1932: 96):

> The actions and reproductions of everyday life come largely by the way, and are incidental to our main preoccupations. We discuss with other people what we have seen, in order that they may value or criticise our impressions with theirs. There is ordinarily no directed and laborious effort to secure accuracy. We mingle interpretation with description, interpolate things not originally present, transform without effort and without knowledge.

The prevailing consensus in studies of memory – be they ecological (such as Neisser, 1982; Neisser & Winograd, 1988) or concerned with information processing (such as Atkinson & Schiffrin, 1968; Baddeley, 1982; Neisser, 1967) – has been a concern with issues of verity in remembering as the indices of structure, content and process – how to sort 'genuine' memories from 'distorted' ones (for example, Loftus, 1979) and there have been heated debates about what has been termed false memory syndrome (Loftus & Ketchum, 1994). However, as we see in the previous extract, Bartlett argues strenuously that issues of accuracy are less important than addressing our 'main preoccupations' – that is, settling current matters at hand as they emerge in communicative action. Indeed, he even goes so far as to argue that, 'in a world of constantly changing environment, literal recall is extraordinarily unimportant' (1932: 204).

What Bartlett then calls for is an understanding of remembering as primarily concerned with how the past is constructed in the present to serve the needs of whatever actions we are currently engaged in. Rather than view what people remember as a window on to the content and structure of individual minds or strident attempts to retell original experience, we ought instead to be concerned with how people construct versions of the past, their position in so doing and their use of the very notion of what it is to remember. Moreover, as Bartlett makes clear in both *Remembering* and, later on, in *Thinking* (1958), this reconstruction of the past is done by means of conversation. Talk is a fundamental aspect of 'everyday thinking' or, as Bartlett (1958: 164) terms it, 'immediate communication thinking'.

It might be argued that this is all well and good, but the real topic remains what people really do with their minds or really can remember, not just what they can report. However, as has been previously argued (Edwards & Potter, 1992), this is an empirically difficult distinction to maintain. Descriptions of experience are endlessly variable. In addition to this, one of the main functions of such talk is to establish what it is that might have actually, possibly or definitely happened. In a sense germane to the psychology of participants, the truth of original events is the *outcome*, not the *input*, to the reasoning displayed in talk. The turn to a discursive analysis of remembering – to understand the way in which remembering is organised for and accomplished within the pragmatics of communicative action – is a legacy of Bartlett's concerns. Conversational remembering is a fundamental aspect of conduct in socially ordered settings, as will be discussed in more detail in subsequent chapters.

The impact of Bartlett's discursive agenda beyond psychology

Bartlett's work has had a significant impact beyond the discipline of psychology. We will now discuss briefly in turn several bodies of work that may be organised according to four key themes from Bartlett:

- commemoration
- conventionalisation
- objectification
- mediation.

Following this we will summarise how these themes converge on the key notion of *experience situated within organised settings*. We will then demonstrate that, in order to pursue this notion within social psychology, we need to turn towards two of Bartlett's contemporaries – Maurice Halbwachs and Henri Bergson.

Commemoration

The *Social Memory* monograph (1992) by anthropologist James Fentress and historian Chris Wickham gives a thorough demonstration of Bartlett's point that memory is reconstructed in the process of its articulation and transmission (or, as Bartlett succinctly put it, the 'effort after meaning' that characterises recollection).

Fentress and Wickham (1992: X) approach memory in terms of the way in which 'individual consciousness' relates to 'the collectivities those individuals make up'. They argue that membership of a social group subtly inflects the form that memory takes for group members. In particular, it inflects the precise manner in which individuals are able to talk or write about the past. For example, in a detailed analysis of the medieval poem 'Chanson de Roland', they show that the structure of the poem sets up a montage of visual images for the listener rather than a clear narrative continuity. The past recalled by the poem is, then, experienced as highly stylised and vivid visual dramatisations of past events.

There are two key points to be made here. First, that the local techniques available for retelling the past – such as poems, stories, legends or folklore – profoundly shape the way in which individuals can gain access to their own history. 'Chanson de Roland', for instance, uses a great deal of formulaic language. This, Fentress and Wickham argue, is the 'mnemonic armature' (1992: 53) that makes the poem memorable and recognisable across the occasions of its telling. So long as the performer retains this armature, precise narrative details can be altered or excised. Second, that, in the process of being told, the poem transmits a set of cultural values and social meanings rather than a clear record of historical moments. Seen in this way, 'Chanson' is a poor record of empirical events, but an excellent vehicle of collectively held ideas. Commemoration, then, for Fentress and Wickham (1992: 59) is 'not stable as information; it is stable, rather, at the level of shared meanings and remembered images'.

This analysis of commemoration clearly follows Bartlett in exploring memory not merely as a faculty with which individuals are endowed – that is, a property or thing (a 'noun') – but also as an activity – a set of social techniques or procedures (as a 'verb'). Fentress and Wickham are concerned with the manner in which social groups make available for members ways of connecting their present lives and concerns with the past. What this means is that 'the way we order and structure our ideas in our memories, and the way we transmit these memories, is a study of the way we are' (1992: 7).

Commemoration is as much about establishing who we are now, as social beings, as it is about settling what happened in the past. Indeed, for Fentress and Wickham, the lesson to be learnt from 'Chanson' is that the power of such commemoration is 'little affected by its truth'. In one sense, it does not matter whether the events recalled did or did not happen in the way in which they are retold. What does matter is that the commemoration takes a form that is sufficiently consonant with the group's collectively held values that members may affirm it without finding it 'strictly believable'. Put slightly differently, 'memory is validated in and through actual practice' (1992: 24).

This appears to suggest that groups can continuously remake the past – at least, within certain limits. Now this may be all well and good when we are considering medieval social memory, as exemplified by 'Chanson', but what of modern forms of commemoration? Michael Schudson directly addresses this point in his 1992 book *Watergate in American Memory: How We Remember, Forget and Reconstruct the Past.*

Schudson begins from a pragmatic position – Watergate is not a myth or a legend, it is a definite historical event. 'Watergate' is the name given to the political scandal resulting from the complicity of the then American President, Richard Nixon, in the cover-up of an attempted break-in during 1972 at the Democrat National Committee Headquarters in the Watergate Office Complex in Washington, DC, with apparent intention to fix a malfunctioning wire tap. Newspaper and then formal Senate investigations led to impeachment proceedings and the infamous eventual resignation of Nixon in 1974. This, Schudson (1992: 55) argues, is 'something [that] happened, and on that, not on interest or values or free interpretation, hangs a tale. Tracing the consequences of "something happened" is what an interest in the past is all about'. The point, for the study of social memory, is to establish not what did or did not actually occur, but to understand how Watergate lends itself to various forms of interpretation and narration over time.

There are, of course, numerous versions of and points of view about 'what happened' around Watergate. For Schudson, it is precisely these kinds of debates and disagreements that constitute what we can term 'collective memory'. He (1992: 50) aims to 'show how different views of Watergate have warred with one another through the past decades and to analyse how different forms and forums have carried these views on in American memory'. What matters is how individuals then orientate themselves to Watergate as a topic, make it salient as a 'memorable' and 'tellable' event and engage with others in such debate. However, one of the peculiarities of Watergate is that, at the time, there were other events – such as the energy crisis of the early 1970s – that would have appeared far more vivid and memorable. Californians, for example, would have directly experienced the spectacle of sitting in 'gasoline lines'. Watergate, by contrast, would have been experienced at a distance, as events reported in a newspaper. If we add to this that there is no formal commemorative practice featuring Watergate (no annual 'Nixon day', for instance) then the persistence of the event in North American social memory is all the more puzzling.

The answer, Schudson claims, is to understand Watergate as a *process* rather than an *event*. Central to this is not what Watergate was, but, rather, what it has now become (and continues to become) as it serves as the source material for a variety of *informal* commemorative practices. For example, Nixon's resignation may be taken as a metaphor for the victory of the common people (in this case, the *Washington Post* reporters who pursued the case) over the powerful (the machinations of Nixon and his White House advisers). As such, Watergate can be used to express or support a variety of projects in the present. Schudson refers to these practices as the 'cultural vehicles' or 'resources' by means of which collective memory is woven. It is via such cultural vehicles that the past comes to us and informs our personal and collective sense of who we are – 'the forms of collective memory, attached to human or humanly constructed vehicles, are an aspect of human culture through which time travels' (1992: 5).

Barry Schwartz's book, *Abraham Lincoln and the Forge of National Memory* (2000), takes a similar approach. Schwartz is also interested in the gap between matters of historical record – in his case, the presidency of Abraham Lincoln – and how that history is reconstructed as social memory – the ups and downs of how Lincoln's 'reputation' and 'legacy' have been interpreted.

Once again, the point of departure is Bartlett's insight that remembering both preserves and transforms in the transmission of the past. If Schudson alerts us to the danger of placing too much weight on interpretation (we cannot change our recollection of 'what happened' on a whim), then Schwartz points out the equivalent danger of imagining that the past determines the present, that we are directly constituted by our history. Instead, Schwartz (2000: 18) argues, we should see the past as acting as a 'model' for the present in two distinct ways – as 'a *template* that organises and animates behaviour and a *frame* within which people locate and find meaning for their present experience. Collective memory affects social reality by *reflecting, shaping* and *framing* it'. Seen in this way, collective remembering is a continuous dialogue between present and past, where what is recalled is used as a 'framework of meaning' for understanding the present without determining the direction of the future.

In Schwartz's analysis, 'frameworks of meaning' are subject to processes of succession and change. Each generation inherits a given framework, but, at the same time, typically recognises potential shortcomings within it and the need for revision. What he (2000: 25) then calls the 'lineaments of commemorative persistence and change' are central to how Schwartz approaches practices of collective remembering. For example, a physical monument may have been erected in order to preserve some past event (such as a war), but the meaning given to that monument by successive generations will pass through a series of modifications. This example also points to the significance of the tools and symbols for commemoration that are passed on in the course of history. We inherit a rich set of materials in which prior choices about which aspects of our collective past are worth preserving are already embedded. Our contemporary forms of collective remembering are then forced to confront these tools and symbols, and are set the challenge of deciding whether or not they have any form of meaning for us, in the here and now.

Conventionalisation

Schwartz's work points us towards a second theme from Bartlett – the manner in which cultural materials are modified and adapted as they are put to use in the work of remembering. It might be argued that this idea is strongly echoed in the approach to memory adopted in the overlapping fields of cognitive psychology and neuroscience. As Schachter (1996) describes it, the emerging view of memory here is as a subjective, multi-level process, where past memories are subtly modified in the present. Thus, in the same way that Bartlett emphasises the contingency between what is granted to us by the cultural materials we use in remembering and what we then subsequently go on to recall, so the cognitive system itself is seen to do the work of reorganisation and transformation based on the way in which the past has been recorded and stored in the neural architecture of the cortex.

   In our discussion of Henri Bergson in Chapter 4, we will return to this critical issue of neural inputs into the activity of remembering, but for now, it suffices to say that, much as an awareness of the contingency of remembering on the part of cognitive neuroscience is to be welcomed, for many critics outside the discipline, the direction and force of Bartlett's argument remains generally misunderstood by psychologists. For example, Maurice Bloch (1998: 69) points out that:

> The problem with psychologists' approach to memory in the real world comes … from their failure to grasp the full complexity of the engagement of the mind in culture and history and, in particular, their failure to understand that culture and history are not just something created by people but that they are, to a certain extent, that which creates persons.

The problem, as Bloch sees it, is that psychologists make an overly firm distinction between the 'inner world' of the cognitive system and the 'outside world' reached via human perception. If one begins to study memory in this way, then attention is quite naturally focused on how the external world becomes represented and encoded by the cognitive system. What we call 'memories' are then subjective symbolic transformations of some external reality, rendered fit for cognitive-neural processing. From here it is only a short leap to imagine that what is called 'culture' is simply a set of techniques that have evolved to assist humans in this process of the subjective symbolisation of the world and the secondary coordination of such symbols in the public domain. As Bloch (1998: 69) has it, standard psychology textbooks on memory (such as Baddeley, 1976; Cohen, 1990) view 'socially instituted practices of memory as merely a primitive form of artificial intelligence' that are tasked with simply translating our private individual representations into public representations and then archiving them accordingly.

Bloch's point is that such a view arrives at the rather perverse notion that 'culture' and 'history' are creations of the cognitive system, designed for its own convenience, rather than the more plausible notion that these terms mark wider processes within which our self-consciousness emerges and has meaning. In fact, it is this direction of influence – from the cultural to the personal – that Bartlett was seeking to elaborate in his discussion of how cultural materials, such as myth, serve to inform and resource our acts of remembering. It is perhaps ironic that it is now anthropologists rather than psychologists who enact the intellectual project of the founder of the Cambridge Psychological Laboratory.

An informative example here is the work of Jennifer Cole (1998, 2001). Drawing on material from her ethnographic work among the Betsimisaraka people, who are located in the small town of Ambodiharina in east Madagascar, Cole (2001: 1) argues for an analysis of how 'individual and social memory are woven together'. For Cole, there is a complex set of interdependencies between personal consciousness and public representations. For example, within Madagascar, there are strong reminders of the legacy of colonial rule in the form of public architecture and other physical symbols. This legacy may be considered painful – Ambodiharina, for instance, witnessed outbreaks of extreme violence and brutality during the transition to the post-colonial period. One of Cole's most remarkable findings was that memories of this period appeared to be almost completely absent from the descriptions given by her informants of their lives and families. Nor were such memories present in the ritual forms of commemoration adopted by Betsimisaraka. Why should this be so? Is it possible that the individual Betsimisaraka have simply 'forgotten' the past?

In fact, as Cole discovered, this was not to remain the case. She witnessed and recorded 'an explosion of memories' concerning political violence and people's emotional reactions to them. These were occasioned by the developing circumstances of a presidential election in the early 1990s. Opposing parties directly invoked memories from political change of previous times when reminding the electorate of differing ethnic groups of the consequences of voting or aligning themselves in one way or another. Anxieties and past rivalries of political and economic ascendancy were used to rekindle the potential for intercommunity violence.

The lesson that Cole takes from this example is that memory is considerably more than simply the storage of past events and experiences. Indeed, the term used by the Betsimisaraka – *mahatsiaro* – translates as 'make not set apart'. This refers to neither a 'thing' nor 'capacity', but rather the activity of renewing some sort of ancestral connection. For example, one family reported an ancestor as having been saved from bandits by the distracting cry of a bird. That bird does not form part of that family's diet. The memory then becomes embedded in a concrete social practice enacted by family members – or, as Cole (2001: 111) puts it, 'memories of those ancestors come to dwell in the very bodies of their descendants'. To use Bartlett's term, we would say that the symbolic properties of dietary ingredients become conventionalised to enable the commemoration of family lineage.

Moreover, this conventionalisation is an ongoing achievement. The Betsimisaraka also engage in a practice of reburial, where individual remains are broken apart and reconfigured into two male and female collected ancestors. Cole (2001: 288) argues that this process provides for a way of thinking about how memories become gathered up together and 'of the transformations that occur as people work to secure their ties to the past, thereby themselves, quite literally, the many who will not be sundered'. By literally rearranging the skeletons of the dead, families reconfigure their relationships to ancestors and knot the present more firmly to a clearly defined version of the past.

Cole uses the term 'memoryscape' (made popular by Geertz, 1973) to denote the two directions pointed out in this work of conventionalisation. On the one hand, there is the constitution of a *diachronic* succession between ancestors and descendants forged by the rearranging of bones. On the other hand, there is a *synchronic* gathering up of relationships between family members as relatives at the burial site argue the significance of which bones should be arranged and the manner and reasons for their selection. Put more simply, the work of revisiting the past is also a work of transforming the present.

A memoryscape is, then, something like a shared space where social and individual memory meet and the identity of family members in relation to a collective past is worked out. This is another way of thinking about the relationship Bartlett identifies between individual experience and organised settings. We see in Cole's work that what is key to an organised setting is how memory is collectively *configured*, and that this configuration involves ways of thinking and acting in concert with one another, along with formal social practices (reburial among the Betsimisaraka).

Finally, Cole also confirms Bartlett's point that participation in an organised setting involves an emotional investment (a mixing of 'affect' with 'attitude'). Recollection, for the Betsimisaraka, is not an abstract cognitive act, but, rather, occurs in a 'fuzzy space between thinking and feeling', as a 'feeling memory' (Cole, 2001: 281). To experience the past in the reburial of ancestors or the ritual sacrifice of cattle is to *feel* the significance of memory within the present, to sense both a connection to what has gone before and an orientation towards the present and what ought to be.

Objectification

Anthropological work, such as Cole's, captures something of what Bartlett is striving for in the various descriptions he offers of 'schemas' as dynamic 'developing patterns' or 'orientations' between the organism and the 'organised mass of past changes'. What such work also underscores is the physical or embodied nature of such an orientation to the past. Now, the experimental psychological study of memory is typically concerned with remembering as a cognitive act, as a work of pure thought (even if that thought is often in 'error'). If the body is invoked in such work, then it is only in terms of the physical state of the cortex, which itself is understood purely as the 'hardware' on which the cognitive architecture is supported.

Consider for a moment, however, what it feels like to take part in a generic memory experiment. One is usually asked to sit in small, barren room for a prolonged period of time and concentrate on a range of meaningless digits or words flashed up on a brightly lit computer screen. This is certainly a most peculiar experience – from the potential physical discomfort of, and ongoing ambiguity about, the nature of the task to the uneasy awareness that one's performance is being monitored and recorded by the unseen experimenter – with whom contact is limited to a few words of greeting, direction and farewell and the signing of consent forms. In short, there are a wide variety of embodied experiences involved in this activity that are simply not registered in formal psychological theories of memory.

In fact, it is rare to find any systematic accounts of these embodied dimensions of remembering. One significant exception is Edward Casey's (1987) *Remembering: A Phenomenological Study*. Casey presents detailed philosophical arguments using phenomenological data for going beyond the analysis of memory as an exclusively mental phenomenon. He argues that a disembodied account of remembering has its roots in the classical Cartesian view of space as an 'empty', homogeneous medium in which our actions happen to occur. For example, the cubicle in which the experiment takes place is simply a convenient space in which subjects can be monitored as they respond to computer-presented stimuli. For the experimenter, the space is considered to have no intrinsic meaning – it is 'dead', so to speak.

However, there are other ways in which to think about the way we inhabit space. We typically find our environments to be rich in meaning, particularly those places in which we routinely work and dwell. Such places are 'alive' – they provide the boundaries and significant markers within which our experiences are contained. As Casey (1987: 182) states, as our experience '*takes place in place* and nowhere else, so our memory of what we experience is likewise place specific: it is bound to place as its own basis'. We have a living, embodied relationship to the places we inhabit – even to the supposedly 'dead' spaces we have occasion to pass through – that affords and shapes our relationship to the past. If this is so, then we must think of memory as extending out into the world (Casey, 1987: 259):

> *The mind of memory is already in the world:* it is in reminders and reminiscences, in acts of recognition and in the lived body, in places and in the company of others.

Our acts of remembering are interdependent on the places and people that make up our everyday experiences. A familiar sight may serve as the basis for a recollection, just as a conversation might afford a particular reminiscence. In both instances, our memories point outside of ourselves. They are part of an ongoing relationship with place and to others. Casey captures this interdependency with his notion that 'adverbs' rather than 'nouns' or 'substantives' best express how we remember. We recollect 'with' the embodied utterances and gestures we make, 'through' the commemorative practices and routines we engage in, and 'around' the significant and meaningful features of the environment in which we dwell. 'Withness', 'throughness' and 'aroundness' then denote three modes of participation that concern, respectively, bodies, practices and places. For Casey, these modes of participation are the relational aspects of remembering that are precisely the ones missing from the disembodied, purely mentalistic study of memory.

Casey is, in effect, arguing that much of what we take to be personal and private is, in fact, embedded in our actual concrete engagement with other people and things. In so doing, the inner character of our experiences becomes necessarily extended outwards and reflected back at us – in other words, *objectified*. What is more, this objectification is part of the full richness of being – our memories become deepened and expanded as a result. However, is it not also possible that certain modes of participation may act to restrict or constrain remembering? Paul Connerton's (1989) book *How Societies Remember* explores this possibility. Connerton is primary concerned with 'ritual' forms of commemoration. He (1989: 59) argues that, as rituals typically involve a highly stylised, repetitive set of movements and actions on the part of performers, this results in a restriction of meanings that arise in the performance, leaving little space for individual interpretation:

> One kneels or one does not kneel, one executes the movement necessary to perform the Nazi salute or one does not. To kneel in subordination is not to state subordination, nor is it just to communicate a message of submission. To kneel in subordination is to display it through the visible, present substance of one's body.

Rituals are, in essence, *performative*. What they seek to accomplish – submission, assent to authority, religious piety – is achieved in the very doing of the act. The space for arguing otherwise or witholding consent is effaced as soon as one begins to participate. Connerton notes that this performative character means that rituals have a compelling effect on participants. To take part in a commemorative ritual is to be recruited into the significance of the event being collectively recalled (particularly when the ritual involves some form of re-enactment, such as when an annual march traces a particular geographical route or flowers are lain at a monument). A principal difference, then, between ritual and the kinds of narrative forms of commemoration studied by Schudson and Schwartz is that, while it always possible to ironise a narrative in the act of its telling, it is extremely difficult, in the course of an organised commemorative ritual, to kneel 'ironically' in submission or perform an 'ironic' Hitler salute. As Connerton (1989: 59) deadpans, 'the limited resources of ritual posture, gesture and movement strip communication clean of many of hermeneutic puzzles'. Moreover, there are, Connerton (1989: 54) argues, 'certain things that can be expressed only in ritual'. For example, the nexus of meanings contained in the transubstantiation of Christ's body within the Catholic ritual of Communion are not adequately expressed in a verbal account given outside of the activity itself.

The key to ritual commemoration is the use of a 'bodily substrate' for the preservation of collective memory. By training and disciplining bodily movements by means of what Connerton calls 'incorporating practices' as diverse as 'good' table manners, 'nice' writing, 'correct' sitting positions or 'proper' marching, a moral order can be established as a matter of habit. Once acquired, such habitual activities all but demand to be performed correctly – we find it troubling to not write properly or eat with our mouths open and are disturbed to see such lapses on the part of others. This is, once again, a reiteration of Bartlett's point that organised settings/schemas create an 'affective disposition' on the part of members. What Connerton adds to this is that, as the habitual activities that accompany such dispositions are freighted not only with their own moral orders but also with a burden of the past (what it means to 'sit nicely', 'smile politely', 'stand to attention properly' and so on), we are more or less impelled to transmit a set of collective values that we might otherwise seek to question. Thus, rituals are particularly well suited to the preservation of those collective memories that are critical for securing group identities (Connerton, 1989: 102):

> Every group, then, will entrust to bodily automatisms the values and categories which they are anxious to conserve. They will know how well the past can be kept in mind by a habitual memory sedimented in the body.

Both Connerton and Casey, then, offer useful counterweights to the narrowly cognitive or mentalist approach to memory by demonstrating how the past becomes objectified in our habitual actions and routine embodied relationships with the world. However, this still leaves open the question of just how this objectification is achieved – that is, the nature of tools or resources that enable the modes of participation. It is to this final theme that we will now turn.

Mediation

As we described earlier, Bartlett's work on remembering is situated within a project of creating a distinctive psychological approach to anthropological issues. Bartlett's concern with the conventionalisation of cultural materials aimed to show that access to the past is never direct – it always passes by way of a set of resources that are derived from the broader cultural and social landscape. These resources then inevitably shape and restructure whatever is remembered.

Although Bartlett's insight has, by and large, not been adopted within the experimental psychology of memory, there is one tradition within psychology that has worked out a systematic approach to the use of cultural resources in higher psychological functions. Sociocultural psychology has its roots in Soviet philosophy from the early to mid twentieth century. The pivotal figures around which this work revolves include Vygotsky (1987), Luria (1979), Leont'ev (1981) and Bakhtin (1981).

In brief, these authors, working within the intellectual space of Soviet communism, deployed techniques of dialectical thinking to analyse human development in terms of collective accomplishments. The central tenets of this work are historical–materialist – they emphasise the grounding of human activity in a historically structured engagement of humans as labouring beings in the transformation of nature. Such activity is structured as distinct social practices that have their own historical trajectories. Individual development, as Vygotsky saw it, is then a matter of the participation of a given person with these already established sets of practices, who becomes transformed as a consequence.

One of the key terms in sociocultural research is *mediation*. Human action is understood as involving the use of tools – both literal tools or artefacts and symbolic tools, such as language – in order to reach its goals. Tools then mediate between action and the objects towards which it strives and, in so doing, expand the range and complexity of what humans are able to achieve. For many sociocultural researchers (such as Engeström, 1987; Daniels, 2001), an 'activity' is then decomposable into a complex of agents, outcomes and mediational devices.

In Vygotsky's work (1978, 1987, for example), the psychological significance of this complex is that mediation not only expands the range of human actions but also has a 'reverse action' back on the human agent. Mediation – notably in the form of signs and symbols – becomes a way in which agents can 'master' their own minds and behaviour 'from the outside' (see Daniels, 1996). What we call higher-order psychological functions are then, in Vygotsky's terms, actions that are first performed publicly and then secondarily acquired as private 'mental operations'.

James Wertsch's (2002) *Voices of Collective Remembering* is a key illustration of a systematic sociocultural approach to memory. Wertsch argues for an understanding of collective remembering where mediated action constitutes the basic unit of analysis. By this, he intends to draw attention to the range of 'cultural tools' that people employ in accomplishing remembering activities. What counts as a tool, for Wertsch, is quite broad – language qualifies, as do written texts and technologies such as electronic search agents. These tools are always relative to the cultural and historical settings in which they are fashioned and produced.

To begin to use a tool is to become connected, in advance of the accomplishment of the act, with a broader sociohistorical collectivity. For example, Wertsch discusses at some length how Russians have traditionally used a particular form of schematic narrative – or 'narrative template' – as a cultural tool that makes it possible to represent their historical trajectory in terms of contemporary circumstances. This template consists of a rudimentary storyline where the peaceful existence of the Russian people is threatened by an aggressor leading to a dire crisis that is only overcome by the heroism of the Russian people. The functionality of this template – which Wertsch calls 'triumph-over-evil-forces' – is that a range of characters and events can be slotted into the narrative without losing the basic plot line. Soviet accounts of the 1918–1920 Russian civil war, for instance, position Western imperialism, in the guise of 'White Russians', as the aggressor, defeated by the valour of the Communist Party, which stands for the Russian people. Post Soviet accounts adjust the timeframe such that it was the initial rise of the communist party in the October revolution that constitutes the tragedy and the Russian people are now seen as distinct actors rather than subsumed by the Party. In this way, Wertsch shows how, despite the successive changes in historical consciousness that have occurred in the transition into and out of the Soviet period, the cultural tool provides for a kind of continuity.

In his discussion of generational differences in collective remembering, Wertsch (2002: Chapter 5, 8) displays how the continuity in the accounts of the past produced by the generation who grew up in post Second World War Soviet Russia can be further indexed to a massive state control of history education where:

> across all 11 time zones of that massive state students in the same grade were literally on the same page of the same history textbook on any given day of the school year, and the official history taught allowed little room for competing voices.

Control over mediational resources is a means of ensuring that what can be collectively remembered is shaped to fit official, state-sponsored versions of the past.

The point Wertsch underscores here is the fit between mediational tools and the contexts in which they are used, such as the history classroom or the 'kitchen table' where alternative underground samizdat photocopied texts were furtively discussed. These contexts are never neutral – they are sites where collective remembering as a practice rubs up against the state production of 'official history'. As Wertsch shows, in Soviet Russia this confrontation was often marked by an all-pervading sense of distrust of the narratives and resources provided by the state. In particular, the regular excision or 'airbrushing' of Party members who had fallen from favour from official historical accounts and even, notoriously, photographic records, was well recognised by Soviet citizens, even if it could not be publicly discussed (Wertsch, 2000: Chapter 4, 8):

> For ordinary citizens as well as for major actors on the Soviet scene, keeping track of which truth was current was a deadly serious task, but it also gave rise to bits of Soviet humour such as the aphorism that 'Nothing is so unpredictable as Russia's past'.

What this cynicism with regard to official narratives reflects is what Wertsch refers to as a more general 'tension' between individuals and the mediational tools that resource their activity. Tools expand the range of what we are able to achieve, but rarely express the intentions of the actors involved in their entirety. Just as the literal act of writing slows down and 'disciplines' the writer, so the narrative tools available for remembering organise and frame what can be remembered. Just as the writer may experience this slowing down as a frustrating inability to get the words out quickly enough, so the individual who is forced to use the official narrative resources may equally feel a tension between what can be expressed via these resources and other 'competing voices'.

The tension between agent and tool can be expressed in a variety of ways, from the efforts by the agent to 'master' the mediational means to attempts at 'resistance' or rejection. It is within the interplay of these activities that Wertsch locates the changing dynamics of collective remembering and, ultimately, the generational discontinuities between the memories of younger post glasnost Russians and their Soviet-educated forebears.

Summary

Our purpose in this chapter was not to provide a detailed summary of the extensive literature on memory addressing sociocultural issues. There are excellent summaries already available in the literature (see, for example, Antze & Lambek, 1996; Irwin-Zarecka, 1993; Klein, 2000; Misztal, 2003; Olick & Robbins, 1998; Wertsch, 2002; Zelizer, 1992, 1995; Zerubavel, 1996). Rather, our aim has been to identify a range of issues that could equip us to develop a social psychology of experience.

Based on our brief review of a variety of work from across the social sciences, it has become clear to us that the kind of social psychology we are pursuing must be capable of addressing at least four sets of concerns. It must be able to show how issues of succession and change in the transmission of collective memory are handled in commemorative practices. In particular, we need to establish the manner in which transformation occurs – how it is that certain elements of the past become reconstructed while others are disposed of. It must also be able to display how individuals and groups engage in the conventionalisation of cultural resources. That is, how they borrow, modify, reconstruct, pass on or destroy narrative, symbols and artefacts as part of their ongoing practices of recalling the past in the present. Moreover, it must be able to provide an account of remembering as objectification of experience. This requires the study of our living, embodied engagement with other people, with objects that hold meaning and with the particularities of the places in which we dwell. Finally, it must provide for a focus on the ambiguous nature of mediation. In other words, how the reach and depth of our remembering activities becomes expanded beyond ourselves by means of cultural tools and, at the same time, how mediation acts back on us as individuals, and the effects this 'reverse action' has on what we can achieve.

We have indicated that all these issues may be seen as deriving from Bartlett's central problem of experience as it is situated in organised settings. Certainly the work that has followed in the wake of his book *Remembering* has helped to define what a psychology sensitive to the concerns of anthropology, sociology and history might look like. However, there remains a sense that this relationship between 'experience' and 'organised settings' is still too vague a formulation. Witness, for instance the difficulty Bartlett himself has in characterising the terms. It is precisely because of this difficulty, we argue, that Bartlett's project has been so profoundly misunderstood within psychology, with the result that 'experience' has been reduced to an operation of recall, while 'schemas' have been simplified as knowledge structures residing entirely within the 'mind'. In order to avoid falling into a similar error, we must try to get as full an account as possible of what these twin notions might actually mean in psychological terms.

To do so, we will turn away from Bartlett himself and towards the intellectual debates around memory that preceded the publication of his work. In particular, we will turn towards the work of two writers with whom Bartlett would have been familiar (even if he did not always adequately represent the true scope of their work in his own writing).

In the next chapter, we will discuss the work of the sociologist Maurice Halbwachs. This work contains, we argue, the most comprehensive theorisation of organised settings in relation to memory that is to be found in social scientific writing.

We will then turn to the thought of the philosopher Henri Bergson. What Bergson offers is the most profound examination of memory and experience on offer in twentieth-century Continental philosophy. Taken together, these two thinkers will provide us with the impetus to crack open Bartlett's problem.

THREE

Territorialising experience:
Maurice Halbwachs
on memory

There is scarcely a single text on social remembering that does not begin by invoking the work of Maurice Halbwachs (1877–1945). Trained initially in philosophy (under the tutelage of Henri Bergson), Halbwachs became a leading figure in the group of French sociologists working on the review journal *L'Année Sociologique* under Emile Durkheim. After Durkheim's death, in 1917, Halbwachs' work continued to expound the sociological programme established in *L'Année*, using social survey data and statistics as the empirical basis for accounts of social cohesion and societal structure. It is during this period, while Halbwachs was at Strasbourg, that the material translated into English as *On Collective Memory* (1925/1992) was published. Halbwachs was tragically denied the opportunity to complete fully further work on this subject. In 1944, he was arrested by the Gestapo and transported to the Buchenwald concentration camp, where he died the following year. A second volume of writings on social remembering – *The Collective Memory* – was published posthumously (1950/1980).

Mary Douglas (1980) argues that Halbwachs' writing on memory occupies a special place in his published work. In it, she claims, the reader may discern Halbwachs settling accounts between his two former mentors – Bergson and Durkheim. The influence of the latter is quite explicit. Halbwachs adopts Durkheim's central dictum of the social origins of thought. For Durkheim, the fundamental categories of thinking are symbols that reflect basic historically grounded 'social facts'. That is, the divisions and contours of a given social structure. Thus social order becomes cohesive when it acquires a taken-for-granted symbolic form in the collective consciousness. Put crudely, the otherwise intangible aspects of social division become symbolic 'things'. Durkheim's much celebrated concept of 'collective representations' – which has been reworked in social psychology within the study of social representations (see Moscovici, 2000, for an introduction) – is, then, an attempt to understand how thinking becomes recruited into the reproduction of social order.

Something like this line of argument appears in Halbwachs' efforts to reposition remembering as a collective activity that is involved in the maintenance of group identity. At times, Halbwachs uses the term 'collective representation' to explain some of the processes that he considers to be at work, but his analysis operates at a finer level of detail – he is concerned with particular groups rather than the social order as a whole. At the same time, Halbwachs clearly strives to offer an account of how the individual fits into this collective arrangement. Indeed, much of *The Collective Memory* is spent developing an account of the relationship between social remembering and the experience of self-identity.

It is in this last respect that Halbwachs engages with Bergson. As Douglas points out, much of this engagement is implicit, as with, for instance, the discussion of the relationship between various conceptions of time. Douglas also claims that much of what is said constitutes a repudiation, which repeats Halbwachs' earlier break with 'Bergsonist' philosophy and turn to empirical sociology. This is certainly one plausible reading of Halbwachs' work. However, as we intend to show in the following two chapters, if one suspends the automatic link to Durkheim, a different reading is possible – one where the links between Halbwachs and Bergson become far more sympathetic and productive.

The 'social' subject

Halbwachs' two major statements of his approach to 'collective memory' are both complex texts that try to address both a sociological and a psychological audience simultaneously. Rather than simply ignore the emerging experimental psychological approach to memory, of which Halbwachs was well aware, both books offer a series of arguments and distinctions that make the case for the impossibility of an 'asocial' approach to remembering. Following a traditional line of argument in the philosophy of consciousness, Halbwachs points to dreaming as a 'hard case' candidate for an activity that might be considered entirely removed from sociality. We dream alone, in private, outside the norms and structures of society. However, Halbwachs (1992: 44) notes that, 'even when they sleep people maintain the use of speech to the extent that speech is an instrument of comprehension'. As language is fundamentally social, the appearance of language in dreams indicates that sociality is at least required in order to organise and understand the images that proliferate in the dreaming state.

Halbwachs argues that language lends *form* to subjective experience, but the argument does not stop here. Dreaming is often considered to be a form of escape in which the individual removes themselves from the social structures of waking life – 'it is one of those rare moments when we succeed in isolating ourselves completely, since our memories, especially the earliest ones, are indeed *our* memories' (1992: 49).

What, though, do these memories consist of? They are of a prior collectivity, such as our early family life, which we are contrasting with that in which we now live, often on the basis that it appears to offer less constraint. This feeling arises of course, Halbwachs notes, from the fact that we simply are no longer bound by whatever constraints or obligations were actually there, which is in stark contrast to the present. We flee from the perceived complexity of the present to a perceived form of simplicity in the past (1992: 49–50):

> So it is that when people think they are alone, face to face with themselves, other people appear and with them the groups of which they are members ... Society seems to stop at the threshold of interior life. But it well knows that even then it leaves them alone in appearance – it is perhaps at the moment when the individual appears to care very little about society that he develops in himself to the fullest qualities of a social being.

By retreating into our images of the past, in effect what we do is strengthen the connections between past and present milieus. We produce an expanded version of ourselves as social beings by bringing into view distinctions only visible by comparing our membership across two different social milieus. Hence, the work that we do to cut ourselves off from public life becomes precisely what makes us sophisticated social characters. Put slightly differently, it is not merely the form but the content of private experiences that is thoroughly social. Our sociality is not grafted on to subjective experience, but, rather, is the very basis on which our sense of individuality is structured. We are always already social beings.

In *The Collective Memory*, Halbwachs restates the point in the face of an intervention by psychologist Charles Blondel. Blondel offers a personal childhood memory of being alone, exploring an abandoned house and 'suddenly falling up to my waist into a deep hole which had water at the bottom of it' (cited in Halbwachs, 1980: 37). This memory, which apparently does not require the presence of another either for its content or recollection, indicates, Blondel argues, that 'we have direct contact with the past which precedes and conditions the historical reconstruction' (1980: 37). Personal memory must, then, be distinct from and prior to collective memory. Halbwachs responds with a series of subtle observations. Although he may have been alone when the recollected events occurred, was the young Blondel somehow 'outside' of sociality? No. He was in fact 'immersed only in the current of thoughts and feelings attaching him to his family' (1980: 39). These thoughts and feelings structured the very nature of the experience (1980: 39):

> That memory belongs to both child and adult because the child was for the first time in an adult situation. When he was a child, all his thoughts were at a child's level. He was used to judging events by the standard his parents had taught him, and his surprise and fear were caused by his inability to relocate these new experiences in his little world.

The tenor of the experience at the time, Halbwachs argues, is provided precisely by its location 'outside' and in opposition to the family. Young Blondel is testing the limits of his familial bonds. The significance of the memory for the adult Blondel is that it marks a first instance of being in an 'adult' situation, forced to rely on himself. However, the sense of all this is given by sociality – the position in relation to the family that the child is exploring. Again, what appears to be the most 'personal' of experiences turns out to be thoroughly social.

Memory 'of' the group?

If an activity such as dreaming – an apparently passive, private experience – can be understood as an active, social process, this merely foreshadows the way in which memory, for Halbwachs, is itself a structured activity that is fundamentally social in character. When we recollect the past, we do not passively open ourselves up to some previously forgotten image, which appears to us as 'ready formed', but, rather, refashion the past on the basis of our current concerns and needs. As Halbwachs (1992: 40) puts it, 'in reality the past does not recur as such … everything seems to indicate that the past is not preserved but is reconstructed on the basis of the present'. How does this reconstruction take place? Here, Halbwachs makes his most famous claim – that reconstruction is a process of mutual elaboration between the individual who strives to recall images and the group of which he or she is a member:

> It is not sufficient, in effect, to show that individuals always use social frameworks when they remember … One may say that the individual remembers by placing himself in the perspective of the group, but one may also affirm that the memory of the group realises and manifests itself in individual memories.

The activity of remembering draws on the resources that become available when we 'place ourselves in the perspective of the group'. We may, for instance, be able to draw on the recollections of others or of key events that have become inscribed in the oral or written history of the group. In so doing, our efforts towards recollection play a part in affirming the nature of the group and strengthening its bonds between present and past. It is at this point in the text, that Halbwachs is often taken – by readers as diverse as Bartlett (1932) and Wertsch (2002) – to be making the wider claim that, given the interdependency of the individual and the group, this latter should at least be considered as an ontological unit in its own right. In short, that groups rather than individuals actually 'do' the remembering (1992: 54):

> Now that we have understood to what point the individual is in this respect – as in so many others – dependent on society, it is only natural that we consider the group in itself as having the capacity to remember, and that we can attribute memory to the family, for example, as much as to any other collective group.

Note the precursor to Halbwachs' claim – we can attribute memory to groups, but only once we have revealed the relational foundations of individuality. Halbwachs is not inventing a new entity, the qualities and attributes of which are modelled on those of the individual, as Wertsch (2002) suggests. Rather, once he has repositioned 'individuality' as a mode of sociality, he then proceeds to unpack the processes on which this sociality itself depends. Halbwachs is not, then, offering a species of sociological determinism. There is not a 'thing' called 'society' that causally determines the actions of a 'thing' called 'the individual'. Rather, there is a process of relating the present to the past by means of which the various modes of social order, including that mode we call 'individuality', emerges – 'it is upon a foundation of remembrances that contemporary institutions were constructed' (1992: 125).

The group is neither the source of memories, nor is it an entity with the capacity to remember. Instead, Halbwachs identifies a 'collective framework' of activities that become embedded – or we might say, 'actualised' – within the permeable boundaries established by a group. Indeed, Halbwachs often prefers to talk in terms of these impersonal 'frameworks' rather than the groups that place limits on their operation. Frameworks are what persist over time, lending continuity to a group, so its 'reality is not exhausted in an enumerable set of individuals' (1980: 118). Groups may survive or be reconstructed when even the greatest majority of their members are absent or deceased. This again militates against the idea, as Bartlett (1932: 296–300) observes, that it is the group itself that is in someway endowed with a miraculous capacity to remember. What matters, Halbwachs states (1980: 118), is that it remains possible for a given person to locate himself or herself within the framework that lent the group coherence, irrespective of whether or not that group is present or currently active: 'when I speak of the individual making use of the group memory, it must be understood that this assistance does not imply the actual presence of group members'.

What, then, is this framework? In essence, it is a series of images of the past and a set of relationships that specify how these images are to be ordered. For instance, with regard to the collective memory of families (1992: 59):

> (e)ach family has its proper mentality, its memories which it alone commemorates, and its secrets which are revealed only to its members. But these memories … are at the same time models, examples and elements of teaching … When we say, 'In our family we have long life spans,' or 'we are proud,' or 'we do not strive to get rich,' we speak of a physical or moral quality which is supposed to be inherent in the group, and which passes from the group to its members … the various elements of this type that are retained from the past provide a framework for family memory, which it tries to preserve intact, and which, so to speak, is the traditional armour of the family.

Family memory, as a form of collective memory, consists of shared images and meanings – that is, categories, qualities, evaluative criteria. Family members use these as a common framework around which individual recollections are interwoven or, rather, such recollections are systematically fashioned around these common elements, which come to act as resources ('models, examples and elements of teaching') for making sense of the present. In this way, the framework supports and reinforces the boundaries of the family – it is like a form of 'armour' that provides support for the fragile familial bonds. Note, once again, that it is memory which seems to be holding together groups, rather than groups determining memory processes. However, the use of the framework does not cut the family off from the wider social order, for, as Halbwachs notes, there are wider sets of cultural 'regulations' (normative procedures) that inevitably insinuate themselves within given family frameworks.

The structure of collective frameworks

Once in a place, a framework effectively governs how remembering is accomplished within a given collectivity. It does this by means of a process Halbwachs calls 'localisation'.

Localisation involves the forging of a network of relationships of meaning, such that, when a given member attempts to recollect some fact, they become aware that 'the thoughts of the others [that is, fellow members] have developed ramifications that can be followed, and the design of which can be understood, only on the condition that one brings all these thoughts closer together and somehow rejoins them' (1992: 54). In other words, the collective framework obliges members to locate their own recollections within this network that stands prior to any given act of remembering. The network then acquires a kind of impersonal status – it cannot be said to originate from any given member. It passes as a commonsense 'mentality', the shared, taken-for-granted background knowledge that makes a member what he or she is.

Halbwachs identifies two particular aspects of localisation. First of all, the tendency to summate recollections from different periods into a composite image. For instance, when we try to remember our parents, what we recall tends not to be a particular fact or episode, but, rather, a prototypical scene, assembled from a variety of elements drawn from different moments. When we recall this scene, 'we compose it anew and introduce elements borrowed from several periods which preceded or followed the scene in question' (1992: 61). Halbwachs (1962: 60) argues that this summative image more effectively conveys the reality of our past than veridical recall of a particular incident: 'the scene as it is represented nevertheless gives, in a gripping abbreviation, the idea of a family'. We may consider these shared summative prototypical images as akin to the knots that hold the network of relationships together and through which our individual acts of remembering are obliged to pass.

The second tendency is to project this ordering of relationships on to the past, such that a 'singularly vivid image' appears 'on the screen of an obscure and unclear past' (1992: 60). For example, in the case of religious collective remembering, the past that is recalled in rites and holy texts, such as the Christian gospels, is a time usually far remote from those who are engaged in recollection. Such a past may be considered ambiguous, as potentially affording multiple sets of historical accounts. However, the collective frameworks of a given religion work around this ambiguity by building up a core unitary account that is continuously rehearsed in rites and ritualised understanding, such that otherwise evident lacunae in knowledge are pushed into the background (1992: 117):

> Theological thought thus projects into the past, into the origin of rites and texts, the views of that past that it has taken in succession. It reconstructs on various levels, which it tries to adjust to each other, the edifice of religious truths, as if it had worked on a single plan – the same plan that it attributes to the founders of the cult and the authors of fundamental texts.

In this sense, religious thought is well served precisely by keeping the past remote, outside of the direct knowledge of any given living person. By doing so, it is able to selectively extract elements that are combined into summative images and ideas, and these, in turn, are projected on to factual events or actually existing places. Halbwachs emphasises that this projection requires some considerable work, a continuous 'adjustment' of heterogeneous elements that, although extracted from diverse sources, are presented as though part of 'the same plan'. He also notes that this practice requires a large tolerance of ambiguity. For instance, it was common in the Christian gospels of the Middle Ages to recognise two or more apparently incompatibly geographical locations as nevertheless involved in the singular story of the crucifixion.

The primary mechanism involved in localisation is linguistic. It is in acts of naming and classifying that individual remembrances become linked to the common framework (1992: 53): 'one cannot in fact think about the events of one's past without discoursing upon them. But to discourse upon something means to connect within a single system of ideas our opinions as well as those of our circle'. For example, when we utter the name of a sister or brother while among fellow family members, we are not using a linguistic token in a purely representational sense to call attention to some person who is absent at the time of speaking. Rather, we are locating our present utterance in a nexus of shared background understandings that delimit the place of our sibling in our kinship network, in shared summative images of her or his character, achievements and so on. There is a prior 'agreement' among members with regard to this framework, which is indexed by uttering the proper name (1992: 72) 'the first name is but a symbol of this agreement which I can experience at each instance or which I have experienced for a long time'. The discursive aspects of the framework then act to 'enlarge my consciousness' (1992: 72) by opening up a rich set of meaningful relationships and prior knowledge simply by the invocation of proper names. These relationships persist even when the contexts in which they were originally learnt have fallen away. In a now unbearably poignant section of the text Halbwachs (1992: 73) wonders:

> What would happen if all the members of my family disappeared? I would maintain for some time the habit of attributing a meaning to their first names. In fact, if a group has affected us with its influence for a period of time we become so saturated that if we find ourselves alone, we act and think as if we were still living under the pressure of the group.

'Physiognomy' as territorialisation

Yet, words alone, despite their power, do not constitute a framework. Another mechanism comes into play in the form of what Halbwachs calls 'particularities' – a shared 'physiognomic' system of gestures, social practices, artefacts, territorial sites and so on.

The term 'physiognomic' denotes the way in which this system, once in place, becomes so familiar that it appears to shine forth from the environment itself. For example, Halbwachs (1992: 123) describes how, under feudal land ownership, 'the noble quality of the lord for his tenant was rooted in his land. Behind the fields, forests and fertile lands the personal face of the lord is perceived'. A set of relationships between people, their purported qualities and the very landscape itself exists (1992: 123):

> Such an assemblage of lands, forests, hills and prairies has a personal physiognomy arising from the fact that it reflects the figure and history of the noble family that hunts in its forests, walks through its lands, builds castles on its hills, supervises its roads – the noble family that brought together its lands acquired through conquest, royal gift, inheritance or alliance. Things would be quite different and would not inspire the same feelings or memories if other persons or another family were in command instead of the present owners.

By way of interpretation, we might say that the landscape becomes 'territorialised' by the nobility (see Deleuze & Guattari, 1988: 310–50; and Brown, 2001). What we mean by this is not merely that the feudal lord owns and exercises control over the land, but, more importantly, every meaningful feature of the landscape and life within that place refers back in some way to the character of the feudal family. The landscape is inscribed with their presence, is 'overcoded' by their family history. Halbwachs describes how we experience this physiognomy as a 'zone of personal relations'. In this view, when the peasant gazes at the feudal land, what they see, first and foremost, is the character of the feudal lord and the obligations, forms of justice and morality that flow from it. In other words, sociality seems to spring forth from nature. 'Seems', because, as Halbwachs is at pains to stress, the 'zone of personal relations' is thoroughly unnatural. It is, we would say, socially constructed and then subsequently 'naturalised' as a result of projection by a collective framework.

Although the feudal example may seem extreme, Halbwachs clearly presents this territorialisation as a generic process that is involved in all collective frameworks. His short text *Legendary Topography of the Gospels in the Holy Land* (to be found appended to Halbwach, 1992), for instance, describes at great length how Christianity seized on sites such as Galilee or Jerusalem and, in processes of summation and projection, established them as critical elements in the gospel stories in such a way that to encounter these sites is to be drawn into the physiognomic structure of the story of Jesus. Wherever we look in the Holy Land, we will inevitably be led back into the zone of personal relations that is bound together by the figure of Christ, who stands at its heart.

In this way, physiognomy (or territorialisation, as we have been describing it) becomes almost indistinguishable from the things themselves. It is as though they could not be other than elements in the dense network of relationships that are projected on to them and, in so doing, have created a lacquer-work of patinated meanings. Halbwachs argues that the predominance of the physiognomic over factual entities even occurs in highly applied settings. The judicial system, for instance, might be seen as a body of practical knowledge. In this sense, it constitutes what Halbwachs (1992: 160) calls a 'zone of technical activity', which involves 'knowing and ... applying the rules and precepts that in every period prescribe for the functionary the general terms of the actions, linguistic forms, and gestures of his function'. These prescriptions become so highly 'attuned to reality' via formalism that they appear almost timeless – 'in their rigidity and generality they imitate the law and forces of matter' (1992: 161). This would place them outside the processes of collective memory. Thus, we might delimit a whole series of practices – including science, law, administration, professional history – for which Halbwachs' account of collective remembering does not hold, but this distinction is only workable so long as we examine the practices in the abstract. The minute we begin to analyse them in their actuality, populated with social beings, then the 'zone of personal relations' reappears to swamp the 'zone of technical activity'. A scientist, a lawyer or a professional historian depends on their familiarity with the collective frameworks of memory that permeate their discipline in order to exercise practical knowledge in the present. Put slightly differently, for Halbwachs, the know-how or informal knowledge that is granted by belonging to a 'zone of personal relations' is more important than the availability of abstract technical formal knowledge.

Duration, memory, history

One of the problems Halbwachs returns to ceaselessly is the apparent con-tradiction between our sense that duration in general – time as it is appears to us to be lived out – seems to flow and change continuously, while the groups to which we belong appear to change very little. At a personal level, then, we are aware of constant change, living our lives in the midst of a 'psychological flux or current' where 'our states of consciousness follow one another in a continuous current, like so many waves pushing after one another' (1980: 125; as we will discuss in the next chapter, this model of consciousness is famously associated with Henri Bergson and William James). However, when we begin to reflect on the past, our memory 'charac-teristically forces us to stop and momentarily turn aside from this flux so that we might, if not reascend, at least cut across a current along which appear numerous branchings off' (1980: 125). The act of remembering seems to arrest the flow of consciousness, turn it back on itself and rediscovers both familiar and novel currents. Indeed, Halbwachs argues, how could memory be otherwise? In order to extract something familiar from the flow of consciousness, it must be necessary for memory to be based on clear differences, resemblances and continuities rather than a ceaseless flow of ongoing change.

This point is central to Halbwachs' argument against what he calls the 'subjectivism' of Bergson and James. In brief, Halbwachs reasons that, as the Bergsonian or Jamesian subject exists as a pure 'stream of consciousness', it must necessarily have its own particular duration that is completely unrelated to anything outside of itself. This renders each subject a 'self-enclosed consciousness' (1980: 96) that is unable to demarcate one momentary state from another as it has no external criterion to draw on to do so. This creates, Halbwachs claims, a number of real difficulties. If the subject is unable to properly differentiate states as they occur, what hope could there be that such a subject would ever be able to recall clearly defined memories? Moreover, how could two such subjects ever hope to communicate something about a common past with one another as the problem is then simply multiplied rather than reduced (1980: 95):

> [i]t is difficult to understand how two individual consciousnesses could ever come into contact, how two series of equally continuous states would manage to intersect – which would be necessary if I am to be aware of the simultaneity of two changes, one occurring in myself and the other in the consciousness of someone else.

Of course, we can and do speak to one another about events that we jointly recollect. To argue otherwise is plainly absurd. We are able to do so by making use of commonly held categories, such as historical dates, names of places and people, terms for types of activities and events and so on. Halbwachs' (1980: 95) point is that Bergson and James are offering a model of the psychological subject that is 'sealed up' in its own consciousness and, therefore, 'cannot go outside' its own duration. If it cannot do that, then there is no way of explaining how these commonly held categories emerge, meaning that not only is communication between subjects impossible but, moreover, it is difficult to imagine how the subject could ever turn around and reflect on its own past.

In the next chapter, however, in contrast to Halbwach, we will show that the Bergsonian subject is most definitely not sealed up inside itself and that Bergson has a comprehensive account of the emergence of common categories that is grounded in the nature of life and adaptation. Nevertheless, Halbwachs' solution to the problem of creating common frameworks is significant on its own grounds. Halbwachs (1980: 98) argues that the precondition for any kind of memory is the joint creation by subjects of an external form of duration that is abstracted from the flow of individual consciousness:

> (i)ndividual durations are able to establish a larger and impersonal duration encompassing them all because they have themselves separated from their foundation in a collective time that provided their very substance.

This abstract and 'impersonal duration' is social in character. It is produced in and by collectivities. In this way, any 'natural' division of time that we might inductively discern by observing the rhythms and cycles of the natural world becomes reformulated within a generalised social conception of time – 'astronomical dates and divisions of time have been overlaid by social demarcations as to gradually disappear, nature having increasingly left to society the job of organizing duration' (1980: 89). Now, as Halbwachs holds that we are always already social beings, and that our very individuality is, in essence, a mode of a prior sociality, it follows that it is this collective time that forms the 'substance' of our own personal duration. Put simply, our own individual duration and sense of time passing is but a modulation of the 'abstract and impersonal' collective time that governs the community into which we have been born.

What forms might this 'larger and impersonal duration' take? The most obvious is that supposed authoritative record of past events we call 'history'. However, Halbwachs makes a clear distinction between time as it is defined by history and duration that is proper to collective memory. The historian, Halbwachs (1980: 80–1) claims, thinks in terms of firm distinctions: 'history divides the sequence of the centuries into periods, just as the content of a tragedy is divided into several acts … simple demarcations fixed once and for all'. Yet, this is in stark contrast to our daily, lived experience as members of collectivities. For us, the world we wake to each morning usually appears fairly stable. We are simply unaware of the epochal differences being introduced by the unfolding of history. To think otherwise would be to act as the 'character in the farce who exclaims "Today the Hundred Years War begins!"' (1980: 82). Our thought is marked not by 'clearly etched demarcations', but, instead, by 'irregular and uncertain boundaries' (1980: 82). These boundaries originate from the collective frameworks in which we dwell and reflect the relationships and images that are sewn together there.

However, Halbwachs notes that this does not mean that our thought is ahistorical. When we try to recall something about our parents or grandparents, we tend to flesh out this remembrance with 'historical significance'. History, in other words, acts as a resource for us that tends to 'shroud' our memories (1980: 61): 'we see radiating from and about the remembrance its historical significance'. However, this resource is necessarily worked up within the immediate context of the collective frameworks that are available to us. It is these frameworks that are primary in relation to memory – a point that Halbwachs famously underscored with the claim that 'general history starts only when tradition ends and the social memory is fading or breaking up' (1980: 78). This primacy arises because, given the inherently collective nature of our existence, our personal fates are tied to the continuity of the groups in which we dwell. The persistence of these groups is, in turn, governed by their capacity to 'perpetuate the feelings and images forming the substance of its own thought' (1980: 86). This thought is, as we have seen, made up of a system of relationships and meanings that establishes resemblances and familiar patterns. Thus, in a sense, continuity is inbuilt within collective frameworks.

The 'implacement' of frameworks

The inbuiltness of continuity within collective frameworks would appear to depend on the collective survival of the individuals who make up the group. However, as we have seen earlier, Halbwachs insists that the essence of the group is not constituted by 'enumerable individuals', but, instead, by a collective framework of shared images and meanings (localised in discourse and 'physiognomy').

How, then, might this framework itself persist in the absence of any living group members? This question is subtler than it appears because, as Halbwachs points out, the very fact that the framework is collective means that it is detached from the duration of given individuals. It constitutes a kind of 'semi-depersonalised medium' in which the common concerns of the group are 'not identical with the particular and transient figures traversing it' (1980: 120). It is this depersonalised aspect that provides the key as 'what is impersonal is also more stable' (1980: 120).

Stability arises because collective frameworks, although impersonal, are not wholly abstract. They have a 'spatial and physical dimension' (1980: 124) that is found in the places and domains within which the group dwells and works. Collectivities inhabit and shape place in such a way that they leave their imprint on it:

Our physical surroundings bear our own and others' imprints. Our homes – furniture and its arrangement, room décor – recall family and friends we see frequently within this framework. If we live alone, that region of space permanently surrounding us reflects not merely what distinguishes us from everyone else. Our tastes and desires evidenced in the choice and arrangement of these objects are explained in large measure by the bonds attaching us to different groups (1980: 129).

The design of our own personal spaces is, then, marked by the systems of value, tastes and desires that arise from the collective frameworks in which we participate. In this way, the framework is effectively 'cut into' a distinct spatial locality. The abstract is made concrete in our activities. This makes it possible to 'read off' the character of groups and their collective frameworks from their efforts at domesticating and fashioning their local environments. Hence, it is possible to discern a 'social type or category' from the description 'Balzac provides of a family lodging or the home of a miser' or 'Dickens gives of a study of a notary public' (1980: 129).

What makes such descriptions truly compelling is the sense that the relationship between humans and their environment is not unidirectional. We intuit that what makes the miser 'miserly' or the notary public 'officious' is partly the nature of the places they inhabit – the tiny damp, ill lit houses or the offices spilling over with countless files and sharpened quills. Halbwachs (1980: 130) presents this as a mutually responsive relationship – we fashion our personal spaces, but are, in turn, shaped by the structure of place:

> The group not only transforms the space into which it has been inserted, but also yields and adapts to its physical surroundings. It becomes enclosed within the framework it has built. The group's image of its external milieu and its stable relationships with this environment becomes paramount in the idea it forms of itself, permeating every element of its consciousness, moderating and governing its evolution.

Place, once fashioned as such by a group, reciprocally acts on the collective. For example, the urban geography of cities, which divides space into distinct districts and communities, reinforces boundaries between groups. Similarly, the distribution of roads and forms of transport powerfully affects patterns of communication and 'neighbourhood relationships'. The image of the local environment then comes to dominate how group relationships are thought of (in some extreme or remote cases, Halbwachs postulates, collectivities have a 'social body with subdivisions and structure' that directly reproduces or doubles the 'physical configuration of the city' that encloses them). Hence, the impersonal aspect of a collective framework is reinforced by the sense group members have that it arises from the very environment itself and not from anything at all social, so deeply embedded does it appear to be in the very things around them (1980: 134): 'this shows us the extent to which a whole aspect of the group imitates the passivity of inert matter'.

Halbwachs refers to this relationship between group and environment as 'implacement'. A group that dwells within a space on which it has 'engraved the form' (1980: 156) of its own collective framework is then 'held firm' by the space, which supports and reinforces that framework to the point that it appears (erroneously) to be its very origin. The process of implacement acts to stabilise the collective by slowing down its common duration. To members, the group appears to exist in a seemingly timeless state where changes, if they occur at all, happen very slowly. This stability comes from the solid presence of the fashioned environment within which their collectivity is implaced. In this way, implacement is an essential support for collective remembering (1980: 157): 'each group cuts up space in order to compose, either definitively or in accordance with a set methods, a fixed framework within which to enclose and retrieve its remembrances'.

Objects as markers of relationships

It might be objected that Halbwachs overstates his case in his theorising of implacement. To what extent do the lived spaces of the group actually serve as the framework for collective remembering? More to the point, precisely *how* do the mundane features of the environment, such as objects and artefacts, 'hold' the memories of the group? Our common-sense experience tells us that objects may serve as useful prompts for acts of remembering – the proverbial knotted handkerchief or the credit card bill left near the telephone, for example. It is more difficult, though, to imagine how things themselves may be 'engraved' with the 'forms' of collective frameworks of memory.

Halbwachs moves between at least three different accounts of how to think of this process. First of all, he posits, in line with the then emerging European phenomenology of the time, that all experience of space is primarily social – that is, space is 'lived' as it is 'perceived'. When we see some object, it is always surrounded by a penumbra of meanings and relationships. Our recognition of an object as such is a matter of experiencing the object in the context of these relationships – a table as something at which a meal might be taken, a cup as something that might be filled with water, tea or wine, for example. It is, of course, possible to 'divest objects of the many relationships that intrude into our thought' (1980: 141), but to do so does not mean that we see the object 'as it really is'. Rather, we adopt the particular 'attitude of another group, perhaps that of physicists' (1980: 141). However, this latter experience of the object is no more real than that of any other group, merely differentially structured.

Next, Halbwachs turns to a Durkheimian reading of objects. As 'things are part of society', it makes sense to consider the way in which they act as symbols for particular sets of values. For example, 'furniture, ornaments, pictures, utensils and knick-knacks "circulate" within the group: they are the topic of evaluations and comparisons, provide insights into new directions of fashion and taste, and recall for us older customs and social distinctions' (1980: 129). Objects, then, are vehicles for the negotiation of social values (the classic modern rendering of this argument is to be found in Pierre Bourdieu's work on 'taste' – see Bourdieu, 1986). A piece of furniture or clothing becomes a symbolic token that is recognisable as such to all group members who are 'in the know'. In this way, objects carry with them a set of associations that resource remembering. The classic instance here would be the kind of nostalgic remembrances that are evoked by encountering objects (say, sweets, toys or clothes) from childhood or adolescence.

It is the final account, however – found in fourth chapter of *The Collective Memory* – that is most suggestive. It occurs during a discussion of 'economic space'. The particular problem for Halbwachs here is how financial value can be attributed to an object by a collective when there 'is no relationship between an object's physical appearance and its price' (1980: 146).

Now, in order for a price to be assigned, it is necessary for a common memory of previous prices and the fluctuations to be established, to which both buyer and seller may refer. This memory of previous prices is index-ically linked to the particular places where it is worked out – typically, shops and markets, but also the whole chain of sites where the goods are grown or manufactured, processed and packaged and, furthermore, in the financial centres where companies themselves are valued and markets regulated (in whatever fashion). There are, then, established social prac-tices grounded in particular spatial locations that 'take charge' of economic memory, with merchants occupying the most visible position (1980: 148):

> Merchants, then, teach and remind their customers of current prices. Buyers as such par-ticipate in the life and memory of the economic group only on entering merchant social circles or when calling to mind previous contacts.

How do merchants achieve this? Halbwachs (1980: 149) notes that the merchant's shopfront acts 'like a screen that prevents the customer's peer-ing into those areas where prices are formulated'. Prices may fluctuate considerably within the length of the infrastructure where they are fixed (think of the way crude oil prices feed forwards in forecourt petrol station prices). However, in contrast to this movement, the merchant is 'spatially immobilised'. This is because he or she is required to stand and wait for the customer. This spatial immobility suggests to the customer that prices themselves are similarly stable. However, Halbwachs (1980: 150) notes, 'not only the merchant but at the same time the merchandise awaits customers'. In order to sell a good, it must be, in most cases, on hand, on display and available for immediate purchase. Now, as the goods must stay in one place, before the watchful eye of the customer, it is necessary for the seller to maintain a stable price (1980: 150):

> In effect, because the merchandise waits – that is, it stays in the same place – the merchant is forced to wait – that is, stick by a fixed price (at least for the duration of a single sale). The customer is actually encouraged to make a purchase on the basis of this condition, because he [sic] gets the impression of paying for the object at its own price, as if the price resulted from the very nature of the object, rather than at the price determined by a complex play of continually changing evaluations.

The intransigence of the object that is being sold – the fact that it rests immobile between buyer and seller – acts to slow down the erratic process of fixing prices. That is, the whole social practice of remembering and setting prices is captured and stabilised (even if only provisionally) by the object. If the problem is how the memory of the buyer and the memory of the merchant – as the representative of an entire commercial infrastructure – are coordinated, then the solution arises when both parties are forced to organise their own memories around the intransigence of the object by which they are forced to wait. It is this object that effectively mediates between the parties and reflects their own experiences of prices back to them 'as if' they originated from the object itself.

We can extend this argument beyond a consideration of price. Objects act not merely as symbolic tokens on which are projected the desires and concerns of groups, but also as mediators of relationships between people. They are markers of social relationships. By this we mean that objects serve as the means of coordinating and stabilising social practices and the remembering activities that are threaded through them. The fluidity of social relationships, then, 'borrows' something of the solidity and stability of the object.

When Halbwachs talks of collective memory being 'localised' in place, what he is advocating is not simply that there is a relationship between a sense of place and the contents of memory, but something altogether more robust. Collective memory is only possible when social relationships are slowed down and crystallised around objects. We will return to this highly suggestive idea of objects as mediators at length in later chapters.

Displacement, disposal and forgetting

Halbwachs' discussion of the inbuiltness of social memory in objects and place has an obvious flip side: what happens when those objects (or even place itself) is destroyed? The answer is, 'displacement' – the destruction of the material supports of collective frameworks – and it occupies a central position in Halbwachs' thought. He (1980: 134) argues that the collective memory can survive such displacement by virtue of active resistance:

> Urban changes – the demolition of a home for example – inevitably affects the habits of a few people, perplexing and troubling them. The blind man gropes for his favourite spot to await passers-by, while the stroller misses the avenue of trees where he went for a fresh breath of air and is saddened by the loss of this picturesque setting. Any inhabitant … who has many remembrances fastened to these images now obliterated forever, feels a whole part of himself [sic] dying with these things … In contrast, a group … resists with all the force of its traditions, which have effect. It searches out and partially succeeds in recovering its former equilibrium amid novel circumstances. It endeavours to hold firm or reshape itself in a district or on a street that is no longer ready-made for it but was once its own.

The collective responds to displacement with more than a 'mere display of its unhappiness'. It sets itself the task of remoulding the space around it, pressing the group form on the 'novel circumstances'. A new housing development, for example, will be rapidly reimplaced by groups, who will mark the redeveloped space in such a way as to make visible once more the boundaries between the groups. Halbwachs suggests that reimplacement will always occur so long as the group remains within roughly the same spatial location. This is because the activities performed by the group 'are driven by an impulse acquired in the past' (1980: 135) that is not easily eradicated. Thus, businesses, such as inns or hotels, re-emerge in a different form on the same location. The group carries on its activities as though driven by a form of 'collective automatism' that refuses to adapt to surrounding changes.

The implication would appear to be that collective frameworks are monolithic in character, vast storehouses of memory that are entirely inflexibly and unwilling to adapt in any way whatsoever, but this is not the case. How could such a structure survive were it simply to keep on unreflectively piling up the past on the present, rather like a 'crowded cemetery where room must constantly be made for new tombstones' (1980: 52)?

Displacement is, for Halbwachs, a visible sign of a more dynamic process of active selection and disposal at work within collective frameworks. All frameworks are selective, in as much as they draw boundaries that demarcate which elements – ideas and images – are to be retained, but this selectivity is also continuously applied to the framework itself. The past is not merely stockpiled, it is subject to continuous review so that existing elements are disposed of at the same moment that new elements are incorporated. For example, Halbwachs (1992: 73) comments on the ancient Greek practice of naming grandsons after grandfathers: 'What is expressed here is the fact that limits are imposed on the interest and attention which gives names to living members whilst eliminating in thought and memory the dead from whom the names are taken'. For Halbwachs, proper names are not simply representational tokens, but, rather, devices for ordering and classifying images and ideas. Thus, the Greek practice is a way of managing the burden of the past by automatically disposing of memory as it ensures that the tools by means of which they might persist are constantly put to new use. Halbwachs (1992: 77) notes that the same process occurs in 'modern' bourgeois societies where marriage partners must deal with the problem of forming a new collective memory system from two potentially incompatible sets of family memories:

> The new family turns from the start toward the future. It senses behind itself kind of moral void: for if each of the spouses were to continue to wallow in their former family memories, they could not think of them in common, since spouses have different memories. To avoid inevitable conflict which cannot be adjudicated through norms accepted by both, they tacitly agree the past is to be treated as if it were abolished.

Here, Halbwachs finds a general model: if old collectivities require a mechanism to deal with the mountainous past that accrues behind them, new collectivities, when they find themselves caught between differing prior frameworks, equally require the same technique of active forgetting in order to break with what has gone before. The very survival of any collectivity, then, seems to turn on their ability to actively forget (1992: 74): 'society is like the woman from Ephesus who hangs the dead in order to save the living'.

Forgetting is not opposed to remembering for Halbwachs, but, rather, its precondition. Forgetting is an active process of disposal that is rigorously applied within the collective framework and subtends collective remembering. We might even go so far as to say that it is the central issue in Halbwachs thought. For example, when Halbwachs describes how groups survive literal displacement (1980: 130), he argues that so long as the image of some place previously occupied by the group remains, then the group itself is able to remain 'united'. Now, this projection of the group on to the past requires a simultaneous disposal of the present. The group must effectively disembed or 'forget' current circumstances in order to shore up the reality of the past. This suggests, as in the case of the gospel stories, that the place being remembered may take on a mythical status that is at odds with the significance that was attributed to the site at the time by the group concerned.

In this way, Halbwachs is able to present collective frameworks as dynamic and intersecting structures. A framework may reach back into the past and 'lock on' to a previous framework, on which it selectively grafts its own values and concerns. This is often how new frameworks emerge, by latching on to the 'landmark' memories and images of established frameworks (1992: 125): 'we might say that new ideas become salient only after having for a long time behaved as if they were old ones'.

The picture Halbwachs sketches is of frameworks woven into one another in a network that extends both spatially and temporally. Within this network, some key images and meanings pass between and are adapted by different frameworks, while others are gradually being disposed of and erased from the collective memory. Remembering is, then, the manner in which the framework is able to extend itself within this network, to expand and distribute the elements it encompasses in order to achieve the effect of an 'expanded impersonal duration' for members. Forgetting – the corresponding dynamic – is the way in which the framework simultaneously contracts within the network, ramifies and consolidates its elements and then redraws the boundaries and intersections with neighbouring networks.

Selfhood as multiplicity

The final aspect of Halbwachs' work on memory that we will discuss is his account of selfhood. As we have mentioned before, it is common to evaluate Halbwachs' contribution to the study of social memory as a species of sociological determinism. However, once we have understood the dynamic and intersecting nature of collective frameworks, we may see that individual acts of remembering cannot be understood as simple channels through which the group exercises its commemorative powers as, in modern societies at least, a given individual commonly finds him or herself passing between frameworks. Indeed, for Halbwachs, this continuous passage of individuals is a necessary feature of how frameworks are organised in relation to one another. The circulation of members between groups allows frameworks to communicate with and enrich one another. The person who participates in numerous frameworks will (1992: 75):

> look for analogies, current notions, and the whole bundle of ideas prevalent in their period outside their group but displayed around it. It is in this way that history does not limit itself to reproducing a tale told by people contemporary with events of the past, but rather refashions it from period to period ... to adapt it to the mental habits and the type of representation of the past common among contemporaries.

In passing between frameworks, the member imports novel ideas – the 'mental habits' of other groups. This is even – or perhaps especially – the case with social figures that Halbwachs (1992: 134) refers to as 'men without a past'. Such figures have long fascinated sociologists (see Simmel's 1908/1997 classic work on 'the stranger' and Bauman's 1998 discussion of 'the parvenu'). The value of this character, for Halbwachs, is that such a person acts as a kind of blank canvas on which the group may project and reflect on its own concerns. However, such 'strangeness' is not merely confined to 'men without a past'. It is, Halbwachs argues, a common experience for us all. It typically occurs at those moments when we experience a distance between two or more groups to which we belong. For example, moments when we feel distanced from the others with whom we are sharing some experience, lost in thoughts and concerns that they are 'neither aware of nor interested in' (1980: 42). We are tempted to consider that this makes for an intensely personal, highly individual experience, but, for Halbwachs, what actually occurs is better understood as an especially complex social experience. We are caught between the collective frameworks of two groups – the one in which we are currently participating, and another in which the concerns that so preoccupy us were originally forged.

This, then, is a restatement of Halbwachs' claim that our most personal and supposedly private experiences are actually entirely social and collective in character. However, here, Halbwachs expands this claim into a model of selfhood. We are never outside of collective life – being alone, being with others, passing between groups, are all modes of sociality. We are then always 'multiple', our selfhood consisting of a heterogeneous mixture of social elements (1980: 23): 'in reality we are never alone. Other men [sic] need not be physically present, since we carry with us and in us a number of distinct persons'. It is this fundamental multiplicity of self that is expounded in the most routinely cited and infamous passage of *The Collective Memory* (1980: 44; see, for example, Wertsch, 2002: 22):

> Often we deem ourselves the originators of thoughts and ideas, feelings and passions, actually inspired by the group. Our agreement with those about us is so complete that we vibrate in unison, ignorant of the real source of the vibrations.

The language of this passage is, admittedly, difficult to follow. The term 'vibration' is sometimes used in a similar way in Bergson's work, where it denotes the manner in which the appearance of stability can mask the reality of movement and change. For instance, Bergson uses the image of a 'chrysalis', which appears to be solid but nevertheless 'vibrates' with the inner transformation of the larvae (1908/1991: 204). Halbwachs seems to be using the word vibration in a similar way here. We feel that our unique and unchanging character structures our personal experiences, our thoughts and passions, whereas, in fact, they emerge by virtue of the varying currents of the social milieu in which we dwell and that rise up within us. Moreover, we mistakenly interpret our discovery that other people think in the same way as we do as further confirmation of the truth of our subjective experience (1980: 44–5):

> How often do we present, as deeply held convictions, thoughts borrowed from a news-paper, book or conversation? They respond so well to our way of seeing things that we are surprised to discover that their author is someone other than ourself. 'That's just what I think about that!' We are unaware that we are but an echo … How many people are critical enough to discern what they owe to others in their thinking and acknowledge to themselves how small their own contribution is?

We fail to see that this miraculous agreement comes about because of our common location in a collective framework that is not of our own making. We agree because we are standing in the same place, so to speak, and have available to us the same stock of cultural resources, so we 'echo' the same material. The point is that, so long as we consider the group to be relatively 'enclosed' on itself, this echoing effect, where each reflects back the same ideas and concerns, will pass unnoticed as we will mistake the echo for intrinsic similarity. We focus only on the chrysalis and overlook the character of the movement. Halbwachs' use of the metaphor of 'vibration' neatly captures this sense of people transmitting a signal to one another at precisely the same pitch and intensity.

The 'overlooking' of movement is central to personal identity. We feel ourselves to be unique, coherent, relatively unchanging beings and, in so doing, forget the essential multiplicity that is derived from the set of loca-tions we occupy across numerous collective frameworks. The more we immerse ourselves in one given framework, the easier this 'forgetting' becomes. However, it is in the process of recollection that 'strangeness' properly returns. That is, the gap between our sense of speaking or acting in a self-consistent manner and the awareness of the heterogeneous social currents that make us what we are. This concept of a 'gap' in our experience of identity is crucial for a social psychology of remembering and forget-ting (see also Bartlett, 1958), but, unfortunately, Halbwachs fails to expand further on it. In order to progress further, we will have to turn, in later chapters, towards Bergson, with his crucial distinction between the 'virtual' and 'actual' aspects of living.

Summary

Despite his reputation as a theorist of how *groups* remember, Halbwachs' real contribution to the study of social memory is his comprehensive account of the structure of the collective frameworks in which recollection is situated.

Halbwachs describes how shared meanings and images create a common 'perspective' within which efforts to recall the past can be located and directed. In our personal acts of remembering, we 'follow the ramifications' of the 'thoughts of others'. Particularly noteworthy is Halbwachs' treatment of language outside of a representational framework. Language – especially the use of proper nouns – is a form of social action that reconstructs past events by invoking the categories and relationships held in a given collective framework. The language of remembering is, then, as discursive psychologists would put it, both 'constructive' and 'action-orientated' (see, for example, Edwards and Potter, 1992). In Chapter 5 we will spell out precisely what it meant by this characterisation of language.

The notion of a 'collective framework' by itself helps us to clarify what Bartlett describes as an 'organised setting' – namely as a structured set of meanings that stands in advance of a given act or remembering. However, Halbwachs adds an additional 'physiognomic' dimension. Frameworks become etched into the spatial locations occupied by communities in such a way that their particular perspective on the past comes to appear timeless – a 'larger and impersonal duration' that marks the thought of individual members. Space becomes 'territorialised' by collective memory. We then see that remembering is profoundly shaped by the mutually responsive relationship between social groups and the places they inhabit. The greater the range of memberships held by an individual, the more complicated the nature of personal memory becomes. For Halbwachs, the complexity of personal memory is to be understood in terms of the spatial complexity of participation in multiple collective frameworks.

A number of threads remain hanging. It is not altogether clear how it is that people 'live out' this 'larger and impersonal duration' and how it becomes modulated as a personal experience of time passing. Nor is it apparent how the 'gap' between a sense of oneself as a unique individual, endowed with a personal and subjective perspective on past events, is managed in relation to an awareness of the interdependency of our experience and that of a diverse range of others. Put another way, much as Halbwachs helps us to grasp the nature of schemas as organised settings, he does not allow us to adequately describe how such settings grant forms of experience. In order to do this, we must pass from spatial complexity to temporal complexity – back from Halbwachs to his former mentor Bergson.

FOUR
Virtualising experience: Henri Bergson on memory

Henri Bergson (1859–1941) was arguably the most eminent French philosopher of the late nineteenth and early twentieth century. The status of his posthumous recognition is nothing like the level he received during his lifetime. Both William James and John Dewey saw their respective versions of pragmatism as being in dialogue with Bergson, whom they regarded as having ushered in a 'new era' in European philosophy.

In 1927, Bergson – who had previously been publicly hailed as both 'the greatest thinker in the world' and 'the most dangerous man in the world' (see Mullarkey, 1999b) – was awarded the Nobel Prize for Literature. His reputation as a major figure in the history of Continental philosophy has been sealed by his influence on the thought of Maurice Merleau-Ponty, Emmanuel Levinas and Gilles Deleuze. In addition, the relevance of his work to theories of psychological development (for example in the theoretical positions of Piaget, Vygotsky and Wallon), particularly his ideas on time and becoming, have been subject to recent reassessment and recognition (Valsiner, 1994).

Why, then – at least until comparatively recently – has Bergson's reputation languished in intellectual circles?

One possible reason is the widespread misunderstanding of the reach and ambition of 'Bergsonism'. A central event in this regard was the publication by Bergson in 1922 of *Duration and Simultaneity*. This is a complex and often highly technical book that opposes what Bergson calls a 'properly philosophical' understanding of time, grounded in human experience, to the way in which time is theorised within modern physics – in particular, Einstein's special theory of relativity. Bergson's professed aim was to open up a dialogue between metaphysics and science. However, that dialogue was curtailed during a meeting the same year with Einstein, who dismissed the possibility of asserting a metaphysical bridge between the multiple times of relativity theory and the subjective time of individual consciousness.

Bergson was subsequently accused of attempting to substitute metaphysical speculation for hard scientific enquiry (a claim repeated in the recent dispute between physicists and social scientists known as the 'science wars' – see Sokal & Bricmont, 1999; Gross & Levitt, 1997; and Callon, 1999; Latour, 1999; Parsons, Long & Sofka, 2003 for two opposing arguments). It has been hypothesised that Bergson's reputation never fully recovered after this (Durie, 1999).

Another reason is the apparent anachronism and sheer peculiarity of the methods and arguments at the heart of Bergson's philosophy. For example, Bergson's first book – *Time and Free Will* (1913/2001) – offers an account of consciousness where mental states cannot be clearly distinguished from one another, thus rendering psychological analysis, as it usually understood, completely impossible. In *Matter and Memory* (1908/1991), Bergson argues for what he calls a 'frankly dualistic' model of the person that refuses to engage in either materialist or idealist reduction, yet ultimately has nothing to do with Cartesian dualism. In later works, such as *The Creative Mind* (1946/1992), Bergson argues for 'intuition' as the most appropriate method of producing adequate philosophical knowledge – an aim that is apparently not contradicted by his claim in *Creative Evolution* (1911/1998: xiii) that a 'theory of knowledge and a theory of life seem to us inseparable'. Small wonder, then, that Bergson's work has failed to sustain an enthusiastic audience outside his native country.

This lamentable situation has changed significantly in recent years, however, with the publication and translation of a number of sophisticated and sympathetic re-evaluations of Bergson (see Ansell Pearson, 2002; Billig, in press; Deleuze, 1966/1991; Lawlor, 2003; Moore, 1996; Mullarkey, 1999a, 1999b). The common consensus among these authors is that, rather than being consigned as an historical relic, Bergson is very much our contemporary in terms of his concerns. For example, Ansell Pearson outlines how Bergson's notion of the 'virtual' offers a powerful tool for thinking about the production of difference in domains as diverse as biology and psychology. Mullarkey teases out the implications of Bergsonism for the renewed engagement of unashamedly metaphysical thinking with scientific rationality at a time when profound questions about the demarcation of claims to expertise and authority dominate contemporary culture. For instance, in the debates concerning 'false' and 'recovered' memory, we may ask who should properly legislate on the nature of remembering – experimental psychologists or therapists, 'victims' of false claims or 'survivors' with recovered memories?

Our own reading of Bergson follows the path opened up by these texts. In this chapter, we will show that Bergson's conception of memory as the dynamic link between action and our experience of time is able to bring us close to the forms of experience that Halbwachs intimates. Moreover, we outline several of Bergson's critiques of psychological analysis and demonstrate that the power of these critiques and their potential implications for the study of psychological processes has increased rather than diminished with the growth of techniques such as neural imaging. Finally, we will describe Bergson's key analytical opposition between the 'virtual' and the 'actual', which will prove critical to our approach to the social psychology of experience and memory.

Reality as process

Bergson is a process philosopher. Understanding the opposition between process philosophy – as exemplified in the work of Bergson, Alfred North Whitehead and William James – and the mainstream tradition of Western philosophical thought – which is currently exemplified by Anglo-American analytic philosophy – is critical to appreciating the innovative character of Bergson's work.

Traditionally, Western philosophy has been concerned with 'substance' – that is, with conceptualising the basic 'stuff' that makes up reality and theorising how that 'stuff' gives rise to the diversity of 'things' we perceive in the world, including 'us' as things capable of perceiving. In this scheme, explaining the nature of things, their essential qualities and so on is more important than exploring the relationships between things or the transformations within things.

This means that much of what we experience in the world around us – activities such as laughing and joking, relationships between people, events such as becoming a parent or losing a job – are seen as secondary to and explained by an account of the real, essential nature of the persons involved. We might, then, characterise Western thought and the kind of psychology it gives rise to as classically concerned with things rather than actions and events or, put more simply, with nouns instead of verbs.

Now, in relation to the psychology of memory, we may see that this classical approach arrives at an understanding of remembering in terms of the structures or systems that underpin the act of recollection. For example, Lashley's (1950) famous use of the notion that memory traces – 'engrams' – are encoded across multiple brain regions makes neural structure the real, essential substance that gives rise, secondarily, to the human ability to remember.

To approach memory in this fashion is to be committed to a search for the number, location and precise nature of these differing neural systems (see, for instance, Hebb, 1949, Tulving, 1983) – but there is an alternative.

This consists of treating the act of remembering as a process, which, once adequately described as such, can then eventually be fitted on to the 'substance' of the brain. Very broadly, this is what cognitive psychologists such as Baddeley (1986), Conway (1990) and Schank, 1982 have all tried to do in their various theoretical mappings of the interacting set of processes that make up human 'cognitive architecture'.

However, from the perspective of process philosophy, the sorts of things cognitive psychologists typically study are not really 'processes' at all. Rather than study process in itself, the tendency remains to subordinate process to its supposed content, ending up back with a 'substance' view of the world (exceptions being Semon's 1923 'mnemic psychology'; Kolers' 1972 critique of the 'trace hypothesis' and Lansdale's 2005 'acropetal memory'). For example, Martin Conway's influential model of 'autobiographical memory' (see Conway & Pleydell-Pearce, 2000) depicts recollection as involving a dynamic set of 'executive processes' and a collection of ongoing goals and values that create a continuity in our self-identity (known as the 'working self'). Conway describes how remembering involves the joint operation of these processes on a knowledge base that stores mental representations regarding experienced events ('episodic memory') and self-knowledge ('autobiographical knowledge') in order to recollect distinct autobiographical memories. Now, while this model certainly emphasises process, the form these processes take is seen as the joining together of relatively stable and enduring representations – that is, process is about creating links between existing mental 'things'.

For a process philosopher, this turning back to the language of substance is unacceptable and, ultimately, creates more problems than it solves, raising as it does questions such as 'Where are these mental things stored?', 'What is their true nature?', 'How do they get "in" the mind?' Instead, the challenge is to understand process in and for itself. On this account, what we usually consider to be 'things' are treated as complex bundles of processes viewed from a particular perspective. In the case of memory, this would mean denying that there is any mental content – be it a representation or a knowledge base – out of which a 'memory' is assembled. Furthermore, as Bergson himself argues, that one would search in vain for the location where such memories might be handled because memories themselves are not 'things' and, as such, are not spatially located anywhere. Such an approach clearly poses severe challenges not only to the psychology of memory but also to our commonsensical notions of remembering!

In order to make some sense of this approach, we must start by clarifying what 'reality' actually is for process philosophy. One of the most ancient distinctions in Western philosophy is between 'being' and 'becoming'.

Being is the name typically given to those essential qualities of a thing that do not change, those aspects that endure despite all temporary changes in appearance. Reality can then be defined by enquiry into the particular kind of 'being' that a given entity has or expresses (this is what is usually called 'ontology').

Becoming is, then, not so much a contrast term, as an entirely different way of considering reality. It refers to a view of the world as being in continuous motion. A river, for example, is defined not by some intrinsic quality, such as the chemical composition of water, but by the particular way in which it flows and changes (this is the grounds for Heraclitus' famous dictum that 'one cannot step in the same river twice'). For process philosophers, all 'things' are actually part of a process of becoming – that is, changing, moving and transforming – so what is real is change itself.

This last is the view of reality to which Bergson subscribes. He describes the matter out of which our worlds are formed as an 'undivided flux' or a 'fluid continuity of the real'. Here, there is no other reality than that of a continuous, ongoing flow of change (1998: 302): 'what is real is the continual change of form: form is only a snapshot view of transition'. Those forms that we perceive are akin to 'snapshots' or provisional viewpoints on the 'open whole' of a ceaselessly changing world. Although fundamentally we exist in a 'fluid continuity of the real', we are, nevertheless, able to actively 'cut out' or 'isolate' discrete forms within that flux. The crucial point for Bergson is that these forms are products or outcomes relative to our particular perspectives – they are not reality itself (1998: 300–2):

> From our first glance at the world, before we even make our *bodies* in it, we distinguish *qualities*. Colour succeeds colour, sound to sound, resistance to resistance, etc. Each of these qualities, taken separately, is a state that seems to persist as such, immovable until another replaces it. Yet each of these qualities resolves itself, on analysis, into an enormous number of elementary movements. Whether we see in it vibrations or whether we represent it in any other way, one fact is certain, it is that every quality is change. In vain, moreover shall we seek beneath change the thing which changes: it is always provisionally, and in order to satisfy our imagination, that we attach movement to a mobile ... In short, the qualities of matter are so many stable views that we take of its instability.

What seems real to us are qualities – sounds, colours, the feel and weight of objects – but these are themselves condensations or snapshots produced by our *intellect* and reflect our concerns ('satisfy our imagination'). For example, colour is not a fundamental property of things, but, rather, an effect of the complex reflection of light waves. If this is so, Bergson argues, we would be mistaken to imagine that it is possible to arrive at a once-and-for-all definition of the essential qualities of something, because those qualities are entirely relative to our current viewpoint. Also, if we properly consider what this relativity implies, we must conclude that, rather than there being 'things which change', properly speaking, there is 'change provisionally grasped as a thing'. For instance, our perception of some object as 'unchanging' is entirely relative to the time that we are able to spend gazing at it. Were we able to stare for several millennia, subtle processes or ageing and transformation would doubtless become visible to us. Equally, if our perceptions were capable of penetrating into the subatomic structure of the thing, rapid processes of motion and vibration would appear that are otherwise entirely indiscernible.

The initial challenge of Bergsonism, then, is to think of reality as a process of change that does not require 'things' or 'substance' for its explanation. Indeed, it may well be inappropriate to think of reality as something that needs explanation, as we will see later on. In order to grasp the relationship we as living beings have with this 'fluid continuity of the real', it is necessary to examine the viewpoints we take on reality and, in particular, the role that time plays in their constitution. It is in this context that Bergson's major concept of time as 'duration' ought to be understood.

The time of living: duration

Consider for a moment the character of a world that is subject to perpetual change. It would be impossible to detect any pattern, any rhythm to this change. Events would occur in a seemingly random yet fleeting fashion. In fact, it would be impossible to say where one event ended and the next began as there would be neither continuity nor grounds for marking an apparent difference.

In order to restore some sense of succession, it is necessary to hypothesise a conscious observer who is able to preserve the past in such a way that it can be synthesised with the present moment. The prolonging of the past into the present, and the forms of experience that are thereby granted, is what Bergson calls 'duration'. In his first work, *Time and Free Will* (1913/2001: 100), Bergson defines duration in the following way:

> Pure duration is the form which the succession of our conscious states assumes when our ego lets itself *live*, when it refrains from separating its present state from its former states. For this purpose it need not be entirely absorbed in the passing sensation or idea; for then, on the contrary, it would no longer *endure*. Nor need it forget its former states: it is enough that in recalling these states, it does not set them alongside its actual state as one point alongside another, but forms both the past and the present states into an organic whole, as happens when we recall the notes of a tune, melting, so to speak, into one another.

Duration is the experience of time passing. It involves a succession of conscious states that enables the conscious being to 'break' their absorption in the present moment (in *Creative Evolution*, Bergson refers to the domination of consciousness by immediate, present sensation as a matter of *instinct*; it is by virtue of the relative complexity of our neural organisation that humans are able to pass beyond a purely instinctive relationship to the world). However, the succession of conscious states is not a simple matter of one state following another, such that each is 'set alongside' the current. If this were so, then it would be necessary to engage in a further explanation of how these separate states became joined together into continuous experience. Rather, consciousness is constituted as an 'organic whole', where states blend into one another (1913/2001: 111): 'we are thus compelled to admit that we have here to do with a synthesis which is, so to speak, qualitative, a gradual organisation of our successive sensations, a unity resembling that of a phrase in a melody.'

The musical metaphor is instructive. In listening to an unfolding melody, we hear the notes 'melt' into one another, forming an indivisible whole. This is not to say that the melody cannot be divided – clearly it can be arranged as a set of notations on a score or played one note at a time. Bergson's point is that in these latter cases we do not have the same experience. To be 'in the music' as it is played is completely different from reading the score or hearing the individual notes. Similarly, our conscious experience of time passing, where moments prolong into one another, is entirely different to the retrospective attempt to divide those moments apart and consider them individually. Bergson then insists that duration, as we live it, be considered as an indivisible, continuous flow of conscious states. Indeed, properly speaking, it may not even be possible to consider psychological life as having 'states' as such. As he notes in *Duration and Simultaneity* (1999: 30):

> There is no doubt but that for us time is at first identical with the continuity of our inner life. What is this continuity? That of a flow or passage, but a self-sufficient flow or passage, the flow not implying a thing that flows, and the passing not presupposing states through which we pass; the thing and the state are only artificially chosen snapshots of the transition, all that is naturally experienced is duration itself.

This is a classic statement of a process philosophy approach to consciousness. The ongoing flow of conscious existence is considered without invoking either states or a 'thing that flows' as explanatory principles. 'States' and 'things' are treated instead as products or outcomes arrived at by artificially cutting into the flow. Such products enable the person to gain purchase on his or her own duration – they are in no sense 'natural'. If this all sounds peculiar, then it is because, Bergson (1913/2001: 13) claims, 'our language is ill suited to the subtleties of psychological analysis'. We are not well equipped to speak of duration – our language favouring substantives over relationships, nouns over prepositions. We will discuss the consequences of this in more detail in the empirical chapters.

A language that is structured in this way operates primarily as a tool for enabling speakers to organise the world around them. For Bergson (1992: 80), the original function of human language is to 'establish a communication with a view to cooperation. Language transmits orders or warnings. It prescribes or describes'. Our utterances, then, point out aspects of the world and instruct others in relation to them ('do this', 'watch out', 'look at that'). This view of language as a tool always used 'with a view to action' (1946/1992: 80) is to be contrasted with notions of language as simply a neutral medium for representing our experience or, alternatively, as a creative, poetic means of elaborating experience. Now, while Bergson certainly has some sympathy with the latter 'poetic' approach to language, he nevertheless emphasises a view of speech as 'communicative action'. In this sense at least, Bergson is close to both Halbwach's 'non-representational' treatment of proper nouns and the more general approach to language found in discursive psychology (for example, in Edwards, 1997; Edwards & Potter, 1992; Middleton, 2002) and social constructionist psychology (such as Curt, 1994; Gergen, 1985, 1999; Shotter, 1993).

That said, Bergson's true interest in language is with the manner in which it reflects a general human tendency to think of the world as an empty, homogeneous medium in which entities occupy unique spatial positions – that is, no two things can be in exactly the same place. It makes sense to us to consider differences in terms of spatial juxtaposition, to think of the qualities of objects as distinct and measurable properties. We can then divide the world up along whatever lines seem to offer the most practical use to us, each division marking 'calls made by the thing to a human activity' (1992: 80). This even applies to 'inner' psychological qualities, such as emotions, which we consider to be comparable in terms of their measurable 'intensity' and 'strength'. In *Time and Free Will*, Bergson argues that, in order to measure some psychological quality, it is typically considered necessary to think of it as either made up from distinct components, which might be isolated and set alongside one another, or as occupying some particular spatial location. In either case, this means treating quality in spatial terms that are borrowed from our practical experience. Because we can divide up the world into parts, we imagine that it is possible to do the same to our own psychological constitution. In short, our *intellect* and the language in which it is expressed have an entirely practical bent that is modelled on the use we make of objects (1998: ix): 'our logic is, pre-eminently, the logic of solids'. This stands in sharp contrast to duration – our experience of the 'fluid' continuity of time passing.

Bergson then identifies a central tension between two forms of human experience – our experience of time and our experience of space. On the one hand, we have a 'natural' immersion in a 'self-sufficient' passage of unfolding time, where our inner life is a continuous flow of heterogeneous change. On the other, our intellect leads us towards a practical engagement with space, understood as a homogeneous medium that can be divided ad infinitum in accord with our needs. The key to understanding Bergson's work on memory is to grasp the full implications of this tension for psychological life.

Halbwachs (1980: 93–4) is quite right when he characterises Bergson as insisting that we must 'discard and erase whatever reminds us of space and external objects' in order to gain purchase on the fluid continuity of duration. At a fundamental level, our experience of 'pure' duration must not be confused with our experience of 'pure' space. However, at the practical level, inevitably for us, these two experiences do become intertwined (and it is this intertwining that Halbwachs appears to ignore).

In *Time and Free Will,* Bergson refers to the commingling of these two forms of experience as 'endosmosis'. This is an 'exchange' where 'real duration' is brought 'into relation with a state of the external world', giving rise to a 'symbolical representation' of time (2001: 110). Put crudely, something of our experience of time passes into our experience of space and vice versa. The net effect is to breathe life into our otherwise inert conception of space and allow for divisions to be made in the otherwise continuous passage of time. The crucial point Bergson makes is that we simply will not adequately understand this mixing of experience, this commingling, unless we have first understood the nature of 'pure duration' and 'pure space' – that is, matter. In order, then, to approach memory, we must first set it in the context of this fundamental division.

Pure perception

In the introduction to his major study of remembering, *Matter and Memory*, Bergson calls his approach 'frankly dualistic' (1991: 9). As we have just seen, the basis for this claim is Bergson's insistence that pure time must on no account be confused with pure space. However, in the same way that *Time and Free Will* culminates in an account of the commingling of these two forms of experience, so *Matter and Memory* also arrives at an account of how time and space are conjoined in psychological life. Nevertheless, Bergson begins by making a distinction between what he calls 'pure perception' and 'pure memory'. We will discuss each in turn.

Perception occupies a very special place in epistemology – that is, formal accounts of knowledge and knowing. It occurs at the point of contact between person and world. It is in perception – seeing, hearing, touching and so on – that a 'sensuous engagement' between the human organism and its environment becomes possible. The classic question then posed to perception is the terms on which this occurs. Do we engage directly with the world? That is, do we see things as they really are or does our prior knowledge and experiences instead mediate our engagement? What we see would then be structured in advance by our expectations. The first position is typically referred to as 'realism', while the latter is a version of 'idealism'.

Realist epistemologies assume that, in principle, perception is capable of allowing humans access to 'things in themselves'. We may then aspire to know the world objectively 'as it really is'. The kind of psychology that follows from this position is best exemplified by J. J. Gibson's (1966, 1979) 'direct realism'. For Gibson, perception involves the unmediated picking up of information that is directly afforded by the environment. Idealist epistemologies counsel instead that perception is fundamentally dependent on our prior understanding of the world – that is, perception is subjective. For example, in Kantian idealism, all perception is relative to the basic a priori categories of understanding that define us as human. We can never gain access to 'things in themselves', only to those aspects of things that present themselves under the guise of these categories. The standard model of perception (and, hence, remembering) in cognitivist psychology is, then, a theoretical elaboration of the subjective implications of Kantian idealism.

The challenge Bergson offers to psychology is his rejection of both idealism and realism. For Bergson, both these species of epistemology arrive at the same kind of problem – how to explain the gap between our understanding and the world itself. Idealism, for instance, is forced to argue that it is our own 'belief' that sustains our perception of apparent order among things as we are denied access to things as they 'really are'. Realism, by contrast, ends up with the near impossible task of explaining how individual representations are formed as these can only appear 'miraculously' if perception is entirely driven by the character of the environment (Bergson, 1991: 22–8).

The solution Bergson proposes is deceptively simple. What we see is neither things as they really are nor a simple reflection of our a priori understandings, but merely 'images' (1991: 9–10):

> Matter, in our view, is an aggregate of 'images'. And by 'image' we mean a certain existence which is more than that which the idealist calls a *representation*, but less than that which the realist calls a *thing* – an existence placed halfway between the 'thing' and the 'representation'. This conception of matter is simply that of common sense.

For most of us, when we open our eyes what we see is a unified, continuous panorama of images, made up from a complex array of colours. These images are precisely what they appear to be. They are not fantasies that we produce, which appear and disappear on our whim. However, they do have a kind of hidden depth – we are aware that what we are seeing is but a surface, the 'crust'. At the same time, images are not what we would usually call 'representations' – that is, copies or models of the 'things themselves'. Instead, images are extended throughout space – they are experienced as 'out there' in the world. Moreover, as Bergson notes, they are independent of our acts of perceiving (1991: 35): 'it is true that an image may *be* without *being perceived*'.

In spite of this independence, images are not – and cannot be for Bergson – 'real' in the proper sense. Reality is a 'fluid and mobile continuity', an 'undivided flux' consisting of 'innumerable movements' or 'vibrations'. An image is, then, a snapshot or provisional stable view that is artificially cut out of this ongoing flow. Bergson speaks of images as being 'contracted', 'selected', 'discerned', 'isolated' or otherwise 'cut out from' reality by perception. In this way, perception extracts images as so many parts from the fluid whole that is reality itself. This part–whole relationship has a great many implications. It means that, contrary to idealist epistemologies, perception is treated as fundamentally adding nothing to the world (1991: 37):

> There is nothing positive here, nothing added to the image, nothing new. The objects merely abandon something of their real action in order to manifest their virtual influence of the living being upon them. Perception therefore resembles those phenomena of reflexion which result from an impeded refraction; it is like an effect of mirage.

Pure perception is a process of subtraction. Nothing is added – rather, a part is isolated and extracted from the whole. Yet, that part still remains connected to the whole, which is the 'fluid continuity of the real'. Beneath the 'crust' of the cut-out image, the ceaseless movement of 'real action' remains present. This is the source of the chrysalis metaphor we encountered in the last chapter. Bergson argues that any objectivity we might be tempted to attribute to an image – that is, what the image contains 'over and above what it yields up' to perception – consists 'precisely in the immense multiplicity of the movements which it executes, so to speak, within itself as a chrysalis. Motionless on the surface, in its very depth it lives and vibrates' (1991: 204). What we perceive, then, is not this movement in its totality, but, rather, properly speaking, a 'virtual image' that is projected back on to the world.

To understand what Bergson means by 'virtual image' we must follow through the claim that the world, as we perceive it, consists of nothing other than images. If this is so, then our own body is also an image, but a part of it that is only artificially 'cut out' from the real, with which it is otherwise continuous. However there is one important difference. Unlike other images we see, we know our bodies 'from within' and can thus grasp something of the movement within its depth. This means that our bodies occupy a 'privileged position' in relation to other images. What does this privilege consist of? All of the images that we see 'act and react upon one another' in accordance with 'constant laws' that, in principle, render this action calculable and foreseeable (1991: 17). However, the images that act on our bodies do not always produce automatic responses on our part – there is a gap or delay. Bergson describes this as akin to a 'central telephonic exchange'. Actions directed at our bodies are coordinated, sorted and held in a waiting pattern, like so many incoming calls, before being redirected to 'this or that motor mechanism', which is 'chosen and no longer prescribed' (1991: 30).

Now, at first glance, Bergson's description of the body – in particular, neural activity – appears to be rather quaint and unsophisticated and has certainly been superseded by the knowledge provided by modern cognitive neuroscience, towards which he appears to be groping. Indeed, Bergson does describe the body as a complex set of neural mechanisms and, moreover, situates this description in an evolutionary account of the intellect. Our evolved ability to divide up reality, cut out images and grasp them as discontinuous elements in a homogeneous space is partly what allows for the sorting and coordinating of incoming action directed towards us (see *Creative Evolution*, 1998: 151–65). However, there is one crucial caveat. In opposition to cognitive neuroscience, Bergson insists that the image we call the brain is, by itself, incapable of producing representations. The brain is merely a complex 'centre of action'. To argue that it is able to generate newly formed representations on the basis of perception is to have 'conjured up' a 'transformation scene from fairyland' (1991: 39). Moreover, this suggests that the brain is somehow outside of the natural world – that is, it has the frankly miraculous power to contain the entirety of nature within itself in this novel form. As we have seen, this 'container' metaphor is misguided; it is the body that is 'part' of nature, rather than the reverse. For Bergson (1991: 31), perception is not a speculative contemplation of the world, nor the input phase in the process of transforming reality into representation, but is, instead, in its pure form, in the service of action:

> the nervous system is in no sense an apparatus which may serve to fabricate, or even prepare, representations. Its function is to receive stimulation, to provide motor apparatus, and to present the largest possible number of these apparatuses to a given stimulus.

Perception, then, is what occurs in the interval between action and reaction. As this interval expands, the more detailed perception becomes.

This is why Bergson places so much emphasis on vision in human perception. When an immediate reaction is called for, perception is compelled to 'resemble a mere contact' (1991: 32), like a touch. However, vision allows humans to enter into relationships with more 'distant influences', the action of which may be 'deferred'. The field of vision is then a field of possible actions. This is to say that perception gives us the measure of our degrees of freedom to act – it 'expresses the power of action in the living being, the indetermination of the movement or of the action which will follow the receipt of the stimulus' (1991: 64). Ultimately, then, perception is a thoroughly practical matter that secures, for the living being, a foothold in reality in such a way that its many and varied needs can be addressed (1991: 198):

> Our needs are … so many searchlights which, directed upon the continuity of sensible qualities, single out in it distinct bodies. They cannot satisfy themselves except upon the condition that they carve out, within this continuity, a body which is to be their own and then delimit other bodies with which the first can enter into relation, as if with persons. To establish these special relations among portions thus carved out from sensible reality is just what we call *living*.

A 'virtual image' is just that. It is selected aspects of the image grasped in terms of *potential* actions and *possible reactions*. The living being initially 'cuts out' or 'isolates' a distinct body in the continuity of the real in accord with its needs – 'Is this a threat?', 'Is this edible?', 'Could this be a source of pleasure?'. However, this image only gains proper definition when it is related to a field of possible of reactions – 'Can I repel this?', 'Can I eat this now?', 'Could I desire this?'. Put more simply, 'the objects which surround my body reflect its possible action upon them' (1991: 21). We see things in terms of what they may or may not do to us and what we may or may not do to them. Hence, we perceive neither objectively (we do not see the 'fluid continuity of the real') nor subjectively (what we see is most definitely 'in' the image), but, rather, 'virtually' (we extract aspects of image in accord with the demands of action).

By way of summary, we should note that Bergson's account of 'pure perception' avoids both idealism and realism by emphasising its practical character. Perception is not a means of getting the world 'inside' the brain, as though it were some form of container. It is, instead, the means by which the 'fluid continuity of the real' is artificially divided in such a way as to afford a foothold for the living being. This is why Bergson (1991: 64) describes perception in a relational way, in terms of parts and wholes: 'perception, in its pure state, is, then, in very truth, a part of things'.

However, Bergson's efforts to describe perception in a 'pure' form – which are essential to avoid lapsing into precisely the kinds of problems regarding representation that continue to haunt contemporary cognitive neuroscience – come at some cost. We are left with a picture of the living being inhabiting a world without time, without succession, without the possibility of progress. Memory must necessarily be reinserted into this picture, but, as with perception, Bergson does this by first describing memory in all its 'purity'.

Pure memory

Bergson uses three terms in relation to remembering: 'habit memory', 'recollection memory' and 'pure memory'.

We will start with 'habit memory'. Bergson illustrates this with the common example of what is usually called 'rote learning'. Say that one is seeking to 'learn by heart' some text, such as a script or a poem. This is typically achieved by repeatedly reading and rereading the text, perhaps in small chunks, such that a 'decomposition and then a recomposition of the whole action' (1991: 80) is achieved. Consequently, we consider that, with each successive reading, a 'memory' of the text becomes more fully 'imprinted'. The question that Bergson asks is are we correct to describe the operation in this way?

In fact, there are two ways in which 'learning by heart' might be said to give rise to memory. We can, for instance, seek to recall each occasion on which we read the text. This would be a memory of a particular time, which might include details such as the time of year, the place in which the text was read, the discomfort or boredom experienced on that occasion and so on. This kind of memory is very different to the memory we believe to have been 'imprinted' as a result of the successive readings – that is, our ability to spontaneously repeat the script or poem.

This latter form of recollection is not, for Bergson, really 'memory' at all, or, rather, it is memory in its most degraded form. Essentially, it is a 'habit' – that is, a 'closed system of automatic movements which succeed each other in the same order' (1991: 80). What Bergson calls 'habit memory' is, then, the result of training the body to reproduce a set of 'intelligently coordinated movements which represent the accumulated efforts of the past' (1991: 82) or, put more simply, an unconscious 'motor diagram' that supports perception in the service of current action.

Habit memory encompasses much of what psychologists typically refer to as either 'procedural memory' (that is, knowledge of how to do things) or the rubric of 'working memory' (see Baddeley, 1976). For Bergson, the 'learning by heart' example is in some ways exceptional. Much of what becomes established as 'habitual' and 'spontaneously recollected' is acquired via accidental repetition. For instance, when we walk confidently through streets we know well, the habit memory that is in operation is not likely to have been deliberately established. Bergson insists that this form of 'memory' be considered purely a physical (that is, neural) phenomenon. It is the bodily means by which 'useful effects' of previous experiences are 'prolonged' into the present moment (1991: 82).

In this sense, habit memory is highly adaptive, being fitted to our ongoing living needs. We might say that it is the unconscious, physical component of a corresponding psychological phenomenon that Bergson calls 'attention to life'. This could be characterised as our conscious involvement in present actions. For instance, in following a speech or lecture, we are trying to grasp not merely what is being said right now but also how these present utterances relate both to what has been said and what is likely to follow. This involves a habitual familiarity with forms and relationships. The school pupil who knows that his or her teacher is about to dictate a fraction will draw a line before knowing precisely 'what numerator and what denominator are to come' (1998: 149).

Attention to life is, then, the expression of our practical concerns – what interests us, what we are trying to achieve and so on. Bergson's point is that attention to life is typically highly focused (or 'tense') – the more caught up we are with our practical concerns, the more our perceptions become structured with a view to immediate action. In theory, we can expand our attention to life almost infinitely, but in practice this is limited by the extent of our perception – that is, the range of the 'virtual' field of action we are able to perceive, able to gather up as 'virtual images'.

The expanding of attention to life covers further instances of the 'trivial' uses of memory that interest psychologists. For example, if we lose our keys, we can retrace the actions that led to the present moment and recollect likely points at which we may have put down the keys. What Bergson would emphasise is, again, that this example really has very little to do with memory in the proper sense of the term. What we strive to bring to consciousness is likely to be not a specific memory of a past event, but, rather, the chain of well established habitual actions that we would have performed. To 'recall' this sequence, it is necessary merely to expand our attention to a field of possible actions. This is, for Bergson, essentially a spatial, perceptual and, ultimately, neural activity.

By contrast, 'memory', in the full sense of the term, has nothing whatsoever to do with space, perception or, indeed, the brain itself. This is an extraordinary claim! In order to make some sense of it, consider the following definition of duration that Bergson offers in his *The Creative Mind* (1992: 179):

> There is no mood, however, no matter how simple, which does not change at every instant, since there is no consciousness without memory, no continuation of a state without the addition, to the present feeling of the memory of past moments. That is what duration consists of. Inner duration is the continuous life of a memory which prolongs the past into the present ... without the survival of the past in the present there would be no duration but only instantaneity.

Bergson here repeats his familiar claims about duration: it is continuous, it involves the prolonging of the past into the present and it is what enables the living being to experience succession rather than be doomed to live out perpetual 'instantaneity'. What is striking, though, is that Bergson uses 'memory' as a synonym for duration. This also occurs in *Creative Evolution* (1998: 4–5):

> Duration is the continuous progress of the past which gnaws into the future and which swells as it advances. And as the past grows without ceasing, so also there is no limit to its preservation. Memory, as we have tried to prove, is not a faculty for putting away recollections in a drawer, or of inscribing them in a register. There is no register, no drawer; there is not even, properly speaking, a faculty, for a faculty works intermittently, when it will or when it can, whilst the piling up of the past upon the past goes on without relaxation. In reality the past is preserved by itself, automatically. In its entirety, probably, it follows us at every instant; all that we have felt, thought and willed from earliest infancy is there, leaning over the present which is about to join it, pressing against the portals of consciousness that would fain leave it outside.

This extract brings together a number of the assertions that illustrate the novelty of Bergson's approach to pure memory. First of all, we must treat memory wholly in terms of duration. As duration is continuous, heterogeneous and an ongoing movement of change, it follows that 'memory' – and here we are really concerned with the wider body of memories that psychologists traditionally call 'long-term memory' – is, similarly, an ongoing flow of past images that never repeats itself. Memory is, then, 'unlimited'. We must imagine something like a continuous melody that, although it may pass through characteristic phases, never ends up becoming identical with itself at any two points we choose to consider.

Second, as memory 'is' duration, it can no more be located in the brain than it can in any other place as, by definition, it is not spatial. This argument is a direct result of Bergson's division of space and time. In Chapter 2 of *Matter and Memory*, Bergson argues at length against treating the brain as a 'storehouse' for memories. Crudely put, his argument is that such a view lacks an adequate explanation for the conversion of perception into representation and vice versa during 'recall'. This subsequently violates materialist principles as it requires a leap of faith on our behalf to believe that, at some point, neurological signals can be transmuted into a unique, subjective, non-physical mental form. It should be noted that, notwithstanding the strange beauty of the 'coloured pictures of the brain' produced by contemporary neuro-imaging techniques such as MRI and CAT scanning, contemporary brain science still fails to deliver a compelling explanation of this process.

Third and, again, as a consequence of the continuous passage of duration, there is never any 'start' or 'end' to the recording of memories. Memory is 'always on'. For experimental psychologists of memory, this is an extremely challenging conception of memory because it suggests that memories do not have a discrete, clearly defined form. Lansdale (2005) offers a rare experimental modelling of an 'always on' approach to memory. He (2005:) argues for an 'acropetal' conception of memory, where all aspects of our experience of some past event prove important for recall: 'this is similar to saying that our memory of a book is more than recalling the final sentences or that our memory of a symphony is more than the recall of the final chords'.

Fourth, if the recording of memory is automatic, it follows that the 'storage' or 'spatial preservation' of memories is no longer a significant issue. Simply put, asking where memories 'are' is the wrong sort of question. We maintain a continuous, unbroken and indivisible relationship to past experience. However, this raises a very different concern. How, then, do we prevent our consciousness from being overwhelmed by this unlimited form of experience that is perpetually 'pressing on the portals' of the present? If we follow the implications of this problem, we will be led, as Bergson (1992: 153) claims, to entirely reorientate our approach to remembering and forgetting:

> if we take into consideration the continuity of the inner life and consequently of its indivisibility, we no longer have to explain the preservation of the past, but rather its apparent abolition. We shall no longer have to account for remembering, but for forgetting.

Put another way, a psychology of memory that assumes memories to be fragile, discrete representations encoded within the brain will find itself absorbed in generating ever more complex models of how such representations are brought back and restored to consciousness. A psychology of memory that assumes, instead, with Bergson, that our experience is, in principle, unlimited and indivisible, will concern itself with how this form of experience is held outside of consciousness – that is, 'forgotten' for present purposes. Its task will then be to describe how an experience of duration intersects with habitual experience and the experience of present action.

The virtual and the actual

'Pure memory' is Bergson's term for the ongoing, automatic preservation of the entirety of the past. It is worth stressing this latter point. For Bergson, it is impossible that we could ever truly 'forget' any part of experience or, for that matter, 'redo' it. However, as we will discuss in a moment, it is entirely possible that, under certain circumstances (for instance, the acquisition of brain lesions), we will be unable to restore past experience to present action. If the past is not 'forgotten', it is certainly held outside of consciousness. This 'apparent abolition' is what ensures that our current actions are not overwhelmed or determined by the burden of past experience, which is to say that memory, in the pure sense, is 'unconscious'. Conversely, consciousness, for Bergson, is concerned with action; it is primarily our 'attention to life'.

Bergson's treatment of the relationship between the past and present is, then, cast in terms of a distinction between 'action' and 'passivity', or, put in slightly different terms, between 'matter' and 'memory'. Much depends on the side from which we wish to view this division. Seen from the perspective of our ongoing engagement with the world – that is, 'matter' – the past is 'that which no longer acts'. The past is passive, inert, a burden that weighs heavily on us. As Bergson (1991: 68) puts it, 'the past is only idea, the present is ideo-motor'. However, seen from the perspective of the entirety of our experience (memory), the present is only the 'tip' or 'cutting edge' of an indivisible, unfolding experience (or 'becoming') that constitutes our particular existence. The present is, then, an instance, an 'actuality'. It is akin to the note just played in an ongoing melody. From this perspective, we see that the present is not that which *contains* the past (the whole of the melody is not 'in' the note just played), but, rather, a given portion of a totality of experience that is continually 'gnawing' into the real.

There are, then, two ways in which to define the present moment. Seen in terms of action, the present moment 'is constituted by the quasi-instantaneous section effected by our perception in the flowing mass' (1991: 139). This is the field of action cut out of the real by our perception, imbued with habit memory (that is, 'attention to life'). Seen in terms of memory, the present 'represents the actual state of my becoming, that part of my duration which is in the process of growth' (1991: 138) – that is, the leading edge of the 'invisible progress of the past gnawing into the future' (1991: 150).

These two definitions mark what Bergson would call a 'difference in nature'. Our efforts to secure a foothold in the 'fluid continuity of the real' are entirely distinct from the 'invisible progress' of duration. At the same time, however, these two aspects of experience are united in what Bergson calls the 'actuality' of living.

The distinction between 'virtual' and 'actual' is pivotal to Bergson's account of lived experience. Whenever Bergson uses the term 'actual', he is referring to action, to what is being done, what is being perceived in the here and now. By contrast, the term 'virtual' refers to what does not act, what could be or has been perceived or done. 'Virtual' is synonymous with 'potential'.

At first glance, we might be tempted to translate these terms into the more familiar language of 'possibility' – that is, for any given action there is a range of possibilities that might have been adopted instead. Now, this way of thinking is entirely appropriate if we are considering purely mechanical, causal relationships between objects – as with the classic example of billiard balls colliding. However, as Bergson argues in *The Creative Mind* (1992: 99), it invites us to assume that the 'possible is *less* than the real'.

We are tempted to believe that in our actions we 'realise' these possibilities and, in so doing, breathe life into them. Our actions are, then, a matter of making real or adding life to a set of predetermined options. However, as Bergson points out, outside of 'closed systems', such as the billiards table, what counts as a 'possibility' can only usually be established *after* accomplishment of the act. For example, literary critics can point to a range of 'possible' factors that might have inspired Shakespeare to write *Hamlet*, but this amounts to retrospective speculation. To argue that *Hamlet* was always a possibility that was eventually realised by the genius of Shakespeare is to do violence to what is meant by 'possible'. We would do better to speak instead of 'absence of hinderance': '*Hamlet* was doubtless possible before being realised, if that means there was no insurmountable obstacle to its realization ... but the possible thus understood is in no degree virtual, something ideally pre-existent' (1992: 102).

There is a serious point at stake here. If the possible is, as Bergson claims, 'only the real with the addition of an act which throws its image back into the past, once it has been enacted' (1992: 100), then it follows that there is *less* and not *more* in the present than in the past. In the same way that pure perception subtracts from the 'fluid continuity of the real', so pure memory involves the reduction – or 'actualisation' – of the 'unlimited experience' that is our duration. Moreover, if our actions do not breathe life into pre-existing possibilities, then whatever becomes actualised must necessarily change in the process, such that 'reality is created as something unforeseeable and new' (1992: 101).

To summarise briefly, the virtual is that which does not currently act. The virtual is potentiality, rather than possibility and so is no less real than the actual, in the way that a seed is no less real than the tree that it may potentially become. There is always 'more' in the virtual than the actual, meaning that 'actualisation' is a diminution or 'contraction' of the virtual. The virtual necessarily changes in the process of becoming actual, which, again, reflects the reality of constant change. Virtual and actual are, then, really another way in which Bergson (2002: 147) describes the splitting of experience between time and space:

> The memory seems to be to the perception what the image reflected in the mirror is to the object in front of it. The object can be touched as well as seen; acts on us as well as we on it; is pregnant with possible actions; it is *actual*. The image is *virtual*, and though it resembles the object, it is incapable of doing what the object does. Our actual existence then, whilst it is unrolled in time, duplicates itself all along with a virtual existence, a mirror-image. Every moment of our life presents two aspects, it is actual and virtual, perception on the one side and memory on the other. Each moment of life is split up as a when it is posited. Or rather, it consists in this very splitting, for the present moment, always going forward, fleeting limit between the immediate past which is now no more and the immediate future which is not yet, would be a mere abstraction were it not the moving mirror which continually reflects perception as a memory.

Bergson asserts here that the virtual is not that which precedes the actual – as we might erroneously assume if we understand potential as possibility – but, rather, our existence 'unrolls' simultaneously in each register. One upshot of this division is that we must understand present actions – the actual – as standing alongside, rather than succeeding, the past – the virtual. This entirely counter-intuitive idea is part of Bergson's wider contribution to the philosophy of time (see Ansell Pearson, 2002; Deleuze, 1991 for proper explication). We may crudely summarise it in the following way. As what we perceive is always imbued with memory, it follows that our perception is never really of the 'here and now', but, rather, of what has just been and what might be (or, as Bergson, 1991: 151) puts it, 'we never perceive anything but our immediate past'. Indeed, if we grasp time as duration, it follows that there really is no point that we can definitively call the present as we are confronted with a continuous unfolding that is always both an 'immediate past which is now no more and the immediate future which is not yet' (think again of the melody, where the notes 'melt' into one another). However, this division does make sense if it is reformulated in terms of what is currently acting and what may (or may not) act. We must, then, think of existence as a process that involves a continuous 'actualisation' – the enacting of potentials – coupled to a ceaseless 'virtualisation' – as the present is preserved as duration.

'Pure memory' is the name Bergson assigns to the 'virtualisation' of experience, as the present becomes automatically preserved in an unconscious or virtual form. By contrast, 'recollection memory' is the opposite movement of 'actualisation', where the past is restored or 'reinserted' into present action. Bergson (1991: 168–9) describes the operation of recollection memory in the following way:

> memory, laden with the whole of the past, responds to the appeal of the present state by two simultaneous movements, one of translation, by which it moves in its entirety to

meet experience, thus contracting more or less, though without dividing, with a view to action; and the other of rotation upon itself, by which it turns toward the situation of the moment, presenting to it that side of itself which may prove to be most useful.

In order to understand this difficult passage, we must clarify a number of things about the 'virtual' nature of memory. First, Bergson emphasises that pure memory is 'laden with the whole of the past'. This means that every 'moment' of experience is preserved in its singularity. This is in sharp contrast to Halbwachs' view – which is shared in some experimental approaches – that memories are essentially prototypes or generalisations.

Second, as pure memory is synonymous with duration and duration is a process rather than a structure, memory must also be considered to be a 'flow not implying a thing that flows'. In this respect, Bergson's use in *Matter and Memory* of the diagram of an inverted cone to depict the operation of recollection is not entirely helpful. We must, as Lawlor (2003) recommends, consider the cone to be in motion, defined by the twin movements of 'virtualisation' (preservation) and 'actualisation' (recollection).

Third, in the same way that psychological states 'melt into one another' in duration, so singular memories must also interpenetrate one another. From *Time and Free Will* onwards, Bergson insists that it is nevertheless possible to consider duration (and, hence, memory) as preserving differences. However, these differences are 'qualitative' or 'intensive' – they admit of no proper measurement beyond confused notions of 'more or less' (2001: 72). This characterisation of duration as a 'virtual multiplicity' (to use Deleuze's 1991 term) – that is, interpenetrating singularities that differ qualitatively – is not a flight of fancy on Bergson's part, but well grounded in a geometric distinction made by the mathematician G. B. Riemann (see Ansell Pearson 2002: 15–18). The key point is that 'virtual' memories are not clearly defined. It is only by means of 'actualisation' that they gain definition.

Bergson (1991: 146) then describes 'recollection memory' in the following terms. When we encounter some difficulty, our consciousness turns towards the past, towards the 'whole of our lived experience', in search of that part of it that can usefully inform current action, that can 'share in the final decision'. This search is not progressive, but entirely direct. Consciousness leaps or 'jumps' the 'interval of time that separates the actual situation from a former one' (1991: 146) to find itself directly in that region of our past that best fits present circumstances. Having made this link, memory – in its indistinct virtual state – becomes actualised. This involves the 'two movements' described above. Memory becomes progressively defined in terms of those aspects that appear to best inform action. For example, from a whole plethora of childhood experiences, only those episodes that inform a parental dilemma will be actualised by the concerned parent. At the same time, these memories become increasingly 'contracted' or abbreviated. We do not recall all of the details, but tend to translate those details into increasingly general terms – for example, what it means to be 'angry at one's parents' rather than specific episodes of childhood frustration.

Actualisation, then, involves a transformation of memory. Memories only become actual by virtue of altering their form, such that they become like perception. This is why Bergson (1991: 134) refers to the outcome of recollection as 'memory-images':

> Little by little it [a memory-image] comes into view like a condensing cloud; from the virtual state it passes to the actual; and as its outlines become more distinct and its surface takes on colour, it tends to imitate perception.

Bergson's claim for 'memory-images' sets up an odd puzzle that we will have cause to return to in subsequent chapters, as what is recollected (rendered actual) does not have the same form as what was experienced (preserved virtually). However, the form that recollection acquires does enable it, Bergson claims, to insert itself into action. This means that recollection enters into the 'centre of action', comprised of the brain and nervous system. Bergson (1991: 236) is not denying that there is a neural component to recollection, merely that this component provides the material means to 'prolong and convert into action' a recollection that it 'cannot give birth to'. The brain is, then, a *mediator* of memory, rather than its *container*. As Bergson (1998: 263) puts it elsewhere, 'the brain is the sharp edge by which consciousness cuts into the compact tissue of events, but the brain is no more coextensive with consciousness than the edge is with the knife'. This position allows Bergson to reinterpret clinical evidence of neurological damage. In all such instances, he claims, what is damaged is not memory itself, but, rather, some aspect of the material means by which it is restored to consciousness and inserted into action (see 1991: 108–31).

In summary, the notions of 'virtualisation', 'actualisation' and 'recollection memory' provide a way for Bergson to re-establish contact between space and time – that is, matter and memory. This contact happens within the body – or, more properly, within the brain. However, in stark contrast to cognitive neuroscience, Bergson sees the pivotal importance of the brain as lying in its role as a mediator between two processes that extend far beyond the individual. The brain is, then, akin to a 'hyphen' (it is the 'and' in *Matter and Memory*, as Worms, 1999, astutely notes). On the one hand is perception, which is 'always, in very truth, a part of things', and, on the other, memory, which is our 'unlimited experience' of the 'whole of the past'. It is the relative complexity of the human brain that allows it to open up an 'interval' or 'gap' between action and reaction. Within this gap, habit memory thickens perception and recollection memory inserts general remembrances. These two forms of 'memory' are, ultimately, what enables humans to operate as 'zones of indeterminism' – that is, as living beings who have acquired the power, by virtue of memory, to extract themselves from the otherwise determinate order of the physical world.

Intuition

We opened this chapter with the claim that Bergson provides the means with which to articulate the form experience may take in relation to Halbwachs' treatment of collective remembering. One obstacle to this goal is the persistent characterisation of Bergson's intellectual position by Halbwachs and others as 'subjectivism'. Now, as we have seen, it is difficult to reduce Bergson's work to any single position. In particular, his strenuous efforts to cut across both realism and idealism (this latter being the bedrock of subjectivism) render such a characterisation problematic. Nevertheless, much of Bergson's thought seems to valorise the personal over the collective and, correspondingly, the psychological over the social.

To dispel this illusion, we will have to return, for a final time, to duration. Every time we have spoken of 'reality', we have used Bergson's formulation of 'fluid continuity' or 'continual change of form'. Similarly, when we have invoked duration, we have been careful to refer to a 'self-sufficient flow or passage' – a flow 'not implying a thing that flows'. To say that the individual, as a living being, is endowed with duration is to say that the individual is fundamentally neither a 'thing' nor a 'stable form', but, rather, a process, an unfolding passage which is part of the wider whole, the undivided flux that is reality itself. Indeed, it is precisely in these terms that Bergson discusses 'personality' as a term for the particular pattern of change that defines our own individual duration. We must think of 'individuality' as a 'trajectory' or, better yet, a characteristic melody extracted from the cacophony of reality. The term 'extraction' is important because it underlines that our own duration contracts within it a variety of other 'rhythms' (Bergson, 1991: 228):

> By allowing us to grasp in a single intuition multiple moments of duration, it [memory] frees us from the movement of the flow of things, that is to say, from the rhythm of necessity. The more of these moments memory can contract into one, the firmer is the hold which it gives us on matter: so the memory of a living being appears to measure, above all, its powers of action upon things.

Duration is what allows for the 'cutting out' of forms. For instance, we are able to perceive differences in hue instantly. Yet, we know that, in reality, such differences are the result of complex patterns of light falling on the tens of thousands of receptors in the eye. Bergson argues that perception must, then, involve the 'contraction' or 'condensation' of these complex patterns into a relatively narrow portion of our experience. Thus, the rhythm of our particular conscious existence is interdependent with and, in some sense, built on the durations of others. To demonstrate this interdependency, we need only imagine what would happen is we were to live our own duration 'at a slower rhythm'. Our relationship to the world, or foothold within the real, would gradually fragment as we would experience reality directly as an 'undivided flux', a constant movement of innumerable changes, with the result that we would be unable to perceive or act in an effective way (1991: 201–8).

Bergson's best-known example of 'contraction' is discussed in *Creative Evolution* (1998: 9–10):

> If I want to mix a glass of sugar and water, I must, willy nilly, wait until the sugar melts. This little fact is big with meaning. For here the time I have to wait is not that mathematical time which would apply equally well to the entire history of the material world … It coincides with my impatience, that is to say, with a certain portion of my own duration, which I cannot protract or contract as I like. It is no longer something *thought*, it is something *lived*.

What is 'big in meaning' in this example is the interdependency of our duration with that of another – in this case, the dissolving sugar. We are forced to wait for the sugar to dissolve. For the time this takes, our own duration is hooked into that of the sugar and water mix in such a way that we cannot 'protract or contract it as [we] like'.

Bergson's point is that the growing impatience that we feel is an emerging and irreducible property of the hooking together of durations. Now, it would have been perfectly possible to have mathematically calculated in advance how long we would probably have to wait for the sugar to dissolve, but this 'mathematical time' is not the time we live; our experience is not reducible to it. Indeed, what is most interesting here is the uncertainty of unfolding duration – perhaps we will become too impatient and drink the water before it is ready, perhaps we will be disturbed and the drink will be left untouched, perhaps we will realise that, after waiting, we no longer desire the sickly sweet water. For Bergson (1992: 93), life must be characterised by the 'uncertainty' found in this small example of being made to wait: 'time is this very hesitation, or it is nothing'.

Properly speaking, then, our own particular duration is not really singular – it is always conjoined with others. At times, these other durations 'envelop' our own, such as when we are forced to wait. Equally, our duration can envelop others, as in the following example (Bergson, 1999: 36):

When we are seated on the bank of a river, the flowing of the water, the gliding of a boat or the flight of a bird, the ceaseless murmur in our life's deeps are for us three separate things or only one, as we choose.

There is a distinct resemblance between this passage and similar examples used by Halbwachs in *The Collective Memory* and the message appears to be very similar, too. It is that our experience is never singular, it is always an irreducible mix of coexisting planes of experience. Halbwachs points out that each plane of experience can be indexed to a specific collective framework. By contrast, Bergson's observation is characteristically about time – that each experience (such as the flowing river, the gliding boat, our personal thoughts) unfolds in its own particular duration. Nevertheless, in our experience, seated on the riverbank, these distinct durations may mutually envelop one another, just as the duration of the sugar and water mixing enveloped our own duration to produce the experience of impatience.

Bergson, then, supplies a novel way of understanding Halbwachs' claim that the personal is but a mode of sociality. If what we call 'personality' is the unfolding of the very particular duration of our life, then that duration condenses within it innumerable other durations. So, as Deleuze (1991) notes, memory is the virtual coexistence of all these intersecting planes of experience, these durations that have become hooked into our own. This is the source of the 'strangeness' we experience in relation to memory. Our conscious experience, dominated by the needs of action, is but one aspect of innumerable coexisting threads of virtual experience.

Bergson uses the term 'intuition' to describe the kind of knowledge we gain from reflecting on these intersecting durations. In common parlance, 'intuition' is the name given to a highly subjective, immediate and non-rational form of knowledge. This has led critics as eminent as Mary Douglas (1980) to dismiss Bergsonism as ultimately subjectivist. Given all that we have just seen regarding Bergson's complex account of consciousness and memory, it should be self-evident that this is not all that Bergson means by intuition. His own, better, definition is that it is simply 'to think in duration' (1992: 34). In other words, intuition is the sort of knowledge that we acquire when we attempt, as far as possible, to situate ourselves within the unfolding of lived experience. However, as our perception and, indeed, our intelligence, is directed towards action, this proves difficult to do. Intuition, then, involves the attempt to 'get back into duration and recapture reality in the very mobility which is its essence' (1992: 31).

How is it possible to 'get back into duration' when, in Bergson's terms at least, we are never outside of it? The problem lies with our lack of conscious awareness of duration, of change, as it unfolds. Indeed, it is only really at those moments of relative detachment – such as when we are made to wait by, for instance, the dissolving sugar – that we are able to adequately reflect on our duration. So, we 'get back into' our duration when it is juxtaposed with or hooked into that of another. Something of our own time of living is disclosed to us when it becomes enveloped by another duration. The kind of knowledge that we gain is then 'intuitive' in so far as it is granted as a real, lived experience.

For Bergson, intuition is a superior form of knowledge because it involves neither artificial distinctions nor imposes a spatial, unchanging form on the 'fluid continuity' of the real. Intuition results, instead, in what Bergson calls 'fluid concepts' – that is, concepts that capture, as far as possible, mobility and change. Moreover, what intuition uncovers is that our duration, our memory, is not singular, but consists of 'virtually coexisting' planes of experience that make our own particular existence entirely interdependent with that of others. To sum up, to get back into duration means recognising that the supposed uniqueness of our own personal experience, our own memory, is illusory – we are always simply a part of a larger whole, as Bergson tirelessly points out. Our memory is necessarily collective, in so far as it envelops and is enveloped by other durations.

Summary

In this chapter we have described how Bergson offers a unique process philosophy approach to remembering. Process philosophy of this sort certainly presents a significant challenge to commonsense understandings of memory. It demands that we try to think of process in and for itself, without recourse to structures or content as the driving factors. In relation to psychology, this means a move away from spatial metaphors (for example, considering the brain as a 'storehouse' or 'filing cabinet' for memories) and the corresponding treatment of memories as mental representations. What Bergson offers instead is a description of memory as 'uncontained', as a dynamic set of intersecting experiences. Bergson insists that we study memory in a way that does justice to a genuine experience of time as duration. He provides a powerful set of conceptual tools for analysing the relationship between memory and action.

In the last chapter, we claimed that Bergson illuminates two problems that haunt Halbwachs' work. The first is the link between individual and collective duration, the second the gap between our sense of the overall consistency of our past experience and the corresponding awareness of the interdependency of our memory with that of others. Bergson's demand that we not confuse space with time, and his further encouragement to 'think in duration', provides the key to unlocking these problems. In the twin processes of 'virtualisation' and 'actualisation', we have the means to understand how our own duration resources our practical needs and, moreover, is fundamentally hooked into the duration of others. Bergson, then, provides a highly effective vocabulary for describing experience in relation to organised settings.

In Chapter 2, we pointed to four themes that emerge from Bartlett's work – commemoration, conventionalisation, objectification and mediation. In turning towards Halbwachs' ideas, we found a comprehensive set of terms for describing how collective frameworks structure commemorative activities and conventionalise cultural resources as they 'engrave' themselves within social space. In Bergson's writings we found an account not merely of the necessary objectification of experience, as duration is inserted into action, but also of mediation as a pervasive feature of how remembering and forgetting are accomplished.

Having reviewed the work of both Halbwachs and Bergson, we are now in a position to turn towards empirical studies of remembering. In what follows, we will not be applying the work of either thinker directly. Rather, we will be attempting to think through the issues and problems they address in relation to the varied settings in which remembering and forgetting occurs – such as families, institutions, workplaces, websites and so on. Our goal throughout will be to see if it is possible to arrive at a distinctively social psychological understanding of experience as it is afforded in the process of recollection.

FIVE

Communicating experience: interactional organisation of remembering and forgetting

How can we begin to study memory in a way that does justice to the issues and concerns raised in the sources we have discussed in the first few chapters? The work of Bartlett, Halbwachs and Bergson presents a number of challenges to way in which psychologists typically understand memory and experience. It is fair to say that, until comparatively recently, psychologists have overwhelmingly thought of memory in terms of the storage of past experience. This container metaphor has dominated psychological research in the same way that talk of 'wax tablets' and 'theatres' (see Yates, 1966) was common for more ancient discussions on the topic. The problems that arise from treating mind as a vast warehouse wherein individual memories are catalogued and retrieved have been much rehearsed, not least by psychologists themselves (see Draaisma, 2000; Schachter, 1996). Such a view leads us to expect a kind of clarity and order to exist in human remembering that is simply absent from empirical evidence. Container metaphors, then, may provide us with the wrong basis for approaching memory (see Danziger, 2002). One very eminent memory researcher – Elizabeth Loftus – describes her personal difficulties with conceptualising memory in the following way (Loftus & Ketcham, 1994: 3–4):

> 'Think of your mind as a bowl filled with clear water. Now imagine each memory as a teaspoon of milk stirred into the water. Every adult mind holds thousands of these murky memories … Who among us would dare to disentangle the water from the milk?' I like this particular metaphor because it defies the oft-heard explanation that memories reside in a certain part of the brain, like coded computer disks or crisp manila folders carefully placed in a file drawer for safekeeping. Memories don't sit in one place, waiting patiently to be retrieved; they drift through the mind, more like clouds and or vapor than something we can put our hands around.

This extract is taken from a book that popularises (and also polemicises) Loftus' work as an expert witness in court cases in relation to what she regards as 'false memory syndrome'. Here, Loftus and Ketcham contrast the relative merits of container metaphors – including the deeply unhelpful conflation of computer 'memory' with human memory – with other, more innovative, metaphors – such as milk stirred into water. They see the advantage of this metaphor as drawing attention to the fluid and diffuse nature of 'memories'. Memories, they argue, are distributed throughout the mind in an inchoate form. Clarity is the result of the process of restoring memories to consciousness – it is not intrinsic to the memory itself.

Now, there is a great deal of resonance between the way Loftus characterises memories and the way Bergson speaks of remembering. However, there is also an important difference. Cognitive psychological analysis, such as Loftus and Ketchum's, persists in presenting the mind – or, rather, the cognitive architecture of memory – as, ultimately, mapping on to the brain. Whether one thinks in terms of a bowl filled with clear water rather than crisp manila folders in a filing cabinet, it still remains the case that the brain is being treated as a place wherein entities called 'memories' are contained. In other words, Loftus and Ketchum are presenting spatial rather than temporal analyses and treating the process of remembering as the transformation of these entities rather than the turning around on experience that Bergson is trying to envisage.

So, what is at issue for us initially is this accordance of an 'entitative' or 'thing-like' status to individual recollections in contemporary psychology of memory. It is in this respect that discursive work in psychology makes an important contribution by rejecting the container view of memory in favour of an understanding of remembering as social action (for example, Billig, 1996, 1999; Edwards, 1987, 1997; Edwards & Potter, 1992; Harré & Gillet, 1994; Mercer, 2002; Middleton & Edwards, 1990a).

Work in this area argues that psychological phenomena such as memory are better understood as *accomplishments* that occur in the course of communicative action, whether this be talk or text. Memory, in this account, is something that speakers/writers *perform* rather than simply *possess* in the course of routine interaction. These performances are informed by cultural understandings of what is to be counted as adequate and felicitous recall (as Bartlett, 1932, himself argued).

It is immediately evident that this reformulation of memory entails a major shift from viewing memory as some entity, in the mind or the world. Instead, we focus on remembering and forgetting as social acts, as ways of accomplishing some activity in the present by invoking the past in an appropriate and resourceful manner. This approach approximates more closely with Bergson's view of memory as informing action at every turn than the contrasting cognitive approach, for which we have given Loftus as one exemplar.

The discursive approach also draws inspiration from Halbwachs' prioritisation of language as the principle means via which collective remembering is organised and coordinated. Halbwachs' concern with the use of proper names, for example, is something that we are able to further illuminate by displaying how all manner of categories – including names – are deployed as discursive resources in acts of social remembering. The discursive approach, then, enables us to develop a whole empirical programme around Halbwachs' respecification of memory as a collective phenomenon.

In this chapter, we will introduce that programme in the following way. If we treat remembering as a situated and contingent communicative act, four key issues immediately emerge. First, as speakers must necessarily act towards and respond to one another in 'real time' in order to sustain an interaction, we are led to attend to the way in which remembering is 'sequentially organised' (Middleton & Edwards, 1990b).

Second, given this sequential organisation, we may analyse how it is that speakers co-opt one other into projects of remembering and forgetting (see, for example, Edwards & Middleton, 1986a, 1988; Goodwin, 1987).

Third, that co-option into such projects involves the realisation of 'memberships' that are made relevant in the social occasioning and organisation of remembering and forgetting (see Bellah, Madsen, Sullivan, Swidler & Tipton, 1985; Orr, 1990; Middleton, 1997b; Wertsch, 2002).

Finally, we may explore the manner in which we interactively commit others to the individual and collective relevance of our experience claims within the contingent 'pragmatics of communicative action' (such as Buchanan & Middleton, 1995; Middleton, 1997a).

These discursive issues – sequential organisation, co-option, membership, and pragmatics – open up promising lines of empirical research into the accomplishment of memory in the discursive contexts of talk and text. The aim of this chapter is to discuss and illustrate these key concerns. In addition, we aim to highlight some of the challenges to the discursive position, especially with regard to how this approach deals with the durability or otherwise of past experience of events.

Interactive and sequential organisation of memory

An early exploration of discursive remembering involved a transcribed conversation in which a group of eight people had been asked to remember everything they could about the film *E.T.* (Edwards & Middleton, 1986a). The analysis focused on the conversational devices participants used in producing a joint version, how they built a taken as given (default) continuity as part of the sequential organisation of their talk concerning the film's narrative sequence. In doing this, they shared the burden of recall, comparing recollections, inserting out-of-sequence reminiscences and commenting when the account ran into difficulty on meta-mnemonic features of what they were doing, such as what it is to remember and forget, as is shown by the dialogue given in Example 1.

Example 1

Diane:	it's very confusing 'cause there's not really a basic story it's all just the fact [that
Lesley:	[little things that [happen
Diane:	[yeah little things that happen that don't really make that much like er they met he met the other children
	(....)
John:	he's trying to explain first of all where he is from do you remember
Diane:	yeah he's
Karen:	that's after he has met all the [children because (&)
John:	['cause he says Ell-i-ott like this
Karen:	(&) all the children were there
	(....)
Diane:	so he meets the older boy um because doesn't he bring him in and says you know what I told you because before he'd been telling everybody that [he'd (&)
John:	[that's right
Paul:	[yeah
Diane:	(&) got some sort of monster or whatever

The study demonstrated the usefulness of conversational data in making visible the ways in which people provide explicit formulations of inferential links and rationalisations concerning their accounts of experience. In the course of such 'public thinking' (see Billig, 1996), we often explicate such links and causal inferences ('so he meets the older boy um because doesn't he bring him in and says ...', 'he's trying to explain first of all where he is from do you remember (...) 'cause he says Ell-i-ot like this'). In addition, we justify and warrant versions against alternatives and the possibility of refutation ('its all very confusing', 'because doesn't he bring him in'). That is, our acts of remembering are always cast in an anticipated argumentative context. We are aware that we may be called on, almost immediately, to justify, warrant or produce supporting evidence for the claims we make about the past and, therefore, 'build in' to our claims rhetorical features (such as reporting mundane detail – 'because all the children are there', and taking up the voice of another – 'he says Ell-i-ot like this') that are designed to address possible objections.

These initial findings derived from conversational action within groups deliberately set up for the purposes of studying joint recall have been demonstrated in a wide variety of everyday contexts, including family, work and leisure situations, where participants talk to each other in the social creation and justification of 'memories'. What these studies are able to provide are real-time instantiations of Halbwachs' description of collective remembering. However, the joint recall of events is a familiar and well-practised activity that may occur across a wide range of settings.

We can illustrate in more detail the range of specific linguistic devices using material recorded in reminiscence sessions by Faith Gibson (1989) and published as part of a guide to the use of reminiscence groups with elderly people by the UK Charity Help the Aged. The group consisted of nine older persons and two 'reminiscence workers' who were co-organisers. According to the details in the manual, the participants had all lived in a residential home in Northern Ireland. A video recording was made as they met each week for four weeks and entered into a series of conversations prompted by resource materials, including objects, music and pictures depicting a range of local and general aspects of life and work spanning the times that they had lived through. The specific linguistic devices for accomplishing reminiscence can be illustrated with reference to Example 2 (Gibson, 1989).

Example 2

From the second session – a slide of a ballroom had just been shown and taped dance music played.

Co-organiser:	what does that take you back to
Mr Jones:	the old-fashioned waltzes they used to call it or the quickstep
Co-organiser:	well tell us about when you used to go to dances
Mr Jones:	well the main thing was to get your arms around a girl (.) nowadays it seems that they want to keep as far away as possible (.) but the music was all much more tuneful than it is today plus the fact that you had a certain amount of rhythm to do different dances (.) there was the waltz a quickstep a slow foxtrot and a military two-step and there's one that I have been trying to remember for quite a while (.) can you remember Mrs Craven what you called it? you took partners and danced middle and arse about
Mrs Smith:	The Lancers
All:	The Lancers
Mrs Rogers:	yes that's right
Mr Jones:	I've been trying to remember that for a week the Lancers
Mrs Rogers:	I know that sort of thing happens

As in previous data (see, for example, Middleton & Edwards, 1990b), specific linguistic devices are indentifiable for remembering jointly, such as:

- tags and overt requests for assistance that signal or invite ratification – 'can you remember Mrs Craven what you called it?'
- overt agreements – 'yes that's right'
- ratification by repeating the previous speaker's contribution – 'The Lancers (…) The Lancers'
- meta-mnemonic formulations of the process of remembering itself and, in this case, the specific problem of remembering – 'I've been trying to remember for quite a while; I've been trying to remember for a week'

All of these linguistic devices contribute to the sequential unfolding of recollection, as each speaker's utterance dovetails with the last. A default continuity is constructed where each contribution builds on and adds to the last.

Reminiscence groups provide a context in which older people – who may experience not only a 'predictable' decline in their powers of recall, but also the increasing loss of interlocuters with whom they shared experiences in common, can be supported. However, rather than concentrate on loss, what this material allows us to bring into focus are the achievements or social accomplishments of the participants. These include the joint construction of meaning about past events, the collaborative realisation of complex narratives and establishing a vocabulary to account for difficulties that appear to be associated with getting older and 'being able to remember' effectively. For example, Mr Jones uses a meta-mnemonic formulation to express the difficulty that he had been having in recalling the name the Lancers: 'I've been trying to remember that for a week.' Mrs Rogers then attends to and socialises that difficulty as being part of the normal problem of trying to recall something: 'I know that sort of thing happens.' Here, individual difficulty is relocated to being part of a 'common experience', rather than an aspect of the vicissitudes of individual cognition.

Meta-cognitive formulations are, then, more than public expressions of our personal understanding regarding the nature of our own mental processes (Flavell & Wellman, 1977). In fact, to understand these expressions solely in this way is to commit the same error as treating a 'schema' as purely a mental representation. Meta-mnemonic formulations arise in an occasioned manner, in particular discursive contexts, typically at points of difficulty – for instance, when speakers claim not to be able to remember something or are suddenly reminded or attempt to remember and try to fit a putative version of events with what another speaker is saying. On all these occasions, a public reflection on one's own mental processes may strengthen or warrant a subsequent claim.

Instead of treating conversational action as a window on mental processes, we can see that conversations act as significant environments in which thoughts are formulated, justified and socialised according to how other speakers talk about mental processes. As has been argued previously (Middleton & Edwards, 1990b), we do not need to know whether or not the claims people make about their mental processes – their 'memory' – are actually correct or not in order to study how remembering and forgetting are socially accomplished.

Goodwin (1987) points out that displays of uncertainty in conversation are typically glossed over in talk as remembering or forgetting. Orientations to uncertainty and forgetfulness can provide speakers with 'resources for shaping their emerging interaction' (1987: 116). Put simply, saying something like, 'I don't remember' is a good way for speakers to leave options open in the conversation. This is an instance of meta-cognitive construction – acquiring a conventional vocabulary and discourse for mental life designed to serve the social pragmatics of conversation (Edwards, 1997). Group reminiscence provides an environment for such formulations.

Co-option in socially organised settings

Discursive analyses can also demonstrate that remembering and forgetting are fundamental aspects of the social ordering of the settings within which they occur. Indeed, their occurrence appears to be functional to the continuing integrity of not only the psychological functioning of people in those settings but also the settings themselves. For example, Edwards and Middleton (1988) examined conversations between parents and young children talking about family photographs. Such conversations frequently turn on establishing just what it is that people are looking at. However, the issue rarely stops there. In working out what is depicted in such snapshots, in jointly remembering, children are drawn into conversations that provide the basis for elaborating issues of identity, relationships and emotional reactions to previous experiences. The sequence of conversation quoted in Example 3 provides an instance of this. A young boy and his mother are looking at a family album. At the time of recording, 'Paul' is just over fours year of age. He is busy examining the pictures with a magnifying glass, engrossed in how the images can be enlarged (Edwards & Middleton, 1988).

Example 3

Mother:	it must have been a sunny day in that photograph (.) mustn't it?
Paul:	yeah (.) oh let's (.) see (.) see that comes (.) bigger
Mother:	mm (...) where were you then? (.) can you remember?
Paul:	there and there's Rebecca look at (.) her ugh ((laughs))
Mother:	she's pulling a funny face (.) isn't she?
Paul:	yeah (.) she thinks it it's so mm let's see let's see what that boy done let's see if there's any (.) agh (.) it's big (.) do you like (.)
Mother:	you didn't like that bouncing castle did you? (.) do you remember?
Paul:	yeah
Mother:	it kept falling over (.) you couldn't keep you balance
Paul:	no:oh:h ((laughs quietly))
Mother:	do you like them now?
Paul:	yeah.
Mother:	do you?

The most obvious difference between Paul and his mother is that, while Paul appears to be concerned with magnifying parts of the image and remarking on what his sister Rebecca looks like, his mother makes persistent efforts to get him to see it as a depiction of a memorable past. She draws his attention to the depicted scene by invoking memories of things contextual to it – the notion that the bouncy castle was something he did not like, that he could not keep his balance and so on. She presents the past as rational and connected and as memorable on that basis – not liking the bouncy castle related to the fact that it kept falling over and made Paul fall over. In the way that she talks about the picture, Paul's mother presents it to him as both a depiction of recognisable and memorable things from a shared past and as a clue to or reminder of things not actually depicted. The route into these non-depicted memories is via affective reactions and personal involvement – how Paul felt about things, how they affected him and their relevance now, to the present by asking if he still does not like bouncy castles.

Throughout the sequence, past experiences are offered as a meaningful part of a continuing biography and development of personal identity. This is more than accessing the contents of memory, it is part of the ways in which what it is to remember and forget are used in communicative action. For example, right at the beginning, Paul's mother demonstrates something important about both remembering and taking meaning from pictures – the role of inference: 'it must have been a sunny day in that photograph (.) mustn't it?' Photographs can be read for clues about the scene depicted. Sunny days are associated with pictures with sharp contrast and deep shadows, with sea and sand, blue skies, summer activities and clothing and so on. None of those clues are explicit in what the mother says, but the implication is clear – that the photograph in some way permits or affords inferences about the weather. In fact, in later sequences, some of these 'affordances' were made explicit. The mother managed to elicit from her children the notion that you can tell how warm it must have been from the clothes (or lack of them) that people were wearing.

The mother demonstrates how remembering can be done by displaying how to read the photographs for clues to the contextual circumstances depicted. The children are taught to treat past events as memorable in terms of how they affected them and how they reacted to them as a family. Inference serves as a basis for reconstruction. Paul, as a child, is then inducted into two sets of procedures. First, the use of artifacts, such as photographs, as inferential 'puzzles' that may resource acts of remembering and, second, the 'resolution' of such puzzles as a way of displaying a continuity between past and present. For instance, by establishing a continuity of personal experience over time – 'it kept falling over (.) you couldn't keep you balance' and 'do you like them now?' Paul's past experiences and preferences, as they are inferred from the photographs, is constructed as relevant to a discussion of the sort of person he is now.

The discursive approach makes visible how we recruit or co-opt one another into social activities. Remembering can be achieved by talking to people. Paul learns how this is accomplished from his mother's efforts to actively involve him. She addresses him directly, inviting his participation and agreement by the use of tags, such as 'You didn't like that bouncing castle did you? do you remember?' They are having a conversation, looking at pictures, recalling past events, scenes and people.

In the course of such conversations, there are particular points at which the participants seem to 'stand back' from what they are doing and put into words that they are remembering or trying to remember or had forgotten. As we have already discussed, such meta-cognitive discourse very often arises at problematical points, where the process of remembering, perception or problem solving runs into difficulty (Edwards & Middleton, 1986a; Norrick, 2000, 2003). When the difficulty is a joint one, the dialogue shifts to a meta-cognitive level.

The collective accomplishment of remembering appears to be functional to the continuing – and, indeed, developing–lives of children and parents as members of family groups (see also Eisenberg, 1985; Fivush, 1994; Miller, Potts, Fung, Hoogstra & Mintz, 1990). As Bakhurst (1990: 211) argues, in settings where remembering is mediated by cultural objects such as photographs, 'we remember by constructing narratives which require the recall of past events for their intelligible completion'. In other words, our narratives set up 'puzzles' that are seemingly completed by the act of remembering, which, as a consequence, does the work of establishing continuities in identity. Such narrative puzzles then make up and sustain the very setting that entails what it is to be an accountable member of a grouping such as a family where the past is a direct topic of conversational concern.

Membership and recollection

This concern with continuity is illustrated in the next example taken from the conversations between Paul and his mother. As with the last sequence, we can observe in Example 4 the manner in which Paul is constantly positioned as the next speaker and, as a consequence of sequential organisation of talk, thereby co-opted into the project of remembering. However, in this sequence we wish to focus on how the potential significance of Paul's experience is achieved in terms of making his actions and supposed feelings (at the time of taking the photograph) relevant to family relationships, implied identities and emotional significances. This involves the use of a series of contrasts between the interdependent experiences of a series of family members, including his father and sister (Middleton, 1997a).

Example 4

Mother:	oh look (.) there's when we went to the riding [stables wasn't it?
Paul:	[yeah (.) er, er
Mother:	you was trying to reach up and stroke that horse.
Paul:	where? ((laughs))
Mother:	would you like to do that again?
Paul:	yeah
Mother:	you don't look very happy though
Paul:	because I thought I was going to fall off
Mother:	you thought you was going to fall off did you? (.) right misery (.) Daddy was holding on to you so that you didn't (.) did it FEEL very bumpy?
Paul:	yeah.
Mother:	did it make your legs ache? ((Paul laughs)) Rebecca enjoyed it.
Paul:	yeah
Mother:	she's a bit older wasn't she? (.) you were a little boy there.

The mother's talk constantly appoints Paul as the next speaker in the project of remembering. Again, in doing this, the mother provides candidate experiences in terms of Paul's actions and feelings, both physical and emotional, that would count as plausible interpretations of the events depicted and his position within them – 'you was trying to reach up and stroke that horse', 'would you like to do that again?', 'you don't look very happy though', for example.

The interactive appointment of Paul as accountable elicits an explanatory reminiscence from him: 'because I thought I was going to fall off.' Paul is required to produce a recollection in order to 'resolve' the narrative puzzle that the mother has set up for him. In doing this, Paul provides an account occasioned in their talk for the display of unhappiness his mother has assigned to his actions in the photograph. What is more, the particular kind of account that Paul produces is, of necessity, couched in terms of mental states as only this kind of account will adequately address the narrative demands that have been established in the interaction.

The mother responds by putting another question – 'you thought you was going to fall off did you?' – and retakes the initiative of monitoring and displaying the form and content of the interaction in terms of candidate accounts of the actions, motives and feelings of those depicted in the photo. She talks of Paul as a 'right misery', of his father's actions in the account offered of the events – 'daddy was holding on to you', Paul's continued discomfort – 'did it feel very bumpy?' – and for his sister's engagement in the same event – 'Rebecca enjoyed it.' In other words, the interactionally occasioned claims concerning his supposed experience of the events depicted in the snapshot are presented as relevant in terms of family relationships, relative and changing identities – 'she's a bit older wasn't she' and 'you were a little boy there' – and comparative affective reactions of family members – 'Rebecca enjoyed it.'

In summary, the experiences claimed on Paul's behalf are contrasted with those of other family members and with himself in the past. The negotiation of Paul's experience is, then, simultaneously a restating of what it means to be an accountable member of this particular family.

The sequential organisation of such conversational remembering privileges the claims made in terms of their relevance beyond a pure statement of what is depicted in the photo – children, horses, adults, beaches and so on. The mother's pursuit of contextual reminiscences co-opted Paul into justifying the claims being made on his behalf about the nature and consequence of his experience. For example, Paul is in some sense forced to accommodate to the evaluation that he is a 'right misery' because to do otherwise would involve challenging the mother's purported statement of fact, that 'Daddy was holding on to you so that you didn't [fall].' When we use reminiscences in this way, we interactively commit others to the relevance of our experience claims or, as in this case, the claims made by the mother on Paul's behalf. In this way, experience claims are not just an individual concern but also presented as a concern of others and a concern in terms of the collectivities with which people are associated within conversational remembering, be they families, teams, organisations, or any organised setting.

Pragmatics of communicative action

Accomplishing accountable memberships of a setting is no easy matter. The following example was recorded in a reminiscence group run in a health-care setting for older people (see Buchanan, 1993; Buchanan & Middleton, 1995; Buchanan, 1997). In such group reminiscence, older people are gathered together and provided with a forum for retelling – remembering – their experiences of life. This sequence (Buchanan & Middleton, 1995) was transcribed from a series of recordings made at a reminiscence group in a day care setting for older people at a large general hospital where the group's members were asked to discuss examples of their favourite tipple (drink) and a variety of cues had been made available, such as beer bottles, pictures of old pubs in the local area and so on.

We shall focus here in Example 5 on a portion of it where Sue, a woman in her seventies, contributed to the discussion of remembered experiences of drinking, but, up to this point, most of the speakers had made a series of contributions concerning their enjoyment of experiences associated with drinking. Sue's account is achieved within that prevailing conversational context.

This sequence illustrates three things about the conversational pragmatics of social remembering. First, as in the previously presented sequences, her account is constructed in ways that are sensitive to and take account of the prevailing conversational context.

Second, she is doing more than merely retelling a particular experience of the past. Rather, she claims consequences that are relevant and sensitive to the current interactional business and setting.

Finally, we can examine some of the conversational devices she employs in the rhetorical substantiation of her claims that the incident she recounts had particular consequences for her. She uses these devices to illustrate her earlier aversion to drink without compromising the declared position of other group members who have already made claims and contributions illustrating their enjoyment of drinking.

Example 5

Sue:	I mean I've got nothing against drink (.) if people enjoy drink I- I think they're entitled to it (.) but erm (.) it's not for me (.) apart from er (.) lemonade and (.) shandy (.) I don't mind that
	((another conversation intrudes for some seconds at this point, until Sue continues))
Sue:	I remember when er (.) my father was alive (.) he used to like a bottle of stout (.) used [to (…) bottle about like this (.) and (&)
Rose:	[mm (.) <u>stout</u> oh yes (.) stout

Sue:	(&) er (.) where we lived er (.) we had a (.) erm (.) a (.) fire grate with erm [(.) <u>hobs</u> I think they called them (…) hobs (.) and er (.) my (&)
Female?:	[ehh [
Meg?:	[yeah that's (yeah)[
Ted:	[ah yeah [
Female?:	[(…)
Sue:	(&) dad used to (.) drink it out the bottle (.) and er (.) he used to stand it on the hob (.) an- and he used to say it was [<u>beautiful</u> (&)
Ted:	[warming
Sue:	(&) (.) and er ((laugh)) a- you'll think (…) and er (.) I used to go to church in those days (.) and erm (.) the parson (.) we had a parson that used to visit (.) and er (.) I said to me dad (.) the parson- (.) I said that the parson's coming (.) [(&)
Ted:	[is that why he kept it on the hob
Sue:	(&) I said that you won't drink your stout while he's here will you (.) ooh my [(&)
Ted:	[((laugh))
Sue:	(&) dad was disgusted he said I <u>will</u> drink me stout (.) he said you ought to be ashamed of yourself (.) and ther[e it stood on the hob (&)
Male?:	[(…)
Sue:	(&) y'know and in walked the parson with his (.) dog collar on I didn't [know what to do(.) and ((cough)) to make (&)
Rose?:	[((laugh))
Sue:	(&) matters worse this erm (.) <u>stou:t</u> was (.) ch ch ch ch ((imitates noise of stout bubbling)) you could hear it (.) bubbling like (&) ((general laughter))
Sue:	(&) (.) yeah and er (.) me Father said to him er (.) ooh and er (.) this parson's name was a Mr Jackson he was a very very nice man (.) and m-me Father said er (.) I don't (.) I don't think going to church is doing my daughter much good (.) he said er (.) she asked me (.) not to have my bottle of stout (.)' cos you were coming (.) and Mr Jackson said well I've never heard such a thing in me life he said (.) I like one meself occasionally (.) I never felt so bad after tha::t ((laughing tone)) ((general laughter))

In this sequence, Sue makes the claim that the reported incident led her to change her feelings about drinking – a claim that accomplishes a particular identity for her in the present setting. She is making claims concerning *entitlements* to the consequences and significance of her experiences of life in terms of the current conversation. It is worth noting that the issue is set up as a matter of remembering – 'I remember when my father was alive'. However, the significance of what is remembered is that it illustrates and explains Sue's particular position on drinking alcohol. We can see at the start of the extract that she tries to make clear that her abstinence should not be read as a moral judgement on others: 'I mean I've got nothing against drink (.) if people enjoy drink I- I think they're entitled to it (.) but erm (.) its not for me (.) apart from er (.) lemonade and (.) shandy (.) I don't mind that.'

The work of conversation analyst Harvey Sacks (1992a) is instructive on this issue. Sacks argues that it is not enough just to *claim* such entitlements to the consequences of particular experiences – people must *show* them to be warranted in their conversational action. The point is that, when we tell a story about events and describe their consequences for us, what we can say that we felt is closely regulated in terms of the interactions of the moment – in this case, ongoing anecdotes positively evaluating drinking. He makes the point that the experience and its consequences that someone such as Sue claims to have had in virtue of her participation in the narrated events must be one that she is *entitled* to have.

Sacks goes on to suggest that we show such entitlements are accomplished by how we place ourselves as speakers in the events we narrate. In this case, Sue manages her position as a character in the recollection she narrates in such a way as to establish her entitlement to have changed her attitude towards drinking: 'I never felt so bad after that.'

Sue's narrative remembering – her experience narrative (see Schrager, 1983) – sets up claims to have had an experience as a consequence of the event she describes and, both the event and the scene-setting that precedes them, is orientated towards accomplishing her entitlement to this experience. She does this by placing herself in relation to the described events in terms of the characters she introduces, the reported attitudes of those characters and the circumstances of place within which the reported events are represented as occurring. This talk makes available contextual information necessary for understanding the reported interaction. We need to know this 'background stuff' in order to make sense of what occurred between the three characters in the story.

Other work is also done to place her in events as someone with particular kinds of knowledge and attitudes. Her description of her father's drinking habits, as well as informing members of the reminiscence group of those habits, also tells them Sue's knowledge as a *character* (Sue-in-the-past) in the story. For example, she begins this scene-setting by introducing one of the characters and describing his drinking habits: 'I remember when er (.) my father was alive he used to like a bottle of stout (.) used to (…) bottle about like this'. Following this, she adds another piece of information about Sue-in-the-past that turns out to be relevant to the story: 'and er ((laughs)) a- youll think (…) and er (.) I used to go to church in those days'. Again, her identification of Sue-in-the-past as a churchgoer carries implications regarding her attitude to her father's drinking.

The reported interaction can also be seen as working out Sue-in-the-past's place in events. She makes this available in terms of both her claimed access to detail of place and the sorts of things people who matter in the account did in them. For example, she interrupts the description of what her father liked to do to provide a piece of information relevant to understanding it – 'where we lived er (.) we had a (.) erm (.) a (.) firegrate with erm (.) <u>hobs</u>' – and then continues – 'and er (.) my dad used to (.) drink it out the bottle (.) and er (.) he used to stand it on the hob (.) an- and he used to say it was <u>beau</u>tiful'. In addition, in even more graphic ways, the other members of the reminiscence group vicariously experience events from the point of view of Sue-in-the-past. She describes what she claims to have 'heard' at the time, even the stout bubbling on the hob: 'and ((cough)) to make matters worse this erm (.) <u>stou:t</u> was (.) ch ch ch ch ((imitates noise of stout bubbling)) you could hear it (.) bubbling like' – a description that is greeted with laughter.

Sue makes great use of 'reported speech' in her experience narrative. This rhetorical resource is critical to the way in which she makes available the conclusion that, while remaining indifferent to drink herself, she is tolerant of others drinking (see Buchanan & Middleton, 1995). Her reported dialogue voices two opposing positions on drinking. On the one hand, Sue-in-the-past voices a moralising position – 'you won't drink your stout while he's here will you'. On the other, her animation of her father's comments to her – 'he said I <u>will</u> drink me stout (.) he said you ought to be ashamed of yourself' – and to the parson – 'I don't think going to church is doing my daughter much good (.) he said er (.) she asked me (.) not to have my bottle of stout (.) 'cos you were coming' – along with the parson's response – 'and Mr Jackson said well I've never heard such a thing in me life he said (.) I like one meself occasionally' – present the opposing view of drinking as a legitimate pleasure.

In summary, the remembering Sue accomplishes can be seen as an attempt to manage the otherwise difficult position of non-judgemental abstinence that Sue adopts in discussion in the reminiscence group. Sue displays that her past experiences entitle her to feel this way. She then uses the reported dialogue as a means of recruiting the voices of others in support of her declared position of tolerance in the present, while at the same time undermining, even mocking, the moral status of her position in the past. The contrast, which is established by virtue of the rhetorical structuring of the reported dialogue, is critical to establishing the plausibility of her claims to the effects of her experience. We can see that there is something at stake in the act of remembering and how that stake is attended to when producing recollections (see Edwards & Potter, 1992; Edwards, 1997).

Summary

We can see how a discursive approach to psychology (Edwards & Potter, 1992; Harré & Gillett, 1994) looks at how everyday versions of events (including people, things, states of affairs) are constructed and occasioned in talk and text. Because descriptions of events can be indefinitely varied, discursive analysis examines how specific versions are produced and fitted to the occasions of their production (see Heritage, 1984).

Overall, discursive analysis aims to reveal how versions are produced – how events are described and so on – and what interactional business participants accomplish by constructing their descriptions in one way rather than another (Potter & Wetherell, 1987). Any account of events reported is one of an indefinite number of possible reports. Often, accounts are contrasted rhetorically with alternative versions (Billig, 1996). Even the idea of versions being 'wrong' can be treated by considering the ways in which participants orientate themselves to and address issues of accuracy, rather than deciding such matters in advance (as is typically done in experimental studies of memory). The factual and cognitive status of a report, as being offered 'from memory' or on the basis of direct experience or as lies, error or hearsay, are also studied as matters to be established by participants, rather than categories applied by analysts after the event. Psychological concerns are redefined within discursive psychology as those that may arise for participants (Edwards & Potter, 1992).

We claimed at the start of this chapter that the discursive approach allowed us to provide empirical support for Halbwachs' claims regarding the collective basis of remembering. In all the sequences we have discussed, it is possible to see speakers' efforts at recollection as dependent on the contributions of others (Examples 1 and 2) or premised on a collectively held experience (Examples 3 and 4) or, finally, bound up with the communicative pragmatics of maintaining current group membership (Example 5). So, in each instance, remembering unfolds on a *social* and *collective* basis. Moreover, we have demonstrated various facets of the interactional organisation of remembering, such as sequential organisation, co-option, membership and pragmatics. These facets are all integral to how speakers communicate past experience as part of current projects and activities.

What, though, of our other claim – that the discursive approach maps more closely on to Bergson's concerns than does the cognitive experimental approach to memory? This is rather less clear. We have certainly been able to demonstrate how experience is fitted into current action (think again of the complexity of what Sue does in Example 5). We have not found it necessary to appeal to any 'things' – be they mental representations or particular neurological structures – in order to analyse how remembering as a process is accomplished. However, it would be difficult to argue that our analysis captured the 'fluid' and 'indivisible' nature of duration of which Bergson speaks so eloquently. We have proceeded as though our sense of the past, of what it means to 'endure' as a living being, were constructed entirely out of rhetorical resources, (such as recaps, elicitations, repetitions, reformulations (Mercer, 2000) and recontextualisations (Korolija, 1998; Linell, 1998). In so doing, inevitably we have ended up treating 'diachronic durability' – our sense of the ongoing continuity of duration – as an inbuilt relationship to and out of 'a succession of synchronic moments' (Clark, Hyde and McMahan, 1980).

How, then, may we overcome this tendency to treat continuity between past and present as something that is worked up anew every time via the rhetorical bits and bobs of the present interaction? To, put it another way, how is it possible to do justice to Bergson's pithy description of 'the continuous progress of the past which gnaws into the future and which swells as it advances'? As duration and memory are synonymous for Bergson, a relationship to the past is always already given in any particular recollection. Indeed, for Bergson, it is discontinuity – the artificial divisions in memory brought about by 'forgetting' – that stand in need of explanation. To address this, we must find a way of conceptualising how it is that the past becomes 'built into' remembering in such a way that it is possible for us to become aware of both 'continuity' and 'discontinuity' in our acts of recollection.

SIX

Projecting experience: succession and change in communicative action

The primary focus of the last chapter was on the discursive analysis of memory as an explicit topic of communicative concern. We looked at a series of sequences where speakers were gathered together in a collective project of remembering. In Example 1, the speakers had been set the task of recalling the details of a film. Examples 2 and 5 featured older people who were participating in structured reminiscence sessions. In Examples 3 and 4, a mother was systematically attempting to engage her child in a discussion of past family experiences, as inferred from a series of photographs. We argued that it is possible to point to a range of conversational features – such as recaps, elicitations, repetitions and reformulations – that enable speakers to construct some sort of continuity between present and past. If this is so, then it begs the question, to what extent, for practical purposes, is this conversational work the primary psychological process of remembering (see also Edwards, Middleton & Potter, 1992, and associated critical commentaries)?

However, one obvious obstacle to such a claim is the nature of the examples we have discussed so far. As these are all instances where remembering occurs as a structured, collaborative activity, could it be that the conversational features we have described are not really to do with remembering per se, but, rather, with establishing the context in which personal recollection can be achieved?

In order to overcome this objection, we will have to show – in this chapter and in those that follow – that the communicative acts by means of which remembering is expressed are not secondary to 'personal memory' but are, by contrast, intrinsic to our awareness of the past. Moreover, the invocation of the past is not confined merely to those occasions where 'remembering' and 'forgetting' is explicitly flagged as such, but occur instead as routine features of all manner of interactions.

At the same time, we will also have to address the issue that emerged at the end of the last chapter. If the pragmatics of situated, occasioned conversation are integral to remembering, does this mean that, contrary to Bergson's claims for duration, the past is constructed anew in the course of every interaction? Clearly this cannot be the case. For each of us, a sense of the past imbues our awareness of present matters at hand. The past often 'weighs heavy' in the present. One way of conceptualising this continuous relationship to the amassed past is in terms of 'historical consciousness' (see, for example, Bakhurst, 1990; Birth, 2003; Blight, 1997). To be a member of a particular culture or identify with a community necessarily means developing some sort of awareness of the historical circumstances that have shaped and affected that culture or community. In this sense, something of the past is 'inbuilt' in the present. Our sense of who we are and what is to be done, then, arise from a rich mixture of en passant elements of the past (Tschuggnall & Welzer, 2002; Middleton, 2002).

Sociocultural studies of the formation of mind – derived from the work of Vygotsky and Bakhtin – have explored the way in which historicity enters into the organisation of human action. Such work takes as central the assertion that human consciousness is organised within the appropriation, use and generation of culturally evolved resources. These include systems of symbolic representation and communication, artifacts and institution-alised practices for the generation and distribution of knowledge systems (Wertsch, 2002; see also Sylvia Scribner, 1985, for a detailed discussion of Vygotsky's uses of history and Lyra, 1999, for further work derived from Bakhtin).

This approach is well summarised by Brockmeier (2002: 21), who argues that, in order to understand remembering as a 'movement within a cultural discourse that continuously fuses the now and then, the here and now', it is necessary to recognise a number of 'interdependencies'. There is, he claims, no clear separation to be made between 'personal memory' and 'social memory' as the former always weaves itself into the latter. Equally, it is not possible to adequately disentangle 'mnemonic processes' from the discursive contexts in which they occur as these processes are often intrinsic to the very functioning of the context itself. For instance, the way in which 'remembering' is done in court is profoundly shaped by the nature of the legal proceedings and how a diarist records his or her past is structured by the form and constraints of the diary as a rich symbolic artefact.

Brockmeier is not arguing that the psychological dimensions of remembering are reducible to culture or context, but, rather that it is not possible to think one without the other – we are here confronted with interdependent and mutually reciprocal processes. This is exactly the position adopted by

Bartlett (1932) in his description of schemas as 'organised settings'. Here, experience is interdependent with symbolic resources afforded by a cultural setting. What is more, as people conventionalise such resources – that is, borrow, modify or adapt them to serve new purposes – it follows that the relationship between past and present is fluid. The persistence of symbolic resources in cultural history creates continuity, while the modification and adaptation of these same resources allows for the possibility of change. This dynamic of continuity and change is also identified by Bergson, who is similarly concerned with the manner in which people turn around on the continuity of their experience and the use they make of that experience in the present.

In this chapter, we will describe three forms of interdependency of experience that are present in the use people make of sociocultural resources, such as language, artefacts, place and communities of practice. These are interdependencies between remembering and forgetting, experience as incidental or intentional and experience as either *individual or collective.* Our aim will be to explore the extent to which a discursive approach is able to make visible the 'weight' of the past in the present and dilemmas of succession and change that subsequently emerge. We will show how speakers manage these dilemmas by attending to the three interdependent aspects of experience within emergent 'trajectories of participation'.

Interdependency of remembering and forgetting

In the previous chapter, we discussed the use of meta-cognitive formulations in remembering, such as 'I've been trying to remember that for a week'. We noted that these kinds of formulations are typically occasioned by emergent difficulties in the interaction. People make reference to various aspects of their conscious awareness as part of the social pragmatics of conversation. However, these formulations tend to evoke broader consequences that may project beyond the current interaction. For instance, they may help to establish the speaker as having a particular relationship to the past, for which they may or not be held accountable at some future point.

Consider, for instance, the following short excerpt – Example 1 – of talk from Lynch and Bogen (1996: 163), *The Spectacle of History: Speech, Text, and Memory at the Iran-Contra Hearings.* Oliver North – a senior US government official summoned before Congress to explain his conduct in a covert military–intelligence operation – faced problems of accountability in dealing with what he claimed he did not know and what he did not tell the then American President, Ronald Reagan.

Example 1

7 July, 1987, afternoon session, ML/DB transcript, p. 37.

> *Nields:* Were you aware of any (0.5) relatively contemporaneous shipments of Hawk missiles from the United States to Israel.
>
> (0.6)
>
> *North:* I don't think so, I mean uh you may refresh my memory again but, I do not know uh at this point of time that I knew that, no

In this example, what is at issue is whether or not Oliver North was aware of the shipment of military weapons from the US to Israel. As Lynch and Bogen point out, rather than straightforwardly reply 'yes' or 'no', what North does is offer a hedged response – 'I don't think so' – which leaves open the possibility of error. He then goes on to 'topicalise' his own memory, making the issue of what it is to have a memory central to his response. By inviting the congressional panel to 'refresh' his memory, North is formulating a notion that, while he is being truthful in his response, it is possible that the evidence on which this response is based – his memory as it currently stands – may potentially be in error. North's notion of a 'refreshed' memory is critical to the way in which his audience might or might not accept his claims 'as plausible and sincere'. The discursive formulation of a refreshed memory calls up particular consequences. As Lynch and Bogen (1996: 193) argue, it places his immediate reply to the Nields' cross-examination 'as an answer in and for the present; one that has no definitive relation to an actual past'.

We can see that the organisation of talk pre-empts future attributions concerning North's involvement in these affairs. North's display of uncertainty concerning what he may or may not remember, now or in the future, has consequences not only for the immediate cross-examination but also sets up trajectories of future significance and participation for his subsequent life and that of others in the world at large. North's interactional deployment of 'memory' is, then, remarkable for its emphasis on two particular interependencies of experience. First of all, North's apparent uncertainty is founded on the notion of the unreliability of memory, that forgetting shadows remembering. Put more simply, much as one would like to be able to remember clearly, inevitably there is much that one will forget. Now, as we argued in the last chapter, there is little to be gained from treating this kind of meta-cognitive formulation as a window on to mental processes. What matters is the social use of memory – how North constitutes his current access to past experience and the significance this access has for the future.

The second interdependency in North's response is the interactional flagging of past knowledge as acquired in an incidental rather than intentional manner. Questions implying intentional awareness in the past are refuted in terms of the incidental status of past and current knowledge. For example, Nields' request – 'Were you aware of any (0.5) relatively contemporaneous shipments of Hawk missiles from the United States to Israel' – directly addresses the intentional status of North's awareness at the time of certain events. North's reply – 'I don't think so, I mean uh you may refresh my memory again but, I do not know uh at this point of time that I knew that, no' – makes the tension between incidental and intentional knowing the issue. North invokes any knowledge that he might have had in the past – what he knew – as incidental to the status of his current knowing and, by implication, the status of his intentionality, his motives, in the past.

This short example encapsulates the social use of what it is to have a memory and how this is invoked in communicative action. The status of North's memory is the interactive output – not a cognitive input determining what can or cannot be represented in his talk. The very issue of experience as incidental versus intentional is at stake in the interactive organisation of this exchange. This is an important communicative resource for building in the salience of the past for present and future circumstances.

What we have also exemplified is how the future is built back into the past as part of the conversational action. As process philosopher Alfred North Whitehead (1933: 213) pointed out, it is easy to see how the future relates to the present:

> The most familiar habits of mankind witness to this fact. Legal contracts, social understandings of every type, ambitions, anxieties, railway timetables, are futile gestures of consciousness apart from the fact that the present bears in its own realised constitution relationships to a future beyond itself. Cut away the future and the present collapses, emptied of its proper content, immediate existence requires the insertion of the future in the crannies of the present.

It is less easy to identify how the future is built in and 'antecedent to itself' (Whitehead, 1933: 213). As we have just seen, one possible solution to Whitehead's problem is to examine the communicative resources used to build the past into the present and project forward versions of possible futures. To clarify this further, we will now turn to another set of examples.

Interdependency of incidental and intentional experience

As process philosophers, Whitehead and Bergson share a common concern with understanding how artificial distinctions or boundaries are created within the ongoing flow of experience. Our actions and activities cut out channels along which particular versions of the past and the future are brought together.

One way in which to approach how the past is present en passant is to study how we order and take meaning from the creation of arbitrary boundaries. Such boundaries may take on the status of significant points of transition, where events and experiences become marked, 'labelled', as turning points or watersheds in both public and private lives, such as presidential infidelity and impeachments – Clinton and Nixon; royal deaths – Diana; trials of public figures – OJ Simpson; Aids and BSE; international conflicts – first and second Iraq wars.

To take another example, much continues to be made of the 'new millennium'. The very notion of 'the millennium' is a conventionalisation of a calendrical transition. It is a purely arbitrary boundary. Nevertheless, a great many activities were organised around this boundary, including the installation of civic amenities and commemorative activities, the tracking and management of computer bugs and so on. The millennium, then, serves as a point around which the experience of living through the calendrical transition from 1999 to 2000/01 is organised in relation to a complex social choreography of circumstance, objects and relationships to others. This does not, and did not of course, guarantee that the 'millennial experience' would be memorable! However, the processes by which attempts were made to *make* it memorable are precisely what is of interest.

Sociologist of science Michel Callon (1991) uses the phrase 'punctualisation' to describe how artefacts and activities are coordinated in such a way as to generate the appearance of a unitary common 'front'. For example, when we insert a card into a cash machine (an automated teller), it is as though we are simply being given our own money. In reality, of course, this simple act involves the mediation of a staggering range of technologies, protocols and processes. The point Callon makes is that, so long as these 'mediators' function effectively, they can be safely ignored. We only tend to notice them when something goes wrong. Callon has extended this insight to the creation of 'facts' in science and more generally, such as in our social lives – this approach is commonly known as 'Actor-Network Theory' (ANT) (see Callon, 1986, 1991; Latour, 1987, 1999; Law, 1992, 2002). What a scientist or a politician calls a 'fact' is always the outcome of a complex and highly mediated process of research and debate. All of this becomes 'punctualised' – that is, gathered up and rendered invisible, albeit only in a precarious and provisional way – when it is presented as a 'matter of fact'.

We can use the notion of 'punctualisation' to understand how boundaries such as the millennium are produced. What comes to count as 'the millennial experience' is achieved by means of the complex mediation of a heterogeneous array of objects, people and places. However, as with the scientific fact or the cash machine, in order for the experience to become 'memorable', these mediators ought to disappear as they are 'punctualised' within a single event. What is of interest, then, is the work of gathering together past actions and events in order to create the effect of something 'memorable' and the simultaneous work of erasing, or 'forgetting', complexity and heterogeneity in favor of projecting the simplicity and unity of experience.

For example, consider the 1999 total solar eclipse. In the UK, this became a major media event, generating many column inches and hours of airtime concerning the individual and social relevance of the eclipse. Of particular significance was that, for many, witnessing a total eclipse was likely to be 'a once in a lifetime experience'. This need not be the case, given access to global transportation enabling people to 'collect' eclipse experiences. However, as with the millennial experience, we can explore the work required to make the case that the 1999 viewing in the Western hemisphere was, indeed, 'a once in life time experience'. Of particular interest was the way in which the event was reported in terms that set it up as having personal and historical significance for the future. British newspaper subeditors exploited the putative significance of the eclipse to the full in writing headlines, a few of which are gathered below (12 August 1999):

> Totally stunning: from Land's End to the Bay of Bengal they turned out for the sight of a lifetime. (*The Guardian*)

> Two minutes to last a lifetime. (*The Daily Telegraph*)

> The beauty and the terror of a moment that will live forever. (*The Express*)

> (T)he historic moment of darkness. (*The Times*)

Example 2 is a brief extract from the concluding paragraph of the leader article by James Dalrymple in *The Independent* (12 August 1999: 2), published in the UK the day after the eclipse. What is interesting is the ordering of reported experience in support of the future significance of the eclipse.

Example 2

> The young mother who had been upset by the beer drinkers thanked the old Cornishman, and we both patted the head of the blond-haired child in her arms. I had a sudden thought that she might live long enough to see another total eclipse in her

lifetime – and that I would certainly not. But it did not really matter. The child and I, and everybody else who was there on that wondrous morning, including the lager louts, had shared in a moment that none of us would ever forget.

Whether or not the hyperbole of the argument is justified is not the issue. What is significant is how the writer establishes the potential significance of this event for the future. As with Nield's question to Oliver North, the interplay of past experience as incidental or intentional is at stake. It is the permanency or not of the significance of that experience in the future lives of participants that is at issue. This is argued for in terms of the boundary between intentional and unintentional features of the experience that the author claims as being called to mind. The writer uses this boundary in establishing the claims to the future significance of this event in the lives of those who witnessed it and in terms of the way the event is ordered and made available to future readers of the paper. Unintentional witnessing and thoughts concerning commonplace events (offensiveness of beer drinkers, patting a child's head, sudden thoughts and the personal insignificance) are contrasted with and used to establish claims concerning the collective significance of the eclipse as a memorable event (see also Wooffitt, 1992). It is the gathering up of these 'unintentional details' and their simultaneous erasure when contrasted with the lasting significance of this 'once in a lifetime' spectacle that does the work of punctualising the experience and rendering it memorable. The piquancy of this contrast is what enables the projected future significance to be built back into the past.

Historical and personal significance is also at issue. The account attends to what might last or not, what will or will not be forgotten and remembered, what might or might not be attended to in the future. The account is also organised in terms of what might be clear and what obscure of the personal and collective experience of this once in a lifetime event, an event that has the potential to be the topic of conventionalised tropes such as 'Where were you when Kennedy was shot?' Thus, this short account also illustrates the way permanency and change are argued for in terms of interdependencies of experience as individually and collectively relevant. Permanence and change are at one and the same time both individually and collectively significant: 'The child and I, and everybody else who was there on that wondrous morning, including the lager louts, had shared in a moment that none of us would ever forget.'

The interdependency of personal and collective experience is used to argue for the memorability of the event. This 'historical' record (newspaper article) and the historical import of the event are accomplished both in terms of rhetorical contrasts between intentional and incidental features of experience and interdependencies of experience as individually and collectively relevant.

The interdependency of individual and collective experience in remembering

In the examples we have just discussed, setting up a trajectory of continuity and change is at issue. That is, the writers responsible for the texts are keen to project forward into the future a sense of what will certainly change – today's concerns and fleeting irritations, the bounded lifetime of given individual – and what will, in all likelihood, be preserved – the perfection of that single moment 'that will live forever'. It might be argued that what this tells us is simply that newspaper writers are in the business of creating catchy headlines. However, it is possible to analyse this process of establishing trajectories of continuity and change across a range of organised settings. Indeed, as Sumedha Gupta (1996) notes, projecting forward the interdependency of individual and social experience in terms of likely continuity and change is fundamental to the durability of the setting itself. She provides a good example of this in her analysis of parent child conversations. Example 2 is a recorded conversation between a mother and her five-year-old son discussing a family trip that they had taken a few days earlier (Gupta, 1996).

Example 3

(Transcription conventions are the ones used in the original manuscript.)

Mother: oh we got up really early. Were you tired?
Child: no
Mother: you weren't? I could have sworn you were tired you fell asleep in the car.
Child: I was not tired I I go to sleep late in the night I didn't sleep so early I didn't even sleep tiil I never even slept before we went before we woke up.
Mother: oh really
Child: yeah
Mother: oh I see, so you're saying you didn't sleep at night at all
Child: no
Mother: oh I can believe that because Grandma said you were first thing in her room at five wanting to know whether it was time to go, right?
Child: yeah
Mother: you are an energetic kid. You really like to do a lot.

[five minutes later.]

Mother: and what did you do while we were inside the building. You never told me that.
Child: we ran we we did a we did a race
Mother: you had a race?
Child: yeah

Mother:	who won?
Child:	I won all the time
Mother:	oohh
Child:	because I'm faster than him
Mother:	you may be also a little taller than him right?
Child:	yeah
Mother:	so you have longer legs, right?
Child:	yeah
Mother:	so that explains how you were faster than him
Child:	yeah
Child:	but I'm energetic and and faster

As Gupta (1996) points out, in the two parts of this example, we see the mother and child jointly establishing and contesting the significance of past events. The child's mental state, his capacity for mental awareness – tired, awake, asleep – is the subject of some debate. As with North's response in Example 1, there are consequences for both parties dependent on which of these terms is jointly accepted as an adequate description.

The child's resistance in accepting the mother's interpretation of his past mental state, his unwillingness to accept having been tired, provides the mother with an opportunity to elaborate the evidential basis of her claim – 'you weren't? I could have sworn you were tired you fell asleep in the car.' The child moves to counter the mother's 'sworn' evidence in an interesting manner. He makes a general claim not just in terms his putative tiredness on the night in question but also concerning his general capacity for not requiring sleep: 'I didn't even sleep till I never even slept before we went before we woke up.' His capacity for wakefulness (not sleepiness) is located within the general circumstances of other family members. That is, he emphasises the interdependency of his own personal experience with the collective family experience of preparing for the journey.

In what follows, we can see the mother picking up on the frailty of his argument in equivalent fashion. For example, the particular details of his falling to sleep or not the night before are not developed as direct issues of communicative concern. Rather, the mother develops her commentary on his recent past in terms of its reported impact on others: 'oh I can believe that because Grandma said you were first thing in her room at five wanting to know whether it was time to go, right?' The duality of experience, the relevance of the child's claims to a lively disposition, are thus made relevant in relation to others in a different way and with different consequences. In addition, the status of his past experience projects into the future in terms of judging him to be an 'energetic kid'.

The impact of this characterisation is powerfully illustrated in the subsequent dialogue, five minutes later, exploring the significance of the child's claims about his physical capacities. The mother here appears to be trying to socialise or seek normative grounds for the child's claims in terms of his relative stature rather than accept the child's preferred formulation of 'winning all the time' as being due to his exceptional abilities. She does this by, again, setting his past experience in the context of its relevance to others, thus undermining the possible hubris of the child's perspective of his 'superman' status in terms of his physical advantages relative to others. However, in addition, the child deploys the mother's characterisation of him as an 'energetic kid' to account for his claims to superior performance. As the mother is, to some extent, bound by her earlier formulation, this is a difficult claim to counter.

What this exchange illustrates is that claims concerning the past do not just influence each individual's original understanding of the event, they also have effects on future interpretations of experience. Moreover, when these claims are established not merely as a matter of personal experience but also as interdependent with collective experience, they gain an added robustness. As Gupta (1996: 9) puts it:

> in this sense, jointly constructing the past may not only work to form shared understanding but work to reconstruct past knowledge into personalised meaning systems; meaning systems that then may function to canalise the perception of future events.

Descriptions that are worked up collectively become projected into the future in such a way that they become difficult to resist – the mother becomes in some sense 'checked' by her earlier depiction of the child as 'an energetic kid'. Clearly, then, failure to examine such interdependencies would be a significant omission (see also Valsiner's 1994 argument for the study of what he calls 'inclusive separations'). Indeed, such interdependencies are just as much the province of participants in memory work as they are a conceptual tool for analysts understanding the social organisation of remembering and forgetting. Mother and son are engaged in a struggle to establish what the relevance is of the wider collective context against which both are reading the claims for personal experience. Again, it is important to make clear that neither we, as analysts, nor the speakers themselves, in their exchange, are attempting to reduce the personal to the collective. Rather, the interdependency of experience – as both individually and collectively significant – is being addressed as part of the process of establishing the legitimacy of recollections of past experience.

Trajectories of participation

The social organisation of memory is critical to managing issues of continuity and change. As we have seen, attending to various interdependencies in experience is the means by which the significance of the past is 'punctualised' and the future is 'canalised' – or, to put it in Whitehead's terms, rendered 'antecedent to itself'. It is also the means by which an organised setting can attempt to ensure its own durability relative to an uncertain future. By constructing both past and future as in some sense knowable, an organised setting can lay claim to ongoing continuity. Traditionally, 'formalisation' is the generic name given to processes whereby a practice or an organisation will attempt to 'future-proof' its endeavours by creating formal structures – such as standards, procedures, lines of accountability (see Cooper, 1992, for a thoroughgoing exploration of this idea). While that is undoubtedly the case, we will argue that both continuity and discontinuity are actively produced by members within organised settings as they attend to issues of 'remembering' and 'forgetting'.

Example 4 (Middleton, 1997b) was recorded in a meeting of a hospital unit providing intensive care for newborn babies (for further work undertaken in this setting, see Middleton, 1997b; Middleton, Brown & Curnock, 2000; Brown and Middleton, 2005). Rapid developments in the condition of patients are characteristic of this type of unit, as are frequent changes of medical and nursing staff. What this means is that dilemmas around succession and change are ongoing within the unit. For instance, in Example 4, current and projected forms of participation are the topic of concern. The exact details do not matter. What is being discussed is potential changes to the ways in which the authority to dispense a particular drug is managed. The speakers then try to establish what aspects of current ways of working ought to be protected and what changed.

Example 4

Key:
JGD = junior grade doctor
MGD = middle grade doctor
paed = paediatrician
labour suite = birthing room

> *JGD:* I think there's something positive about any doctor can sign it it doesn't matter you're a paed but if a doctor's available sign it
> *MGD:* I think that's open to error it'll be missed I think there's a routine we have to develop a routine whereby it's somebody's responsibility to sign the prescription who's responsibility really lies with the paediatrician
> *JGD:* I don't see how a slip's gonna be any easier than the notes really
> *MGD:* it means you're not looking for the notes and it means that it's done in labour suite they're all born in labour suite =
> *JGD:* = but labour suite are forgetting to stamp the notes so they're gonna forget to do that because they haven't got the well the receptionist
> *MGD:* it's much less likely if it's routine that a slip is available and a sticker's put on it and- for it to be missed

As with Examples 1 and 2, the issue of change and continuity is made visible in terms of the contrast between incidental actions and intentional actions. The problem that the doctors then wrestle with is the status of future actions. This turns on the question of how to make the prescription of the drug an intentional feature of how participants in this setting go about their work.

The middle grade doctor suggests that the answer lies with the formulation of a procedure that makes prescription writing a defined responsibility for a nominated group of doctors: '… we have to develop a routine whereby it's somebody's responsibility to sign the prescription …'.

We also see how interdependencies of actions, as individually and collectively relevant, are at stake. The junior grade doctor suggests that, as all doctors have the authority to write prescriptions for drugs – they all have the individual background and experience that equips them to have the authority to write prescriptions – it does not fundamentally matter whether or not a given doctor is also a paediatrician: 'I think there's something positive about any doctor can sign it it doesn't matter you're a paed but if a doctor's available sign it'.

Note how that proposition is rebutted by the middle grade doctor. We might imagine that the doctor could well have claimed the authority to say what should or should not happen. This is not the case. Instead the middle grade doctor makes a claim concerning the possible outcome of relying on the collective responsibilities of doctors to provide signatures that emphasises the necessity of establishing a routine where it is the direct responsibility of an *individual* to sign a prescription and, moreover, that this individual ought to be a paediatrician.

The moves between individual and collective relevance in relation to changes in practice are used to establish the grounds of the argument concerning the forms of organised settings that would produce continuities in the care of the babies in terms of the dispensing of this particular drug in the future: 'I think that's open to error it'll be missed I think there's a routine we have to develop a routine whereby it's somebody's responsibility to sign the prescription who's responsibility really lies with the paediatrician.' The junior grade doctor's counter-argument is formulated in terms of his or her individual perspective on the advantage or disadvantage of the suggested change in practice: 'I don't see how a slip's gonna be any easier than the notes really.' Again, this is countered by the middle grade doctor in terms of the collective relevance and projected benefits of individual action in using slips rather than looking for notes: 'It means you're not looking for the notes and it means that it's done in labour suite they're all born in labour suite ='.

Ole Dreier's (1997, 1999) concept of a 'trajectory of participation' usefully illuminates something of this discussion. Dreier is similarly concerned with the interdependent relationship between people and the social contexts in which they act. He argues for a model of human action where *participation* in a given social practice or context is taken as primary. As social beings, we are always already participating in some practice – we are never 'not involved' in one social context or another. Indeed, social contexts are themselves organised in relation to the potential ways in which participants will engage with them. A 'trajectory of participation' is, then, a projected series of engagements of people with a particular practice.

In relation to the current example, we can see that the doctors are involved in the formulation of possible trajectories of participation that will ensure, as a given, that someone must, in the end, be responsible for drug prescription, while at the same time, projecting new and innovative features of practice.

The relevance of the putative changes to work organisation are argued for in terms of the interdependencies and effects of these changes for individual and collective action. The argument implies the forms of organisational setting that would make it possible for routinised accountability to occur – the use of stickers.

Conventions and transitions are not so much built in as an emergent effect of the communicative organisation of socially ordered remembering and forgetting in group action. For example, what it is to forget is both reported as a matter of fact – 'but labour suite are forgetting to stamp the notes …' – and used as an argument for the collective position of the labour suite in the future, accounted for in terms of resources available to them: '… so they're gonna forget to do that because they haven't got the well the receptionist.'

We may also use the idea of 'trajectory of participation' to display how persons attend more broadly to issues of continuity and change in terms of biography and history. One final example illustrates this point. Example 4 was recorded in group discussion, with older people reporting their experiences of education in the 1920s and 1930s after listening to recorded school sounds (Gibson, 1989).

Example 5

Key:
MC = co-organiser 2

> *Mary:*   (…) I was a bad writer ((MC laughs))
> *MC:*   well you must have got better you're very good now
> *Mary:*   no not now with my arthritis the teacher used to take me up to ((laughs)) they
>   used to take me to the blackboard before maybe 40 of a class (.) I had to write

(.) the teacher wrote on the top line you see and I was supposed to copy it as near as possible to hers until I got to be a good writer (.) and in the Irish School they had an enormous big certificate it had been awarded by the Vere Foster people for a team of writers from the Irish Society School (.) that was before my time (.) and the teacher took me up one day and she said to me (.) can you read that (.) and I said I can (.) and she said do you see your name there (.) and I said no I don't (.) and she said no and you never will ((other laughter)) (.) and I never <u>did</u> ((laughs))

MC: you weren't good enough Mary

Mary: no that was before my time you see but my grandfather wrote like that

MC: yes

Mary: he was a beautiful writer and so was my father

History and biography are relevant here in terms of what is taken to be the changing status of participation in historically changing traditions of writing. This short example invokes a whole range of trajectories of significance and participation, both now and then. What it is to be or not to be a member of a particular tradition of practice and the implications this has for abilities to participate in cognate activities is a live concern. The way Mary organises her account of learning to write illustrates this. She positions herself in terms of transitions and continuities of abilities, both now and in the past. Tradition and changes in the community of practice of writing are used interactively in the social organisation of her reminiscence. Changes from the writing practices in her father's and grandfather's day are used as a means of establishing continuities and changes in the individual and collective relevance of her shifting identities of competency as a writer. Here we see the interplay of history and biography used as a communicative resource in terms of changes in traditions in a community of practice. In addition, trajectories of significance and participation are deployed in the ironised reported dialogue at the chalkboard with the teacher.

What Mary does in this example is to describe how her future trajectory of participation in traditional writing practices was already mapped out for her at school. She populated a present the future of which, in these terms, had already been established – she was doomed to fail. However, in explicating this trajectory, as set up by the teacher, Mary is able to mark the difference in terms of the lived experiences of previous generations who inhabited a world where such craft was judged differently. The potency of the memory emerges in the way she turns round on that difference and, in so doing, marked out her future as one that was not necessarily determined by the immediate trajectories of the teacher's judgements. Put simply, Mary is able to turn around on the very idea of a trajectory of participation being mapped out for her and use that as a way of making sense of apparent discontinuities between her own biography and that of former generations.

Summary

Bergson's demand that we consider the manner in which the 'past gnaws into the present' has been of central concern to us in this chapter. In order to do justice to this idea, we have had to address how people position themselves via their communicative acts in relation to the 'weight' of the past and the significance of possible futures.

Bergson himself thought that the way to proceed with this problem was to analyse how people mobilise their past experience in relation to current circumstances and how this turning around on experience extends and projects the scope of current actions into the future.

In this chapter, we have been able to demonstrate this process empirically. In the examples we have discussed, we have shown how speakers attend to and manage various interdependencies of experience. These include interdependencies between remembering and forgetting, the incidental or intentional basis of action and the individual and collective significance of experience.

We have argued that these interdependencies in experience are useful in so far as they enable people to construct 'boundaries' in the ongoing flow of their experience (this is our rendering of Bergson's notion of 'cutting out'). Such boundaries may do the work of both 'punctualising' a given event – that is, attempting to preserve it as simple and memorable by means of a systematic 'forgetting' of the complex mediations that make it possible – and 'canalising' future significance – that is, projecting forward the likely consequence of present circumstances in such a way that the future becomes 'antecedent to itself'. The notion of a 'trajectory of participation' neatly captures this work of managing issues of continuity and change by relating them to versions of the past and possible futures.

Throughout this chapter, we have, following Bartlett, been at pains to stress that the interdependency of personal experience and the organised settings in which it occurs means that not only is neither reducible to the other but also that a certain malleability is to be expected in both. Because people are able to conventionalise the symbolic resources within which they find themselves historically located, it follows that we are not victims of our cultural or historical circumstances – change or modification are always possible. However, have we perhaps overemphasised the ability of people to turn around on their own historical circumstances? Is it not the case instead that history exerts a holding power over us that is often difficult to resist? Does not what we take to be historical consciousness often resemble 'false consciousness'?

Susan Rasmussen (2002) points out that a shortcoming of an exclusive focus on interaction is that is risks becoming blind to the real power of broader historical and social dynamics. She elegantly argues that, while it is important to attend to understanding how succession and change are negotiated in a given setting, it is also important to appreciate how settings define the conditions under which such negotiation is possible at all. That is, people are not able to do and say as they like – their sayings and doings are, to some extent, structured by the nature of the settings in which they are obliged to participate. The relationship between past and present is, then, in some sense already 'punctualised' and 'canalised' in advance. We think Rasmussen is right. We are lacking a sense of how people are 'compelled' by certain versions of the past and forced to engage with these versions in order to make sense of their own recollections. In order to illuminate this further, we must now start to excavate further the nature of organised settings. This requires that we start to tack in the opposite direction and go from Bergson back towards Halbwachs.

SEVEN

Localising experience: implacement, incorporation and habit in zones of personal relations

Our concern in the course of the last two chapters has been with understanding how 'remembering' and 'forgetting' allow people to situate themselves in the flow of lived experience. We have seen how this is achieved by means of various rhetorical and conversational features of communicative action. We have also described how experience is 'punctualised' and 'canalised' via the management of various interdependencies, resulting in the knotting together of pasts and futures in the present. This ongoing work is essential in not only making sense of personal experience but also ensuring the endurance of the organised settings that are immanent to such forms of experience. Remembering and forgetting are, then, integral to the settings in which they occur.

Edward Casey (1987: 182) pithily draws attention to this grounding of remembering in his remark that, as experience '*takes place in place* and nowhere else, so our memory of what we experience is likewise place-specific: it is bound to place as its own basis.' Casey is arguing that our relationship to the places and spaces in which we dwell profoundly affects how and what we remember. Bergson (1991) also argues that, while it is necessary to avoid the conflation of memory with space, our recollections are 'called out' by the demands of the immediate contexts in which we are acting. Moreover, he is sensitive to the dynamic relationship between experience and place – the unwinding of experience (or 'virtualisation') occurs in tandem with our efforts to engage with and act on our immediate environment ('actualisation'). Finally, part of what Bartlett (1932) sought to make visible with his notion of a 'schema' or 'organised setting' was the complex mix of 'affect' and 'attitude' that characterises our involvement with a given cultural location. That is, we feel invested in the places in which we dwell, which seem to us to shape the way in which we apprehend the world and relate to our own past.

In this chapter, we will seek to explore further the relationship between remembering and place. We will try to understand how place acts as a source of meaning and significance for our recollections and the ways in which features of place exercise a 'holding power' over memory. Halbwachs provides the guiding thread for our discussion.

As outlined earlier, while Halbwachs (1980) recognised the importance of linguistic resources in social practices of remembering and forgetting, he also identified other important resources that define the particularities of what he calls a shared 'physiognomic' system of gestures, social practices, artefacts, territorial sites and so on. This complex articulates the past in such a way that it can appear as if places 'speak' their history to us. However, what Halbwachs invites us to attend to is the work that is involved in 'territorialising' space, of creating relationships between groups and the material contours of their local world. The immediacy of the past that we feel so strongly in certain places is, then, not some quasi-mystical emanation, but, rather, the outcome of the creation of what Halbwachs refers to as 'zones of personal relations'.

We will examine these 'zones of personal relations' in relation to a range of empirical examples. We want to understand how these zones are produced and sustained, the ways in which they afford remembrance by articulating the particularities of place, practice and objects into discourse. Most importantly, how it is that invoking these particularities establishes a 'feeling for place' that can affectively commit others to the versions of the past that are constructed in our descriptions of place.

Localising the past

Halbwachs argues that, once a collective framework is in place, group members are effectively obliged to situate their own recollections within the 'branchings' and 'ramifications' that it sets out.

This is achieved by means of a process Halbwachs calls 'localisation'. There are two aspects to this process. First, the tendency to 'summate' recollections from different periods into a composite image or idea – for example, bygone times, the 'good old years', the 'dark days'. Second, the 'projection' of these ordered relationships on to the past, such that a 'singularly vivid image' appears 'on the screen of an obscure and unclear past' (1992: 60).

Our initial aim is to illustrate this dual process in more detail. To do this, we will refer back to the sequence concerned with the morality of drinking that we previously introduced in Example 5 Chapter 5 (Buchanan, 1993;

Buchanan & Middleton, 1995). Our concern then was to demonstrate the social organisation of remembering and (re)membering in the course of participating in a reminiscence group. In other words, we focused on claims concerning past experience of drinking and how reported shifts in moral probity provided the opportunity to work membership of a group. However, we ignored key features of both the setting in which the sequence occurs and the setting that is described in Sue's narrative. We will now display in Example 1 (Buchanan & Middleton, 1995) how establishing the relevance of the particularities of these two settings – present and past – is integral to the act of remembering.

Example 1

Sue:	I mean I've got nothing against drink (.) if people enjoy drink I- I think they're entitled to it (.) but erm (.) it's not for me (.) apart from er (.) lemonade and (.) shandy (.) I don't mind that ((another conversation intrudes for some seconds at this point, until Sue continues))
Sue:	I remember when er (.) my father was alive (.) he used to like a bottle of stout (.) used [to (…) bottle about like this (.) and (&)
Rose:	[mm (.) <u>stout</u> oh yes (.) stout
Sue:	(&) er (.) where we lived er (.) we had a (.) erm (.) a (.) fire grate with erm [(.) <u>hobs</u> I think they called them (…) hobs (.) and er (.) my (&)
Female?:	[ehh [
Meg?:	[yeah that's (yeah) [
Ted:	[ah yeah [
Female?:	[(…)
Sue:	(&) dad used to (.) drink it out the bottle (.) and er (.) he used to stand it on the hob (.) an- and he used to say it was [<u>beautiful</u> (&)
Ted:	[warming
Sue:	(&) (.) and er ((laugh)) a- you'll think (…) and er (.) I used to go to church in those days (.) and erm (.) the parson (.) we had a parson that used to visit (.) and er (.) I said to me dad (.) the parson- (.) I said that the parson's coming (.) [(&)
Ted:	[is that why he kept it on the hob
Sue:	(&) I said that you won't drink your stout while he's here will you (.) ooh my [(&)
Ted:	[((laugh))
Sue:	(&) dad was disgusted he said I <u>will</u> drink me stout (.) he said you ought to be ashamed of yourself (.) and ther[e it stood on the hob (&)
Male?:	[(…)
Sue:	(&) y'know and in walked the parson with his (.) dog collar on I didn't [know what to do (.) and ((cough)) to make (&)
Rose?:	[((laugh))
Sue:	(&) matters worse this erm (.) <u>stou:t</u> was (.) ch ch ch ch ((imitates noise of stout bubbling)) you could hear it (.) bubbling like (&) ((general laughter))

Sue: (&) (.) yeah and er (.) me father said to him er (.) ooh and er (.) this parson's name was a Mr Jackson he was a very very nice man (.) and m- me father said er (.) I don' t (.) I don't think going to church is doing my daughter much good (.) he said er (.) she asked me (.) not to have my bottle of stout (.) 'cos you were coming (.) and Mr Jackson said well I've never heard such a thing in me life he said (.) I like one meself occasionally (.) I never felt so bad after tha::t ((laughing tone))
((general laughter))

In the account, Sue provides us with a glimpse of her personal life during her youth and via this, a glimpse of the culture in which that life was lived. The remembered past that she invokes is not the past in some abstract, general sense, but it is a localised and 'peopled' past, a past mapped out in terms of practices that people engaged in, the significance of objects in the domestic spaces of her younger life and in terms of the social relationships of those people mediated by such practices and objects.

We have already discussed how Sue's account works to accomplish situated identities for herself and other participants in relation to the morality of drinking, but the invocation of this localised, 'peopled' and 'objectified' past also displays and draws on an ordering of the place that is taken as standing prior to any given acts of remembering. The drinking habits of fathers, the religious beliefs of young parishioners, the comings and goings of local parsons – all this is laid out by Sue as a commonsensical, taken-for-granted 'zone of personal relations' that is relevant to the elaboration of her identity in the present. The success of her account crucially depends on Sue's ability to establish that her direct experience of these relations entitles her to invoke them in the present and, moreover, that this invocation is of direct relevance to the present assembled company.

Sacks (1992a) examined this working of entitlement in relation to the telling of 'second stories' in conversation. In part, his argument relates to the distinction between 'claiming' and 'showing' understanding – that is, one way of showing that you have understood another's story is to produce one that is similar to it. He goes on to enquire into the precise nature of this similarity and suggests that a common procedure that recipients of stories use to find a similar story is as follows. If the teller appears as a character, find a story in which you appear as the same character (such as witness to a car accident). The teller's 'place' in events, then, is not only significant in terms of working entitlement to experience, but also as something that recipients attend to as a means of finding stories that they can tell in localising them to current circumstances. Put another way, the zone of personal relations, that Sue unpacks in her narrative may serve as an anchor and reference point for similar acts of localisation by Sue's interlocutors.

It is worth dwelling for a moment on just how Sue performs this unpacking. She moves between the first person active voice and the more passive collective 'we' (referring to her family life at the time). Moreover, she introduces her father as a character in the narrative. Schrager's (1983) work on the social organisation of oral history testimony is relevant here. He notes the way in which tellers of narratives move between different 'points of view' or 'places' in the course of the telling – for example, speaking sometimes as 'I', sometimes as 'we'. In doing this, the teller expresses not only her own perspective on events, but also that of others, incorporating their experiences into her account. In moving between the use of 'I' and 'we', we position ourselves as having a place in an orderly set of relationships between people, things and events and we identify ourselves as members of various social groupings, on whose behalf we presume to speak. We display and enter into a coherent and taken-for-granted zone of personal relations, that is taken as standing prior to and extending beyond the immediate circumstances of our telling, in terms of both space and of time. Sue can be seen to be creating a potentially habitable world, one in which the recipients of her story can place themselves and locate, even if only tangentially, their own experiences.

Incorporation

As Halbwachs describes them, zones of personal relations, contain their own sets of values, desirable qualities, relevant categories of things deemed to exist in the world and so on. However, he also points to the peculiar way in which these values, qualities and categories become naturalised. Seen from within the zone, they appear to acquire an almost timeless character. In Sue's account, for instance, it is simply taken as given that fathers drink beer by the fire, that parsons visit young parishioners at home. The dense nexus of values regarding family and religious life that are embedded here are not up for questioning – that is just how things are.

If this is the case, how is it that the recipients of Sue's story are able to locate their own experiences within this most particular zone of personal relations? We may speculate that, for some listeners, this might be an entirely alien world, peopled with peculiar characters and utterly strange practices, yet Rose, Meg and Ted all contribute to the unfolding account. They all 'do' affiliation by reiterating or elaborating on details as the narrative unfolds. It is notable that at no point is there any resistance and questioning. Even requests for clarification – such as 'is that why he kept it on the hob' – are located within the world as it is given.

The three other speakers, then, appear to be incorporated into the zone of personal relations, that is being mapped out, even though it is entirely possible that they might never have known such a world. Furthermore, it is also possible that all three might take issue with the moral order that infuses this zone – that they may disagree in part or wholly with the values that are writ large in the story. Indeed, as we described previously, the apparent point of its narration is to allow Sue to articulate her abstinence from drinking alcohol without appearing to be adopting the 'moral high ground'. This makes the apparent incorporation of Rose, Meg and Ted all the more puzzling.

We can unravel this puzzle a little more by focusing on what 'incorporation' means in this instance. Connerton (1989) points to physical activities – gestures, movements, skilled actions – as the 'bodily substrate' on which commemoration occurs. The embodied performance of certain activities – that is, 'incorporating practices' – does a work of commemoration that differs in kind to the telling of narratives. Thus, in taking the 'body of Christ' in Communion, the worshipper re-enacts and memorialises the relationship between the Son of God and mortal believers, and, in sitting 'nicely' with legs crossed and arms folded, the child performs the historically given relationship of authority between teacher and pupil and ensures, albeit only briefly, its persistence into the present moment. In both cases, the performance of the activity commits the person to the set of values that are being commemorated, without these values needing to be verbally articulated.

Now, as recipients of Sue's story, Rose, Meg and Ted are certainly not required to perform any physical accompaniment. Nevertheless, the thrust of the story is to work up the contours of a physical environment in which the listeners can potentially see themselves as acting. Care is taken to deploy the correct term to invoke the particular kind of fireplace present in the room. The bottle of stout placed on the hob is described in such a way that Ted is able to imaginatively appreciate or savour its reported 'beautiful' qualities – and, hence, taste – as 'warming'. All three are invited to enjoy Sue's embarrassment as she is literally caught between the father and the parson, with all eyes drawn to the 'bubbling' bottle. The narrative places the listeners within its world and carefully directs their gaze back and forth between the characters and 'ch ch ch ch' of the warming stout.

It may, then, not be necessary for the participant to actually 'do' anything at all, but merely for them to experience how it would be to potentially act in some environment for incorporation to occur. Tarnya Cooper (1999) extends Connerton's work in this way in a fascinating account of how nineteenth-century viewers of engravings of Rome produced by Giovanni Battista Piranesi found themselves so deeply drawn into the images that, when they were eventually able to visit the city, they were left with the confusing sense of having 'been there already'. Piranesi's work was remarkable in a prephotographic age for its manipulation of topographical detail. In particular, Piranesi used a variety of pictorial devices to dramatise his views of Rome in such a way that the 'magnificent' character of various architectural features could be seen. Strategically placed figures in the images would, Cooper (1999: 122) argues, act to direct the gaze of the viewer, such that they could imaginatively place themselves in the scene:

> Piranesi's cast of disreputable male characters attempt to clamber up the monument's façade, over rubble and distorted trees ... they act as visual tour guides to the eye or *cicerone*, offering up the pyramid as a cultural circus to be explored, consumed and digested by following the sinuous human forms against the darkened façades.

This vicarious experience allowed the viewer to see the city '*as if* they were themselves already gauging the space of the catacombs, or scaling the monuments' (1999: 119). First-time visitors to Rome who had already experienced the city in Piranesi's prints then found themselves curiously both already familiar with the topography and disturbed by the disjunction between what they were now seeing and their recollections of Piranesi's depiction – 'As Beckford, Goethe and Hazlitt all found, being in Rome became a sort of dialogue between the remembered and the real' (1999: 114).

The detailed description of Sue's former home then acts in a similar fashion to the tour guides in Piranesi's prints. Both serve as the means for incorporating the listener or viewer, allowing them to imaginatively place themselves in a localised set of personal relationships, to vicariously experience what it must be to move through that physical environment. The crucial element to stress is that, following Connerton, this experience is not primarily cognitive or intellectual. Rather, it is a matter of feeling that one could physically engage with the features of the place as described – for example, one could pick up and drink the stout, savouring the warming taste on the tongue and throat or look back and forth between the arriving parson and outspoken father, frame the squirming Sue!

To be incorporated into a localised zone of personal relations, is then to enter into a trap for the senses where one feels physically part of events as recollected.

Summating the past

If Sacks' and Schrager's work draws attention to the way in which talking about the past works to locate us not only in the world in which those events occurred but also in the place in which they occurred, then Connerton and

Cooper allow us to see how participants are physically incorporated into the relationships that constitute place. We may draw together these observations under the rubric of what Halbwachs calls 'summation'. For Halbwachs, summation occurs when a collective framework organises the details of the past in such a way that they become concatenated in a particular image. He points to family memory as a particular instance, where a particular scene, such as a 'typical' evening in the family home, will dominate collective memory. This scene is not a direct recollection of a specific moment in time, but, rather, a prototypical model that is assembled with 'elements borrowed from several periods which preceded or followed the scene in question' (Halbwachs, 1992: 60). The value of this prototype is that it acts as a resource that serves as common currency for all group members – who are able to display their membership by being able to reproduce the scene – and allows for indefinite modification (within limits) on each occasion that it is recalled.

Sue's narrative, then, appears to have something of this prototypicality. Its clear and effective narrative structure suggests that it has been rehearsed on numerous occasions and, we may suspect, contains details that might, in actuality, be drawn from differing instances and subsequently combined together to lend the account its 'singularly vivid' character. Equally, Piranesi's engravings are prototypical in as much as they combine views of Rome and architectural details that would not have been visible to the viewer in the way that Piranesi constructs them. The summated prototypical image is, then, not a direct representation of some event as it happened or some object as it was, but, rather, a compelling construction that draws its power from the ability to incorporate the listener or viewer into the texture of the world it recollects.

Recollections of this type often exemplify a general characteristic of the past as recalled, such as a particular social practice. Example 2 is a typical instance of this. The extract, is as with Sue's story also drawn from Buchanan and Middleton (1995). Mary, the care worker, is asking Enid about the management of domestic chores:

Example 2

Mary: how about you Enid (.) how did you manage in those days

Enid: I used to do about the same you know (.) you used to put em in a tub first (.) an er (.) give em a good punch (.) my mother made us count to a hundred ((laugh))

Mary: did she

Enid: yes ((laughing)) (.) we couldn't stop punching until we'd done a hundred (&)

Mary: o::h

Enid: (&) (.) and then we had to get em out and rub em

Mary: yeah

> *Enid:*   and er (.) put em in a bath at the side of us (.) and then we should get them out then (.) and put em back in the tub (.) give them another little punch (.) and then we used to have to put em in the copper with some soda and Sunlight ((soap))

The formulation of washing clothes 'in those days' summates a whole range of prototypical practices. In response to the care worker's question, Enid begins by speaking as 'I', then mentions her mother and how her demands concerning the way washing should be done defined what it was to do washing at that time – 'you used to put em in the tub first.' The term 'you' in this context is both 'what was generally done in those days' and how this particular family actually went about its business – 'my mother made us count to a hundred.'

It is only after establishing this level of generality that Enid moves to 'we' – 'we couldn't stop punching.' This shift also specifies that the recollection is of Enid's childhood rather than her washday routine as a housewife. The 'we' is invoking a particular zone of personal relations that is exemplified around prototypical 'washdays' as one of a number of children in the family and what it was to have a place in a past where they all worked together and helped in relation to one another.

Again, as in Example 1, this is an occasioned description that works to locate the speaker in relationship with various features of place. This recollected place is made habitable for recipients by means of the extended description of the mundane washday routine. The washing is given a 'good punch', repeatedly, while Enid and her siblings 'count to a hundred', then extracted, rubbed, repositioned, given a 'little punch', transported, placed in a 'copper' tub, treated, mixed and allowed to rest.

This sequence of highly prescribed actions has all the character of the 'restricted' sets of movements that Connerton (1989) identifies with ritual. As with any ritual, these described movements carry with them a set of moral sensibilities about the value of cleanliness and how it is to be achieved, along with an ethic of collective family labour. Enid does not need to articulate these values directly as they are performed in the very act of describing the washday routine.

In Enid's recollection, we see both aspects of summation at work. On the one hand, the linguistic shift from 'you' to 'we' marks out membership and the collective currency of what is remembered – this memory defines Enid as having a place in a family, in an 'organised setting' with its own procedures and so on. On the other hand, the dense description of the washday routine in terms of the physical manipulation of the washing serves both to ground a specific moral order in a way that makes it difficult to challenge directly and incorporate the listener by means of their ability to locate themselves in this pattern of activity – to feel the hard and gentle punches, strain with bending over the tub, smell the soda and Sunlight soap dissolving in the tub.

Example 3 is taken from the same discussion as that used in Example 2 (Buchanan & Middleton, 1995). Here, the speakers Jean and Doris use 'we' in a potentially more general sense.

Example 3

Doris: but I think (.) it's lovely to see them flying in the wind
Mary: washing
Doris: your clean sheets
Mary: that's me (.) I love to see washing (.) I don't like these rotary (.) lines (.) I like to see it actually bl- with a prop=
Jean: =on the line like we did
Mary: with a prop (.) I like it on the line (.) I think they get a good blow
Jean: up on the line (.) yes
Doris: because we had (linen?) sheets then (.) whereas you get nylon sheets now (.) so easy to wash (.) but we had sheets to be ironed didn't we (.) and pillowcases (.) and the lot (.) blankets
Jean: everything
Mary: of course you had blankets then (.) how did you go on with the blankets then washing blankets

As in the previous extract, the speakers here move readily to nominate themselves as members of social groups, as participants in social relationships by using the word 'we'.

Schrager (1983), writes about the openness of reference of 'we' and the way that this enables an account to be at once personal and collective, and collective in varying degrees. 'We', then, may be heard as indexing a group, an age cohort or a period in time. This openness has the effect of potentially extending and conflating the values of the group to which the speaker claims membership with that of a more general historical collective – the 'we' who constituted 'the people' at that time.

What is also striking in the extract is the way that Mary – the care worker – becomes incorporated into the unfolding recollection by attending to specific features of drying sheets and blankets. Her first turn makes a contrast between rotary lines, which, by being qualified as 'these', indicates an object that is currently in use – 'I don't like these rotary lines', – and longer lines, which are supported by a prop. Jean seizes on the reference to a prop and line and claims ownership – 'on the line like we did' – by using the collective 'we', thereby relocating the objects as emblematic features of a recollected prototypical scene of washing.

Doris then further elaborates this prototypical scene by setting up a further contrast between the physical properties of sheets 'then' and 'now'.

This contrast also performs some rather delicate work. Freighted within the contrast of physical properties – that sheets 'then' required ironing, whereas sheets 'now' are 'easy to wash' – is an implied difference in values. Washing, drying and ironing 'then' presented a significant investment of domestic labour for Doris and Jean, as indicated by the three-part list of 'sheets to be ironed didn't we (.) and pillowcases and the lot blankets'. The implication is that Mary – despite her enthusiasm for older drying methods, shown when she says, 'I like it on the line I think they get a good blow' – has no understanding of what this practice actually involved when the materials to be washed were so significantly different. She has it easy, it might be said.

Here we see an interesting example where the incorporation of the recipient of a recollection is accompanied by an implicit critique issued by the narrator. Doris and Jean draw Mary into their collective memory of what it was to dry clothes in former times, but do so in such a way that Mary is obliged to accept a contrast between the values of 'then' and 'now', which also contains an implicit reproach for her 'easy' life nowadays. To paraphrase, it is all very well and good for Mary to like seeing washing blowing on the line, but she has no idea of just what work that pleasant sight meant! We may also discern that Mary picks up something of a possible rebuke as, in her final turn, she orientate directly to this contrast between 'then' and 'now' by identifying Jean and Mary as 'you' – 'of course you had blankets then' – and by going on to topicalise blankets as a particular object of concern – 'how did you go on with the blankets then'.

We will now turn to examine this use of contrasts, and the way in which they set up ineluctable differences in moral orders, in more detail.

Projecting zones of relations into the past

In many discussions of reminiscence work – and, indeed, everyday talk – 'the past' is rarely referred to as such. Instead, phrases such as 'bygone days', 'times gone by', 'the olden days', 'yesteryear' and so on are typically encountered. In this way, the past is gathered up in terms of a singular or vivid image that obscures any heterogeneity of relationships. The past is set forth as though it could be grasped in an immediate and straightforward way without contradiction or indeterminacy. A similar kind of work is done in representing the past as a time that 'belongs' to someone – as 'my time', 'our day' and so on. Projection, then, as Halbwachs describes it, involves this setting out of a clearly presented zone of personal relations that are identified or marked as belonging to the historical experience of a particular group.

Part of this claiming of 'our time' for a particular group is the dual marking of the past as both discontinuous with the present – the past is 'gone', it is irrevocably unalterable – and, yet, still coincident with the ongoing lives of group members who are defined by that shared past. Coincident, that is, not with the mere fact of their existence – the author of such words in the present is clearly still alive – but, rather, with the way in which lives were lived, with the practices by means of which those lives were constituted. What we are now, speakers claim, is a product of a past that we shared. Such projected ordering of past relationships localises the place of the past in ways that makes it available for rendering the significance of experience in the present. Example 4 (Buchanan & Middleton, 1995), shows this in the sequence concerning domestic chores – such jobs as cleaning doorsteps are taken to be emblematic of 'former times'.

Example 4

> *Doris:* I remember it because wasn't there a saying if your front doorstep was clean
> your home was clean and anybody that didn't do their front doorstep
> *Vera:* never see anybody do their doorstep these days do you

Doris refers to the cultural significance of this practice, which was so important that it was formulated as a saying. Vera, then, contrasts this with present practices – 'never see anybody do their doorstep these days do you?'– in such a way as to mark the disappearance of the former practice and, at the same time, to suggest the moral implication that follows from this disappearance – that people care less about cleanliness than they used to.

A unitary or singular view of the past is set in place that effaces any moral ambiguity by ruling out inconsistencies or deviations in the implied routines as a sanctionable matter. Doris does not need to spell out the nature of the sanction levied against 'anybody that didn't do their front doorstep' because, within the zone of relations that she is projecting, such a thing is unthinkable – '*everybody* cleaned their doorstep!' Doris and Vera are working up these relationships to make a strong contrast with 'these days' (indefinite present tense) where 'you' (an unspecified disinterested observer) 'never' (extreme case) 'see' (direct witnessing) 'anybody' (inclusive generalised plural) do their doorstep.

In this way, a simplified and abbreviated past is used as the contrast pair to an equally vivid and reductive version of the present. By spanning both times, Doris and Vera are able to locate themselves as being defined by the values of former times and, thus, entitled to pass judgement on the failings of the present.

Projection and contrast also dominate the sequence in Example 5, from Gibson (1989).

Example 5

FG:	Mr Jones do you look with pleasure on school days
Mr Jones:	well I never had any unhappy moments (.) I never was very clever (.) so they didn't expect too much from me but (.) er (.) the education that I got was very little and I left school before er (.) six and a half months before I was fourteen and worked ever since until retirement (.) but (.) er (.) I was just saying to Mrs Coulter here (.) that we weren't meek or mild and we were up to all the devilment of the day (.) the discipline in class (.) no one would ever think of interrupting your master or mistress as the case may be (.) so it is very difficult for (.) me at my old age to understand the thuggery that goes on in schools now and even masters attacked
Mrs M:	if you wanted the teacher's attention you put up your hand ((laugh))
Mr Jones:	oh golly yes (.) and if- if you had you couldn't do that too often because you weren't allowed out too often (.) (&)
Mrs M:	no
Mr Jones:	(&) you might do it once a day (...)

In Example 5, one of the group's co-organisers, Faith Gibson, asks Mr Jones about his schooldays. After giving her a few brief biographical details, he moves on to an account of the discipline maintained when he was at school: 'the discipline in class no one would ever think of interrupting your master or mistress as the case may be' – and goes on to compare this with 'the thuggery that goes on in schools now and even masters attacked' again, we have a disciplined past of orderly relationships and authority. In making it clear that this contrast is not due to a difference in the nature of children – he says, 'we weren't meek or mild and we were up to all the devilment of the day' – the projected orderliness of the past makes available the contrast with the indiscipline of the present.

As with the previous example, the projection of orderliness effaces deviation and deviancy in the past. The descriptions of the 'ordered past' provides the projected framework for constructing the difference in the morality of times past and present. For example, while, in the past, 'interrupting' was not even thought of, in the present, 'thuggery' and attacks on teachers are allowed to happen. We see here the combination of projection in the coherent description of contrastive past practices and summation in the working up of an abbreviated and unambiguous set of images and values. Present heterogeneity is contrasted with past homogeneity.

Both extracts work to constitute a difference between the cultural and moral order of past and present. The key to establishing such a contrast is the ways in which uniform, vivid images are projected on to the past in a manner that eliminates potential problems of ambiguity and uncertainty. Such a contrast is clearly not uncontroversial. We may imagine that, in principle, recipients might question, attack or straightforwardly reject the implied critique of present values. They might, for instance, choose to topicalise the abbreviated nature of the way 'those days' are presented with 'C'mon now, are you *really* saying that things were *so* much better then?' questioning. However, here we see the power of Halbwachs' analysis. The key elements of zones of personal relations – projection and summation – operate in tandem to actually militate against such critique.

First, by projecting the zone of personal relations in terms of a past commonly experienced by group members, speakers are able to work up a set of entitlements where membership provides a privileged vantage point. It is because members have known a time that was so different to the present that they are entitled to pass judgement on what they see now. Correspondingly, it is because the recipient has *not* known such a past that they *cannot* be said to have achieved a reflexive distancing from the present that entitles them to judge adequately. Moreover, as Halbwachs (1980: 98) notes, the past that is projected has a curiously 'timeless' character as it is 'a larger and impersonal duration', unlike that of the individual alone. Groups, then, have a sense of their own past that does not map clearly on to a definite historical framework. We see this in the use of indefinite terms such as 'these days' and other synonyms. This 'larger and impersonal duration' may then be mobilised by speakers as something far wider than their own individual experience – what they recall is simply how things used to be when 'doorsteps were done' by everybody and no child would ever dream of 'interrupting your master or mistress'. In this way, speakers are able to partially conflate their own recollections with an ahistorical past in general. This places recipients in the difficult position of apparently having to take issue with the entire weight of the past in order to challenge the very particular contrast on offer.

Second, the use of summation is used to construct highly vivid and specific images of the past acts to incorporate recipients. Practices – ranging from sweeping doorsteps to raising hands in class – are detailed in a compelling way that allows recipients to inhabit – if only for the moment – the physical texture of the world being described. Values are not then communicated directly or, rather, they are not presented as abstract goods, but lacquered around the practices being described. Recipients are inducted into a habitable world, their gaze trained in particular way. They are invited to imagine what it must be to physically engage with the practice as described, in the course of which a specific set of values is articulated. Attending an orderly classroom then becomes emblematic of a 'better world', in the same way that cleaning doorsteps becomes a marker of a time when communities were active and orientated towards a sense of pride in their environment. Indeed, so compelling are these images, that the speakers invite recipients to share their disbelief that things could be otherwise – 'never see anybody do their doorstep these days' and 'it is very difficult for me at my old age to understand the thuggery that goes on in schools now'.

In summary, Halbwachs' notion of a zone of personal relations draws attention to the processes whereby people must situate their recollections in relation to a prior nexus of images, ideas and values. In all five sequences that we have discussed, speakers 'remember' by reconstructing the zone of personal relations in such a way that it can potentially recruit the experiences of others. That is, although other speakers may not have direct familiarity with these relationships, they are able to either vicariously experience what it must have been to participate or, alternatively, situate their own experiences as contrasting with those of members.

Habit memory and order-words

As we have noted, enrolment in a zone of personal relations appears to be primarily an 'affective' or 'embodied' matter. Recipients are incorporated via a complex direction of their senses – they are invited to 'inhabit' the zone as it is described to them. Now, this use of the body as the locus around which remembering is performed is described by Bergson in terms of 'habit memory'.

Bergson does not suggest that memories are in some sense 'in' the body (this would be to commit the fallacy of believing that 'memories' are 'things'). Rather, he (1991: 82) draws attention to 'intelligently coordinated movements which represent the accumulated efforts of the past'. In other words, the repetition of certain well-rehearsed movements (learning by heart, knowing the steps, for example) achieves the effect of prolonging something of the past into the present.

What Connerton (1989: 102) then adds is that social groups may exploit this process by entrusting 'to bodily automatisms the values and categories which they are anxious to conserve'. Rituals are the collective means by which individual bodies are recruited into the task of prolonging the past into the present. Now, while the recipients in the five examples we have just discussed are not participating in any 'ritual', they are being recruited into versions of the past by means of their preparedness to vicariously experience that past as something in which they might have participated. Speakers invite recipients to 'hear' and 'taste' the warming ale or 'feel' and 'smell' the pummeled washing or 'gaze' at the washing flapping in the breeze. We might say, then, that this is also a form of 'habit memory' – speakers incite recipients to reproduce or merely anticipate various 'intelligently coordinated movements'. By responding to this incitement, feeling what it would be to act in this way, recipients become bound into not only the past as it recollected by the speaker, but also the moral order with which that past is freighted.

To illustrate this process further, we will look at an extract from the work of Kyoko Murakami (2001a) in Example 6 that investigates the social organisation of remembering and reconciliation. Murakami interviewed a series of British veterans who had formerly been prisoners of war in Japan during the Second World War (Murakami, 2001b). All of the interviewees had participated in a return visit to Japan some 50 years after their experiences of incarceration in a labour camp in mainland Japan. The significance of their post-war experience and the consequences for them of the return to Japan formed the focus of the interview, from which the following extract is taken.

Example 6

Ted:	I haven't worked all morning getting it right for you just to look at it
Audrey:	Well- well I usually eat first and then [I (…)
Ted:	[(right) right. (Now) what would you like to hear about (.) would you like to hear how
Interviewer:	yes, uhm (.) are you finished with all-
Ted:	aye we're all right (.) [we're all right
Mary:	[yes yes
Ted:	[I am all right (.) you are in charge now
Interviewer:	oh (.) no (.) hohoho
Ted:	you give the orders *Kyo:tuske:h*
Interviewer:	hh no no no no I'm not here for that (.) hehh (.) um ((drink))
Ted:	(now hurry up when) (.) Charlie's out and then you might get some (.) order (.) heh he[h
Mary:	[heh heh heh
Interviewer:	well (.) is this a comfortable (.) seating [arrangement for everyone?
Ted:	[get yourself comfortable
Ray:	oh we're lovely and comfortable
Charlie:	are you finished with this plate (.) honey?
Interviewer:	yeah (.) thank you
Charlie:	okay (.) now
Interviewer:	I'll get my notebook then

In this first extract, we see the use of a Japanese phrase – *kyotuskeeh*, which means stand to attention – by Ted – one of the veterans. Murakami (2001a) points out that Japanese words and phrases are a pervasive feature of the interviews with the ex-POWs. For example, terms such as the following appear – *sagyoo takusan*, which means a lot of work/labour, and *ichi-ni-san-shi*, which means one two three four, – counting numbers as in a roll call. Such Japanese phrases are clearly a consequence of the interviewees' experiences of war-time captivity and working in camps under Japanese command. Furthermore, as Murakami (2001a) describes in detail, they are delivered with embodied actions (Goodwin, 2000). For example, with emphases relating to how a Japanese guard in the camp might have addressed them, they say *SAGYOO, SAGYOO*, which means 'work, work', louder than usual and in a commanding deep voice. We interpret the use of phrases in this way as an act of incorporation – the recipient is invited to simultaneously experience what it is to be commanded and what it is to issue commands – such as when Ted says, 'you give the orders *Kyo:tuske:h.*'

It is relevant that the phrase is introduced at the point when the interview shifts from the pleasantries of introductions and refreshments to the 'business' of the interviewees addressing what they take to be the purpose of their discussion with the Japanese interviewer. Up until this point, there has been some delicate discursive management of social relationships. For instance, Ted addresses the mores of eating the food specially prepared for the occasion: 'I haven't worked all morning getting it right for you just to look at it' and the veterans' putative status as reporters of their experience: ('would you like to hear how'). The interviewer then addresses the boundary between the niceties of refreshment and opening up the main 'business': 'yes, uhm (.) are you finished with all-'. Ted responds by orientating conversation towards the delicacies of who is to set the agenda: 'you are in charge now'. Such a potential asymmetry of power is resisted by the interviewer – 'oh (.) no (.) hohoho' – resulting in a declarative reformulation by Ted: 'you give the orders' and in the use of the Japanese for 'stand to attention', '*Kyo:tuske:h*'.

What then is the status of this utterance? The hesitant receipt by the interviewer – 'hh no no no no no I'm not here for that (.) hehh (.) um' – indicates that the utterance creates some 'trouble' in the interaction. Much turns on what is indexed by the term 'that' in the interviewers response, 'I'm not here for that'. We may interpret 'that' as referring to the social relationships and power asymmetries of the camp. It is precisely 'that' that the interviewer is 'not here for'. The interviewer rejects Ted's putative formulation of her position as one of power and authority as, to accept such a role – even if it is willingly offered by Ted – is to risk reproducing the social relationships of the camp in the present and to exacerbate further the obvious dilemmas of managing her identity as a Japanese national in the current interaction.

It is remarkable that such trouble could result from a single word. We would also argue that '*Kyo:tuske:h*' does more than simply demonstrate Ted's linguistic competence. It also does the same work of summation and projection that we have described in the previous examples, albeit in a more compact and efficacious manner. The utterance acts as a switching point, where the two zones of personal relations – those of the camp and those of the present gathering – are brought together. In it, the past is made directly relevant to the present – or, more precisely, the past is 'actualised' in such a way that it forms a penumbra around the ongoing pleasantries. The contrast between the moral order of the present moment – where the Japanese interviewer is treated graciously as a guest – and the moral order of the camp – where the veterans endured forced labour at the hands of Japanese guards – is made instantaneously available. The uttering of the phrase places both interviewer and interviewees in such a way that the contrast between the two zones of personal relations becomes immediately apparent. All who are present in the room are invited to feel the visceral shock of *Kyotuskeh* – what it is to have that word ringing in one's ears, and passing through one's lips. And as with the previous examples, this act of incorporation is difficult to countenance since the interviewer is disallowed the discursive resources of direct argumentation.

Kyotuskeh is, then, a peculiar kind of performative utterance, the affective force of which incorporates the recipient into the recollected zone of personal relations. Deleuze and Guattari (1988) refer to such utterances as *mots d'ordre*, which is usually translated as 'order word' or 'precept'. However, what Deleuze and Guattari are referring to is not merely literal 'orders' – as in the current example – but a whole range of utterances that do the work of ordering social relationships (see Brown & Lunt, 2002). They emphasise that such utterances are typically 'indirect' – that is, rather than treat the utterance as expressing some intentional state on the part of the speaker, what it instead indexes and makes available is some wider context and set of relationships. For instance, if one hears a racist or sexist epithet unexpectedly and casually dropped into a conversation, what is most striking is not what one is then led to think of the speaker of the utterance, but, rather, the sudden emergence of a whole set of categories, practices and relationships with which one is forced to immediately engage. This is 'visceral force' of the utterance. The 'precept' that Ted utters in the present example is not, of course, in any sense racist or sexist. However, like all such utterances, it has the effect of instantaneously making present or 'actualising' an otherwise absent zone of personal relations that contrasts with the present one.

What we arguing, then, is that utterances such as *Kyotuskeh* have an affective force that compels recipients to engage with some aspect of the past that is instantaneously made actual in the present. These kinds of utterances elide the distinction between the discursive and the non-discursive. We may understand them in terms of the situated, occasioned pragmatics of communicative action, but also in terms of the reordering of present relationships that they achieve and the manner in which they recruit recipients in a visceral sense and immediate way into some version of the past. Put another way, these utterances change the way in which we relate to the here and now by creating a sudden juxtaposition with the features of an otherwise absent place.

Summary

In this chapter, we have begun to move away from an approach to remembering concerned with communicative action and towards a concern with how people become committed to or recruited into versions of the past by attending to the features of place. In particular, we have established that the body acts as a crucial site for commemoration, through which people become 'incorporated' into the process of recollection. Halbwachs' notion that, as physical beings, we inhabit zones of personal relations, where memory is 'localised' in the material contours of the world served as the starting point. We then explored the dual aspects of localisation – summation and projection – and discussed how these are achieved in the actualisation of past relationships.

However, it is Connerton's notion of 'inscribing practices' and Bergson's concept of 'habit memory' that have allowed us to begin to understand how incorporation operates. Recipients of a recollection are invited to vicariously experience the material contours of the past as it is described. They are drawn into a potentially habitable world. By either reproducing or anticipating actions that are indexed to the prior zone of social relations – examples we looked at were drinking beer, pummelling washing, standing to attention – the recipient necessarily prolongs something of that past into the present.

Habit memory is not, then, some mysterious storing up of the past within the body, but simply a technique by which the repetition (or anticipation) of certain bodily movements serves to index some aspect of the past. As Connerton observes, this method of prolonging the past into the present has an 'automatic' or prereflective quality. The commission of the act – bending before the church altar, shaking hands, kissing someone farewell – renders visible a set of necessarily pre-existing relationships and an accompanying moral order that the agent is in some sense obliged to 'affirm'. In our final example and discussion of 'precepts' or 'order words', we displayed how this process can be achieved in a highly economical way by certain kinds of utterances and the 'visceral effect' such utterances have on recipients.

Embodiment, then, has emerged as a key mediator of recollection. It is via the involvement of the body, or incorporation, that the past is materialised or prolonged into the present. Is the body the only material means by which this achieved, though? Are there not other material mediators that are every bit as essential?

A small example from Elaine Scarry (1985) provides direction. In her remarkable text entitled *The Body in Pain*, Scarry ponders why conflicts between nation states have typically been settled by war as the results are rarely conclusive or satisfactory for either party. Why not, she asks, settle matters by means of competitive sports or even, she hypothesises a cake bake-off? Working through these alternatives, Scarry concludes that the real aim of war is not to settle matters once and for all, but, rather, to injure one's opponent in such a way that they will physically bear the scars of the conflict. In other words, what war does is force the losing side to remember their defeat by having this inscribed into the long-term physical suffering and injury of the population. Defeat becomes written into the body.

So, Scarry's particular version of the argument for the body as the site of commemoration emphasises how ideology and the moral order of victory and defeat are inscribed into the flesh of combatants. However, this ties the memory of conflict to the longevity of survivors. If this is so, then the memory of war quite literally 'dies' at some point.

War, though, is a doubly instructive example as we can also see that the commemoration of conflict is achieved as well by creating objects that are meant to sustain and preserve certain kinds of relationships. The most obvious class of such objects are war memorials, but there are others, such as works of art, souvenirs, films and so on. In other words, although we might consider the body to be the primary site where the past is inscribed, there are many other ways in which memory becomes 'objectified'. We need, then, to examine how these other forms of objectification occur and the role they play in prolonging the past into the present.

EIGHT

Objectifying experience: mediating, displacing and stabilising the past in objects

'For a long time I used to go to bed early'. So begins Proust's monumental study of memory and its recovery. Proust's (1913/1981, 1922/1992) conception of memory is best captured in the literal translation of the French *A la recherché du temps perdu* – in search of lost time. The time that is 'lost', is not, for Proust, recovered by means of improved literal recall or a more accurate chronological record. In fact, one might say that these practices militate against the sort of recovery of the past that Marcel, the protagonist, finds so elusive. The past that is sought exists outside of historical record. What Marcel seeks is the *potency* of the past, not a mere recalling of 'what happened' or 'who said what'. He wants to find a way of engaging with the manifold possibilities of the past that could never have been visible as such at the time, so that the effects of these possibilities may be extracted, multiplied and prolonged in the present.

In his day, Proust was held to be a Bergsonist author – a broad brush description lent weight by a family connection: Proust was pageboy at the marriage of his cousin to Bergson in 1889. Doubtless there is something in this characterisation. Like Bergson, Proust is fascinated with 'habit', with how the repetition of 'intelligently coordinated movements' prolongs the past into the present. When recalling the Parisian salon of Madme Verdurin, for instance, Marcel – the narrator – peoples his recollections with characters whose mannerisms and physical tics appear to express far more of the tone of the past than the unfolding historical events that serve as its context. This is not because Marcel has no apparent interest in such events, but, rather, because history is grasped as it is mediated by the activities of the salon. Thus, the Dreyfus Affair – a major event in French political and cultural memory – is recalled in terms of how it was expressed in the changing mannerisms of the Verdurins (Dreyfus was a military officer subject to anti-semitic and false accusations of treachery, resulting in wrongful public humiliation and exiled imprisonment – the case is the basis of Emile Zola's famous 1898 '*J'accuse*' letter).

As we saw in the last chapter, habits or embodied actions are powerful ways in which recipients become incorporated into some remembrance. However, what Proust – with his description of an active recovery of a past that is 'outside of time' – and Bergson – with his notion of a leap into 'pure memory' – point to is something different. For both authors, what is actualised in recollection is not exactly what was experienced at the time. Marcel, for example, is able to clearly recollect aspects of Count Charlus' homosexuality ('inversion') that were not readily apparent to him at the time. What occurs here is not the recontextualisation of knowledge, as might be typically theorised in experimental work (see Engel's 2000 discussion of Proust, for example). It is not the case that Marcel simply puts a different interpretation on information that he already possesses. Rather, Marcel recollects a past that he could not have experienced. In a strict sense, this is a past that has never been. This puzzle constitutes one of the main themes of Bergson's *Matter and Memory*, a point unlikely to have been lost on Proust's contemporaries.

How can we make sense of this Proustian/Bergsonian puzzle? How might it move us forward analytically from a concern with the communicative and embodied pragmatics of remembering? Let us turn to the most famous scene in the text, when Marcel's journey into the past is initiated by the taste of a 'spoonful of the tea' in which is soaked a 'morsel' of the 'petites madeleine' offered by his mother (Proust, 1981: 48–51).

This is an unusual event, involving 'a thing I did not ordinarily take' on a 'dreary day with the prospect of a depressing morrow'. Hence, the surprise when an 'exquisite pleasure' takes hold of Marcel, with 'no suggestion of origin'. Memory does not at this point flood incidentally back to the narrator, as is commonly described. Indeed, Marcel is not even clear what is happening. He feels at first 'filled' with a 'precious essence', but then corrects himself: 'rather this essence is not in me, it *was* me'. In confusion, he takes two further sips. Nothing is clear. He then tries to focus on what he is experiencing, but divines nothing other than the presence of an 'abyss of uncertainty', a 'dark region'. How to confront this? How to seek the source of the experience? 'Seek? More than that: create'.

This is Marcel's great discovery. The past can only be brought into the present as a result of the most supreme of efforts. One must journey into the 'dark region' of one's own experience. The tool to make this possible comes from what is currently at hand – the spoon of cake-infused tea. Moreover, what the tool enables Marcel to do is not only uncover something previously hidden but also reinvent, rework what he searches for in the present: 'Seek? More than that: create'.

The process nevertheless remains difficult: 'Ten times over I must essay the task, must lean down over the abyss'. Finally, a scrap of memory appears – of Marcel's childhood routine of being fed a tea-soaked madeleine by Aunt Léonie, memories of whom, along with Marcel's mother, provide a thread through the subsequent text.

Thus, Marcel's journeying after lost time begins. Note, however, that these efforts are initially directed not inwardly, into the depths of Marcel's consciousness, but outwardly, such that the memories appear to emerge from the objects currently at hand (Proust, 1981: 51; see also Casey, 1987, on 'uncontained memory'):

> And as in the game wherein the Japanese amuse themselves by filling a little bowl with water and steeping in it little pieces of paper which until then are without character or form, but, the moment they become wet, stretch and twist and take on colour and distinctive shape, become flowers or houses or people, solid and recognisable, so in that moment all the flowers in our garden and in M. Swann's park, and the water-lilies on the Vivonne and the good folk of the village and their little dwellings and the parish church and the whole of Combray and its surroundings, taking shape and solidity, sprang into being, town and gardens alike, from my cup of tea.

Memory springs into being from the cup of tea, not the 'dark region'. Perhaps the teacup is acting as a contextual cue for the activation of a set of associations stored as mental representations in long-term memory? This explanation, though – couched in the terms of experimental psychology – is problematic on a number of grounds. First of all, it ignores Bergson's crucial distinction between *perception* and *memory*. If the two are conflated in this way, we will be forced to attempt to explain how a perceptual event – the taste of the tea – can be transformed into a kind of protomemory in such a way that it can be compared to other past representations with which it is somehow associated, begging the further question of how such association occurs.

Second, if the cup of tea acts as a cue, why has it not produced this same recollection on previous occasions? What is it about this particular cup of tea that makes it a 'contextual cue'?

Third, how is it possible that the initial recollection of Aunt Léonie gives way to the whole of Marcel's childhood? If the cup of tea really did act as a discrete contextual cue that was capable of triggering off other associations, then we would expect specific, discrete 'episodic' memories to result, not a sense of the entirety of Marcel's past.

In his study of Proust, Deleuze (1972/2000) offers some useful clarification. Deleuze notes that we cannot understand the scene with the cup of tea if we think of it in terms of associations between sensation – taste – and ideas – those of Combray and its – inhabitants – as there really is no direct link between the tea and what Marcel subsequently recalls. What there is instead is a play of similarities and differences. The taste of the madeleine is the same both now and then, but the Combray that 'rises up' within that taste is not constituted in episodic terms. What Marcel recalls is a set of qualities that make up Combray – an array of colours, a sense of the temperature, the shape of the madeleines displayed in the pâtisserie window and so on. This, Deleuze (2000: 61) argues, is a recollection of Combray that is dislocated, different in kind to either a past or present moment:

> Combray rises up in a form that is absolutely new. Combray does not rise up as it was once present; Combray rises up as past, but this past is no longer relative to the present that it has been, it is no longer relative to the present to which it is now past ... Combray appears as it could not be experienced ... Combray rises up in a pure past, coexisting with the two presents, but out of their reach ... 'A morsel of time in the pure state' (III, 872).

Deleuze then claims, drawing implicitly on Bergson, that what Marcel recollects is a 'past that never was'. What could this possibly mean? It is not a question of 'false memory', remembering events that did not occur. Rather, what is at issue is the structure of memory itself. This follows directly from Bergson's approach to memory in terms of duration. If all of our past experiences are, by definition, part of our unfolding duration, and if duration is organised in a qualitative, undifferentiated 'virtual' fashion, then we simply do not possess clear, episodic memories. Our memory of events, then, involves reconstruction – we artificially extract or dissociate past events from the otherwise interconnected tissue of duration in order that they can be reinserted into the demands of current circumstances (this is what Bergson means by 'actualisation'). So, technically, what we recollect is not exactly what we experienced at the time. Moreover, as duration is the condition of any sort of experience whatsoever, it is simply impossible that we could ever bring these conditions as such directly to consciousness – this would be rather like attempting to lift ourselves up by our own shoelaces. So, again, we must necessarily say that what we recollect is a past 'that never was' (see also Lawlor, 2003).

What Marcel recollects is a set of qualities that are extracted from his unlimited 'virtual' prior experience of Combray. This includes not only his former direct experience but also his experience of all the times that he has since reflected on Combray. So, these qualities, while grounded in the totality of his experience, are not really relative to any particular event. Hence, what he recollects is, strictly speaking, relative to neither past nor present, it is Combray 'as it could not [have been] experienced'. Hence, the overwhelming sense of joy that Marcel feels arises from his sense of a difference in kind between this 'new' Combray and the one that he recollected on other occasions. Proust refers to this as the experience of a 'morsel of time' (Deleuze, following Bergson, glosses this as exposure to the 'pure past' – that is, an intuition of duration).

Now, while all of this may sound peculiar when contrasted with the usual language of recollection derived from the experimental psychology of memory, what Proust, Bergson and Deleuze are doing is really only exploring the implications of the theoretical hypothesis of memory being 'always on', as proposed by psychologists such as Lansdale (2005) and Kolers (1975).

The implication that we will be exploring in this chapter is that objects – such as the cup of tea – provide a material basis on which some aspect of duration – that is, the ongoing totality of our past experience – may be artificially divided and reinserted into the present. For Marcel, the qualities of Combray are 'enveloped' by the taste of the madeleine in such a way that they appear to rise up from the cup of tea, like the Japanese flowers unfolding in water. It is the durability of the teacup, its apparently unchanging nature, that provides the material support for Marcel to turn around on his own past.

The argument that we want to make in this chapter is the following. Objects can serve as the mediational means by which we may establish a particular relationship to some aspect of our past. They, in effect, lend something of their apparent stability to the fluidity of our unfolding duration. Objects, then, provide occasions for extracting and reconstructing the past and, at the same time, act as structures or 'envelopes' into which we can insert and develop recollections. Thus, our memories seem to us to rise from the objects themselves.

Objects as mediators

Throughout this chapter we will use the term 'mediation' to describe the role that objects play in practices of remembering. However, there are various ways in which 'mediation' can be understood. Our initial definition is drawn from cultural psychology, inspired by the work of the Lev Vygotsky (see, for example, Cole, 1996; Daniels, 1996; van der Veer & Valsiner, 1991; Wertsch, 1985, 1998). Here 'mediation' is understood as the intervention of cultural tools or artefacts in subject–object relationships. This intervention – or 'mediational means' – comes between the 'subject', as originator of actions, and the end or objects towards which such action is addressed. Mediation fundamentally alters the relationship – the subject is able to expand the range of conceivable outcomes. For example, the emergence of writing as a 'mediational means' restructures the production and mobilisation of knowledge. Vygotsky (1978) emphasised that such mediation results in 'objectification' of human action. The mental becomes 'materialised' in the mediational means used to direct it.

We can illustrate something of this objectification by returning to an example that we discussed previously in Chapter 5 (Example 3). Example 1 from Edwards & Middleton, 1988 below features a mother and son discussing a series of family photographs. In our previous discussion we mentioned, but did not remark on, the significance of the fact that Paul is using a magnifying glass to examine the picture.

Example 1

Mother: it must have been a sunny day in that photograph (.) mustn't it?
Paul: yeah (.) oh let's see see that comes bigger
Mother: mm (.) (…) where were you then? (.) can you remember?
Paul: here and there's Rebecca look at her ugh ((laughs))
Mother: she's pulling a funny face (.) isn't she?
Paul: yeah (.) she thinks it (.) it's so Mum let's see let's see what that boy (.) done let's see if there's any agh it's big (.) do you like (.)
Mother: you didn't like that bouncing castle did you? (.) do you remember?
Paul: yeah
Mother: it kept falling over (.) you couldn't keep your balance
Paul: n:ohh ((laughs quietly))
Mother: do you like them now?
Paul: yeah
Mother: <u>do</u> you?

Seen from the perspective of 'mediated action' (see Wertsch, 1998), we may note that there are two different sets of actions being performed here, both of which use the photographs as mediational means. Paul is playing with the magnifying glass and using the photographs as materials for experimenting with various focal lengths to enlarge the details to create different effects. Paul's mother, by contrast, is engaged in family reminiscence. She uses the photographs as the evidential basis for various inferential claims. Moreover, as we discussed in Chapter 5, she seeks to recruit Paul into a project of joint remembering by instructing him in the use of photographs as the mediational means to achieve this kind of recollection.

At the beginning of the example, these two distinct sets of mediated action do not entirely mesh. The mother's prompts to Paul to reconstruct the scene as a recollection – 'it must have been a sunny day in that photograph (.) mustn't it?' are not picked up on by Paul as his focus is on the technical problems of making various aspects of the scene visible – 'yeah (.) oh let's see see that comes bigger.' However, by the end of the sequence, it appears that Paul has abandoned his experiments with the magnifying glass and been drawn into his mother's project.

There are two points worth making about the kind of mediated action that occurs in this sequence. Vygotsky (1978) argued that mediational means tend to rebound back on the subject who deploys them. He termed this 'reverse action' (1978: 39). If mediation objectifies human action, then the resulting objectification can act as a means by which the subject can reorganise his or her own psychological functioning. For instance, Paul's mother 'objectifies' family relationships by treating the photographs as the mediational means by which the character of family membership can be made visible and discussed. However, the resulting objectification in some sense commits both Paul and his mother to the representation of the family as it may be inferred from the photographs. Hence, they must spend time negotiating the status of the 'funny face' that Paul's sister Rebecca is seen to pull.

We may also detect what James Wertsch (1998, 2002) calls the 'irreducible tension' that is present in mediated action. Wertsch argues that mediation is never completely transparent. Although mediational means typically facilitate and enlarge the scope of what the subject is able to achieve, this comes at some cost. For example, the subject may be finding that the resulting objectification of their action does violence to their original intentions. In the case of remembering, this may mean that personal recollection becomes tied into the structures of the mediational means in such a ways as to render what is remembered problematic. Wertsch (2002) gives the example of cultural narratives used in the former Soviet Union to describe past events such as the Second World War. While these narratives serve as mediational means for the framing of personal recollections, they also come with considerable 'cultural baggage' – not least their association with now discredited Soviet 'official history'.

In the present example, we may interpret some of the difficulties the mother experiences in recruiting Paul to her version of past events as due to 'irreducible tension' that exists between the photograph as a useful way of occasioning talk of past family experience and the photograph as a direct visual record of the occurrence of some event. For instance, the mother uses one photograph as the basis for the claim that Paul could not keep his balance on the bouncy castle – this being part of a wider attempt to establish continuities in Paul's preferences and identity over time. However, as the still photographic medium is unable to capture the whole event, this allows Paul to reject his mother's claim. The irreducible tension here is that the photograph affords collective remembering, but does not capture sufficient detail to allow for consensus to be reached about the recollected events. To put this slightly differently, the past that the photograph makes visible is a past that was not and could not have been experienced as such by all the family members.

Translation and the object

Another way in which 'mediation' may be understood is to be found in the work of the French philosopher of science, Michel Serres (see general introductions by Brown, 2002, 2003). Serres' work is best summarised as dealing with the general problem of communication in relation to 'noise' or disorder.

In his provocative text *The Parasite* (1982b), Serres argues against the possibility of 'unmediated' relationships between communicative partners. The minute we try to establish a relationship with someone else, we must necessarily involve a mediator – be that language, gesture or whatever. This mediator becomes, in effect, a 'third party' to the exchange, contributing its own dynamic, with the result that our attempts to communicate become inflected with the character of the mediator on which we now depend entirely. There is, then, a fundamental paradox involved in communication, which is that to communicate at all requires that we 'trust' in a mediator that is instrinsically 'unreliable'. Serres, then, sees communication as, in some sense, a 'battle' by communicative partners to overcome the difficulties inherent in mediation.

Typically, one way in which this is done is to multiply the series of mediations, such that difficulties in one mediator are 'rectified' by the deployment of a second and so on (see Serres, 1982a). For example, we may decide that what we say to one another in a meeting is insufficiently conclusive and, therefore, we require a second written record – minutes. However, then, we have the further difficulty of establishing the adequacy of these written minutes and require a further procedure to 'ratify' them and so on and so on. Serres envisages communication as extending itself into ever more lengthy chains of mediation in order to achieve its ends.

Serres' work has been developed by writers such as Michel Callon (1980), Bruno Latour (1987; Serres with Latour, 1995) and John Law (1994, 2002) into an approach known as 'Actor-Network Theory' (ANT), mentioned earlier. Although this approach was primarily designed to study communication in scientific settings – in particular, the production of scientific 'facts' – in recent years, it has been applied more generally across a range of social science problems (see contributions to Law & Hassard, 1999, and Law & Mol, 2002).

ANT uses the idea of chains of mediation as way of analysing how complex forms of organisation are accomplished. It also draws out an important point about the *identities* of the 'actors' involved in such chains. In Serres' original work, 'mediators' are not seen as secondary to a communicative exchange, but, instead, are treated as 'agents' or 'actors' in their own right – 'third persons'. Moreover, the identity of the original communicative agents is defined by the relationship that they necessarily adopt with mediators. Serres calls this process 'translation' (see Serres, 1982a). Our identities, as actors, become defined by the shifting chain of mediators that extend, ramify, amplify, displace and transform our actions. ANT uses this notion of 'translation' to argue that the identity of actors (both 'subjects' and 'objects') depends on the place that they hold in a network of mediated activities (see Callon, 1986).

How might this notion of 'translation' allow us to understand the manner in which objects 'lend their stability' to recollection? Consider the following sequence in Example 2, which is again drawn from Buchanan and Middleton's (1995) work on reminiscence with older people. Here, a lengthy description is provided of a piece of clothing that appears central to the plausibility of the memory.

Example 2

Vera: my mother used to wear erm (.) sack apron (.) cos years ago they used to make the aprons out of a (.) sack bag hadn't they?
Doris: [ooh that's right
Enid: [you could buy[the sack bag (…)
Vera: [can you remember (.) I can remember
[my mother (.) and she used to-
Jean: [yes (.) yes (.) used to make aprons out the sack bags or a black one (.) and you'd go and change after dinner and she'd put (.) you know (.) a new pinafore and a clean dress or something like that
Enid: we used to buy ours from the Beehive
Vera: ye:s (.) I can see my mother (.) she used (…) sack bag y'know (.)
[of her back and her front-
Jean: [yeah (.) that's wash day

Vera introduces a 'sack apron' as a particular kind of home-made garment worn while engaged in domestic labour and then invites ratification of her claim: 'cos years ago they used to make the aprons out of a (.) sack bag hadn't they?' Doris, Enid and Jean offer immediate ratification, displaying awareness of this practice, and assist Vera's claim by means of further elaboration: 'you could buy the sack bag.' These supporting contributions then act to work up a commonality of experience, which, in turn, constitutes membership. This building of membership by talking about past practices and associated objects is common in reminiscence groups (see Buchanan & Middleton, 1995, for further discussion).

However, this is not all that the invocation of the sack apron achieves. Note how it is subsequently related to a range of other objects – sack bags, from which the aprons are made, 'black' aprons, which are a similar, alternative hand-made garment, new pinafores and clean dresses – fine garments, the value of which comes from how they contrast to sack aprons – the Beehive, which is a local shop where the other garments were purchased. The sack apron is, then, one element in a network of relationships between objects that is unpacked as the conversation unfolds. Each element becomes defined in relation to this overall historically grounded network of mediated activities around domestic labour. The past is then localised in relation to the network, such that, in describing the contours and elements of the network, the speakers are able to construct common experience. That is to say, describing the objects – the mediators – becomes a way of describing the people whose identity is in part 'held' by the relational place they occupied in this network of mediated activities. For instance, it is following the invocation of the Beehive that Vera finally claims to catch sight of her mother as she was then: 'ye:s (.) I can see my mother (.) she used (…) sack bag y'know (.) of her back and her front.' The past seems to rise up from the objects as they list and describe them in turn.

We may use the notion of translation to note three aspects of what is collectively recalled here. First of all, the objects, as they are recollected, 'translate' what the speakers are able to collectively recall. To put it another way, the speakers are obliged to pass by way of the objects in order to establish a commonality of past experience. Vera introduces her mother as a topic of reminiscence by way of the sack apron, inviting contributions from Enid and Vera. Their contributions, focused on aprons, enable Vera to tie her own recollection to the progressive working up of the collective experience of the practice: 'can you remember (.) I can remember.' Tracing the relationships between objects then allows Vera to 'see' her mother – that is, to be able to extract a clear image of her mother wearing the bag 'back' and 'front'. We might then claim that Vera's ability to adequately recall her mother is translated into the descriptions of the objects that she produces with the support of her three interlocutors.

Second, the relationships between objects also translate a set of collective values. The 'sack apron', for instance, is clearly a cheap, home-made garment that is emblematic of a time when finances are tight and homemakers are forced to rely on their own resourcefulness to manage domestic labour. The sack apron also ties the wearer into a local community of activities – note, for instance, the reference to the Beehive as the local shop where other items could be purchased. Furthermore, the contrast between the sack apron and the new pinafore or clean dress brings with it a set of values about the place of domestic labour in the running of a household. Mothers would 'change after dinner' into a fresh set of clothes, thereby marking a break between daytime chores and evening activities. Now, all of these values – which are ultimately transitory and belong to a time that is now past – are 'held' in the relationships between objects. The values are, in effect, translated or inscribed into the very material form of the objects themselves, thus acquiring a kind of durability. The invocation of the object allows speakers to unpack these values as they unfold the network in which they were embedded.

Third, as a collection or network, the objects described 'punctualise' the recollection as common experience. In Chapter 6, we used this term to refer to the coordination of activities in such a way as to give the appearance of a common 'front' or as marking a particular boundary, such as the millennium. In ANT terms, 'punctualisation' is the effect of a common identity that is generated when a network appears to be cohesive. For instance, when Jean sums up the mediated activities as collectively recalled in the prior turns in the words, 'yeah (.) that's washday' – what she does is indicate how that stretch of the past can be packaged together or 'boxed up' as a single, compound category of past experience, 'washday'. Of course, what is punctualised in this way is a whole variety of specific experiences, people, artefacts and practices that have been translated into a common network of activities.

The notions of punctualisation, translation and networks of mediated activites provide us with another way of restating Halbwachs' concerns. When Halbwachs describes past experience as summated into a singularly 'vivid image', what he points to is also the 'packaging up' of a whole variety of activities and events into a compound sense of the past. Furthermore, Halbwachs' idea of a zone of personal relations that is structured in a 'physiognomic' manner – such that relationships extend into and become objectified in the artefacts and environment in which a community dwells – is enriched if we understand that process as one of 'translation'. For instance, when Halbwachs describes the automatic recognition by the reader of a literary character as a 'miser', this happens because the identity of the miser is held by the objects by means of which he or she translates his or her activities, such as ill-lit offices, quill pens thrust into drying ink wells and so on. 'Miserliness' is, then, not so much a character trait as an effect generated by the particular configuration of the subject in relation to a network of mediated activities. It is enough to situate ourselves – either as readers, speakers or listeners – within such a network to grasp the character of those who typically populate it.

In summary, we may say that objects mediate our activities in such a way that our concerns and identities become subject to translation. What we are, then, becomes defined, in part, by the place we occupy in relation to these chains or networks of translations. Now, in the case of remembering, we may begin to reconstruct past experience by using the apparent stability of an object as the basis for unfolding our recollections of people and events. By describing the supposedly unchanging character of the object, we gain a foothold on the activities that this object – such as the sack apron – previously mediated. These activities then also appear to gain a kind of durability by virtue of the relationship that they have to the object as described. In other words, the object lends something of its material durability to the people we wish to recall – it projects something of its stability into the fluidity of our past experience. This is how Marcel is able to recall Combray by taking a sip of the madeleine-infused tea. The durability and apparently unchanging character of the cup of tea provides him with a foothold on which Combray may reconstructed in the present.

Now, unlike Marcel, Vera and her interlocutors do not have a sack apron to hand in the present (although eliciting memory by means of direct contact with objects is a feature of some forms of reminiscence work with the elderly – see, for example, Bornat, 1994; Gibson, 1989). However, they too borrow something of the stability of the sack apron and other objects that mediated the washday activities to reconstruct past experience. It is by virtue of projecting this apparent stability on to the past that Vera is ultimately able to recollect her mother. Now, in the same way that Marcel recollects not some definite event, but, rather, a set of qualities that summate the entirety of his past experience of Combray, we would speculate that what Vera claims to 'see' is not an image of her mother on some particular occasion, but, rather, a compound 'sense' of her mother – her way of standing, the shape of the sack apron as it lays on her front and back, the contrast between the colour of the sack and her mother's bare arms and legs and so on. This, too, technically, is a 'past that never was' as such. It is a 'morsel of time' experienced in the present.

Objects as markers of relationships

To say that objects mediate remembering is, then, to argue that objects provide the means for the past to be created anew in the present. This creation may produce a version of the past that was not and could not have been experienced as such at the time. It is 'time regained', to use Proust's compelling term.

Translation involves establishing the identity of some artefact in relation to a network of other artefacts, people and practices. Indeed, the identities and properties of all the elements gathered up in such networks appear to be exchangeable (see Latour, 1994) or interpenetrate in such a way that they may be 'punctualised' in a particular form or 'singularly vivid image' – such washday.

To recollect or reconstruct this network in the present, we may project the apparent stability of the artefacts involved on to that stretch of the past that it localises. What might otherwise be fluid and transitory acquires a kind of durability when recollected by way of objects. Thus, Vera can 'see' her mother, having first invoked the sack apron she typically wore on washdays.

Although we have been using the vocabulary of Vygotsky and ANT to understand how artefacts afford recollection, Halbwachs' (1980: 156) original insight that groups render their own past as memorable by 'engraving their form' on their immediate material world remains a good basis on which to understand this process. Halbwachs (1980: 130) argues that a collective 'transforms the space into which it has been inserted' – that is, objectifies its images of itself in such a way that the identity and particular past of the collective territorialises social space. Collective memory is literally written into the places and artefacts in and through which the group dwells.

This objectification of the collective secures the durability of its identity, which now takes on a 'natural' appearance – the group comes to 'imitate the passivity of inert matter' (1980: 134). In other words, the structure of the social relationships that define the collective comes to resemble the artefacts and environment it has previously fashioned.

We may see something of this 'imitation' in Example 3, which is also drawn from Gibson (1989). The speakers here are discussing farming practices that were common in the community in which they all grew up.

Example 3

Brenda: [we never (.) we didn't have that many sheep (.) at <u>that</u> time
Beatrice: [wh = wasn't there arrangements (...) (.) and a bath (.) great big bath and
              then the (...) (.)   [and they put the sheep down after (&)
Mary: [(aye that was)
Beatrice: (&) one another   [
MM: [Hughes's had that in Ballycairn (.) Hughes's had that in
              Ballycairn
Beatrice: mm
Mary: and they put them down (...) (the other side)=
Beatrice: =in there and out the other side (.) (...)
Mary: we used to go in school to watch- (.) watch (...) ((laughing))
Brenda: you tried to do it on a dry day so's that they'll dry out
Beatrice: mm

As with the last extract, the speakers here are drawing on considerable shared experience, acquired by dwelling, for most of their lives, in the same community. We can pick up quite a few mundane details about everyday life in this community as it was then, by following the recollection. For example, farming is clearly a major occupation 'we didn't have that many sheep' – supported by a local infrastructure – 'Hughes's had that [a sheep bath] in Ballycairn' – but children were, nevertheless, attending school 'we used to go in school to watch' – although the nature of farming work required that seasons and climatic conditions determined the structure of local activities 'you tried to do it on a dry day so's that they'll dry out.'

The speakers here reconstruct the qualities and dynamics of the community to which they belonged by invoking embedded material practices. They recollect particular places (Ballycairn), artefacts (sheep bath), institutions (the local school) and the local ecology (dry days). It is as though it were possible to 'read' the character of the community from the contours of the place in which it dwelled. For instance, the Hughes family is described not in terms of family lineage or the character of individual members, but in relation to their ownership of a particular piece of equipment – 'a great big bath' – which is essential for the mass dipping of sheep. The relationship between the Hughes family and the community, as it is recalled here, is, then, mediated by the bath. This artefact becomes, in the recollections of these speakers, a marker of the social relationships between the Hughes's and the broader community.

Serres offers a useful account of this role played by artefacts. He claims that, when objects mediate between subjects, they act to 'slow down' or stabilise social relationships (1995: 87):

> Our relationships, social bonds, would be as airy as clouds were there only contracts between subjects. In fact, the object, specific to Hominidae, stabilises our relationships, it slows down the time of our revolutions. For an unstable band of baboons, social changes are flaring up every minute. One could characterise their history as unbound, insanely so. The object, for us, makes our history slow.

The difference between humans and the great apes, Serres claims, is that, for primates, social relationships require constant attention and maintenance (see also Latour, 1994, 1996). A baboon cannot afford to ignore what his or her fellow troupe members are doing as relationships are constantly being remade. Thus, social change is a given. For humans, however, social change is, typically, a more prolonged process. We do not have to pay the kind of intense concern to our social relationships that characterises primate life. This is because, Serres argues, humans use objects to mark out and stabilise their relationships to one another. For instance, the use of enclosed shelters enables us to create a division between the public and private, to choose whether or not and with whom we spend part of our time. To take another example, in the extract above, we see how, as a collective activity, sheep farming is made routine – and, hence, predictable – by the use of the bath. Without the bath, farmers would be forced to make complex negotiations with the community to mobilise a workforce able to manage the task. With the bath, however, a given farmer now only has to negotiate with the Hughes family. As Latour (1996) points out, mediation via objects makes social relationships less complex and protracted, but, at the same time, these relationships become denser and more complicated – for example, ownership and access to the bath must now be addressed.

It is precisely this kind of complication that Halbwachs (1980) is alluding to in his description of collective remembering in economic transactions. The problem, for Halbwachs is that of understanding how transactions are possible given fluctuations in prices that require both buyer and seller to remember past pricing patterns. The solution is that buyers must be artificially sheltered from such fluctuations at the point of sale. As we introduced in Chapter 5, this is achieved by the apparent durability and unchanging nature of the object for sale (Halbwachs, 1980: 150):

> In effect, because the merchandise waits – that is, it stays in the same place – the merchant is forced to wait – that is, stick by a fixed price (at least for the duration of a single sale). The customer is actually encouraged to make a purchase on the basis of this condition, because he [sic] gets the impression of paying for the object at its own price, as if the price resulted from the very nature of the object, rather than at the price determined by a complex play of continually changing evaluations.

Crudely put, the relationship between buyer and seller – which, in principle, is characterised by constant changes in price – is stabilised by a mediating object. The seller is forced to stick to a given price, which the buyer is then encouraged to see as arising from the 'very nature' of the goods in question. One cannot exclude these mediating objects from a definition of the collective as they are precisely what lends relationships between people their stability and form. So, in the case of Example 3, we must think of the collective being recalled as entangling objects (bath, sheep), procedures ('after one another', 'in there and out the other side') and the associated features of place ('we used to go in school to watch').

Much of the confusion surrounding Halbwachs' use of the terms 'collective' and 'individual' stems from the assumption that a collective consists of unmediated relationships between subjects that are 'as airy as clouds', to use Serres' phraseology. By contrast, Halbwachs clearly describes collective remembering as being located in the complicated and highly mediated relationships between humans and artefacts and the social spaces that are thereby 'territorialised'.

Attachment and displacement

We have seen how objects stabilise not just remembering, but also the collective via which recollection is accomplished. As Halbwachs outlines, this stabilisation occurs because the apparently unchanging object acts as a point at which changing and otherwise highly variable relationships between people can be brought together. In this way, Marcel navigates Combray as it was then and Combray as he now recollects it in the timeless taste of the madeleine-infused tea and Vera catches an otherwise elusive glimpse of her mother in the childhood home in the collective elaboration of the qualities of the sack apron and, finally, a joint recollection of bygone days in a farming community are held together by the apparently mundane necessity of a sheep bath. In each case, the solidity of the object restores fragile bonds to people and places that are the subject of remembrance.

However, we should not lay undue emphasis on this solidity. It is not given by the 'very nature' of the object itself, but, rather, is an effect of its ability to hold together social relationships. We might speculate that not all madeleines taste exactly the same, sack aprons were not used in precisely the same manner in all households and, perhaps, somewhere the sheep bath now lies rusting and covered by weeds.

What matters is not the qualities of the object itself, but the manner of its *attachment* to the people whose social relationships are thereby mediated. Gomart and Hennion (1999) note that, while mediation certainly increases the scope of what a given person is able to achieve, it also means that, in some sense, we as agents have to 'give ourselves over' to the mediator. That is, we need to recognise our interdependency with the mediational means via which we act or grasp that we no longer really master their actions, that our actions 'act back' on us (this is perhaps another way of understanding Vygotsky's notion of 'reverse action'). Attachment, as Gomart and Hennion define it, refers to this ambiguity of extending our action and submitting to the mediator or, more simply, of 'action' and 'passion' in mediation. To be 'attached' to a mediator is to experience something of this ambiguity – this is what lends our attachments their piquancy, such as the cigarettes we know we will 'one day' give up, the favourite outfit we hope to be able to fit into again, the car that seems to choose the mornings on which it 'refuses' to start.

The converse of attachment is *displacement*. When a mediating object becomes detached from its original conditions of use, it may acquire another role as a 'memento'. For example, Radley (1990: 51) notes that the sorts of artefacts that typically serve as occasions for remembering are likely to have been kept and arranged in a haphazard fashion: 'a silver cigarette lighter from one's smoking days, a cribbage board from the times when the family came round to play cards'. What is striking about the displacement of these artefacts from their 'proper time' is that they act as reminders of what we once had, what we once could do and what we have now lost. The provisional and, ultimately, transitory, nature of attachment is, then, intrinsic to the significance we accord to mementos. Seen in this way, the artefact opens up an ambivalent relationship to the past.

This can be illustrated further by considering Example 4, from Helen Hewitt's (1997) investigation of life story work with profoundly handicapped people. It is a transcription of part of an interview with a father concerning the life of his profoundly learning disabled adult son, Lance, before his life in long-term hospital care.

Hewitt was concerned to establish features of the early lives of clients that could form material for 'a life story book'. This book featured as a key resource in Lance's move from hospital care to long-term care within the community, which would entail a whole range of new personnel coming into contact with him. The aim was to provide a resource concerning significant details of the individual lives of those in long-term care relationships that might otherwise be lost to future carers.

Interviews with a whole range of family and previous carers were conducted to gather resource material to include in the life story books (see also Hewitt, 2005, for further details of the development and use of life story work for people with learning difficulties).

In the following example, Lance's father discusses two events, separated by ten years in time, both of which involve the same kind of object. What is at issue is the displacement of this object and the significance it has in terms of Lance's attachment to it.

Example 4

Father: (…) (.) <u>this is basically it</u> (.) all I can literally <u>add</u> to it (.) or say (.) there's not much I know but (1)

Interviewer: oh no I'm sure there's a lot more rea::lly I mean (.) there's special memories that you've got of sort of (1) of isolated events that (.) you know (.) I mean I'm sure you must have a lot of photographs haven't you?

Father: oh yes if you want photographs but uh (.) he was a (.) wheelchair case (or should a say pramulator) and (.) most of the time he sat in his chair (.) one of those chairs like that and he became quite (paralyzed) but he has a memory (.) that's one thing that I would tell you (.) and the reason that I know this is becau:se in Australia (.) he used to have a chair that used to (stand) (.) and have these springs that went across (.) and he used to put his hand on one of these things and twang them (.) and of course with it being on a wooden floor (.) because there they have wooden floors (.) it was just like a double bass

Interviewer: (laughing) like a digeree-doo

Father: and he used to love this (.) you know (.) he'd <u>really</u> get excited by it (.) well (3) we took him away (2) and it must have been <u>ten years later that</u> we bought a chair that was similar to that (.) and <u>do you know</u> the first thing he did his hand went straight underneath

Interviewer:	and twanged it
Father:	<u>ten years later</u> (.) so <u>he's</u> got a memory (.) now if he thinks about that what other memories has he got about other (.) so:: (2) he wasn't a cab-bage (.) there was something in there ((points to head)) that was (.) func-tioning somewhere (.) although he couldn't <u>express</u> it (.) it was there (.) but he uh (1) we were amazed he just sat in this chair (.) we sat him in this chair never never (thought of) and the first thing he did his hand went straight under (2) well he tried to do it (.) he didn't quite make it but that's what he wanted to do because he used to like (…) and that was <u>ten years</u> earlier (1) he was quite grown up then (1) so honestly he thought about this <u>noise</u> (.) or music or whatever and he wanted to do it again (1) and he knew how to make that (.) that sound so he could put pieces together to make something which was functional to to himself

The father sums up at the beginning of this sequence what he has to say about his son's life prior to long term hospital care: 'this is basically it (.) there's not much I know but.'

In order to accomplish the interactional work of the interview, the inter-viewer then introduces the notion of memories as being interlinked with objects, such as photographs. Memory is then worked up as an issue by the father as he establishes continuity across two sets of events separated by time and place. This results in a respecification of the issue, such that the father's concern becomes that of displaying that his son, despite his profound learning difficulties, has the ability to remember things across this lengthy period of time.

In building his claim, the father does not simply interpret or project meaning on to his son's actions. Rather, he points to Lance's attachment to a particular object – the chair with springs 'that went across'. He then describes in some detail how Lance was able to engage with the chair and the particular properties it gained as a result of it being positioned on a wooden floor: 'and of course with it being on a wooden floor (.) because there they have wooden floors (.) it was just like a double bass.' Because of his attachment, Lance was able to extend the range of his actions and, as a consequence experience the pleasure of being able to do so: 'and he used to love this (.) you know (.) he'd <u>really</u> get excited by it.' The account then shifts to what happened ten years later under equivalent circumstances. Here – amazingly – Lance encounters the same kind of object, displaced in time from the earlier experience and attempts to 'reattach' himself: 'and the first thing he did his hand went straight under.' However, on this occa-sion, unfortunately, the effect is not the same: 'he didn't quite make it.'

What is significant about the displacement of this artefact is the provi-sional and 'fortuitous' nature of the attachment that Lance was able to sus-tain on both occasions. In Australia, ten years ago, Lance's chance act of twanging the springs allowed him to not only to extend his repertoire of actions via the mediational means of the chair but also demonstrated to his parents his ability to reflect on and enjoy his own capacities. Ten years later, when Lance encounters a similar chair, the significance of this attachment, for his parents, is that it displays that Lance must have the capacity for long-term memory: 'so *he's* got a memory ... he wasn't a cabbage'. A coherent linkage of the two events is now possible. However, this linkage – which is only possible by virtue of the 'fortuitous' mediation of the artefact – is ambivalent. On the one hand, Lance's parents are now able to construct a different kind of identity for Lance that is built around his thus far 'hidden' capacities that have now been revealed: 'now if he thinks about that what other memories has he got about other'. On the other, they must also accept that these capacities appear to be dependent on the particular and highly provisional mediation of the chair, as it alone has made this discovery possible. Moreover, they must accept that Lance's recent attempts at attachment were not successful and that his previous love of the act of twanging the springs will not be reproduced. The significance of the displaced chair is, then, a bittersweet mixture of revelation and loss.

The more general points we would wish to make here are threefold. First, that Lance is produced as an individual, as a subject, via his attachment to the chair. It is by virtue of being able to extend his powers to act via the chair and by displaying his pleasure at the exercise of these powers and, finally, by an apparent display of the memory of this initial attachment, that Lance is accorded an increased status of subjecthood by his parents: 'he wasn't a cabbage'. Again, we must say that social relationships – indeed, the very condition of being accorded subjecthood itself – is entangled with the objects that mediate our actions. This has some bearing on Halbwachs' claim that individuality is a mode of sociality, except that we must now understand sociality as interdependent with the mediational means via which it is rendered cohesive. Second, that the relationships between the family members come to be marked out in relation to the artefact. The chair becomes a way for Lance's father to describe his relationship over time with his son and, in particular, his realisation of his son's capacities. The artefact, then, facilitates and marks out social relationships in the family. Third, that the displacement of the artefact is precisely what enables a linkage between two otherwise entirely remote points in time. The chair opens up a kind of 'envelope' of time where a continuity that was previously absent is now immediately apparent. In a sense, Marcel's experience of a sudden connection between past and present – made possible by the displacement of an artefact that is equally at home then and now – is comparable to what Lance's father experiences with the chair. In both cases, an entirely fortuitous displacement of an object becomes a way of not only recollecting the past but also entirely reconfiguring the totality of that past. For Marcel, this is the beginning of his exploration of the character of Swann and of the Guermantes; for Lance's father this is the beginning of his realisation that Lance is and always has been capable of far more than he ever suspected: 'now if he thinks about that, what other memories has he got ...'

Summary

In this chapter, we have moved on from a discussion of how the features of place enter into collective remembering towards a concern with the particular role of objects. We began with the puzzle that Proust, Bergson and Deleuze offer of a 'past that never was'. As we have seen, this is not so much a piece of fancy metaphysical speculation as a genuine attempt to engage with the implications of the recognition that memory is 'always on'. As conscious beings, we live with the entirety of our past, which advances at every moment and does not easily resolve into neatly bounded recollections. However, the fluidity of duration may be managed by the relative stability of objects. We may 'borrow' something of their apparently unchanging nature to gain a foothold on our prior experience. What is significant about Marcel's encounter with the madeleine-infused tea, then, is not anything to do with 'association' – in the traditional psychological sense – but, rather, with the persistent way he systematically uses the apparent durability of this artefact as a means of engaging with the totality of his past experience of Combray.

The mediation of objects is, then, critical to our management of experience. We have explored this mediation by drawing on a range of approaches. From Vygotsky and cultural psychology, we have drawn the notion that mediational means to 'objectify' our experience and that such objectifications 'rebound' on our subjectivity, or set up an 'irreducible tension' between the agent and cultural tool. From Serres and ANT, we have taken the notion that mediation – or translation – is 'unreliable', as in extending our actions we are committing ourselves to the mediator. In fact, if we follow through on this line of thought, we will end up finding a clear-cut distinction between agent and mediator unhelpful as the identities of each are reciprocally defined, their apparent properties 'interchangeable'. For this reason, we have preferred to speak of 'networks' of mediated activities, where people, artefacts, procedures and places are entangled together. Now, if this account holds, we will see that one is able to recall a past community by describing the mediating artefacts that mark out the social relationships between community members. In other words, by focusing on what is seemingly durable over time – the structure of the object – one is able to adequately recollect what otherwise seems to be fluid and changeable, which is the structure of human relationships. Seen in this light, Halbwachs' remarks on the 'implacement' of the collective in its social space take on renewed pertinence.

We have, then, arrived at a recognition of the pivotal importance of the 'attachment' of people to the mediational means via which they act. This attachment is always, to some degree, ambivalent. We must accept our inderdependence with that which allows us to extend our powers of action and, consequently, submit something of ourselves to the mediator. It is in this sense that the detachment of mediating artefacts gains its particular power. When we re-encounter the artefact, we are reminded of not only what was, what we are able to do via former attachment, but also what was purely transitory and is now lost.

However, this does raise a further possibility. What if the artefact is never lost, but, rather, grows in importance over time? What if the mediational means by which the collective 'engraves itself' on social space becomes ever more expansive? What if our 'objectifications' come to seem more important than the experiences that they are supposed to render durable?

The further we move in this direction – towards the embedding of experience in concrete formal structures – then the more likely it is that, at some point, the ambivalence of mediation must give way to a sense that our objectifications 'overtake' us. What, then, is the fate of personal recollection when it becomes dominated by impersonal and highly stratified versions of the past? We address this problem in the next chapter.

NINE

Technologising experience: infrastructures in remembering and forgetting

Example 1

(From Brown, Middleton & Lightfoot, 2001)

Interviewer:	I guess what I am hearing is that one use of the e-mail seems like it is very formal – to report on action points from the meeting?
ReadyAds Project Manager:	yes but also as a record of where … ((they both look at a computer screen)) (.) if you look down this side it has everything that I am working on and each one – whatever it is about – will go into, so it is also a filing cabinet and I never really (.) I hardly ever cancel mails until a project is over (.) so everything is important as it could have something important in it (.) every one has got bits that are important (.) the other thing that I do (.) for example with that person – the supplier I said that does not come up with the goods – I set up a contact straight away in journal and automatically keep mails when I have sent them or received them so I know that I have got a record (.) for example (.) 'you sent me an e-mail saying that you'll do this so (…)' (.) it seems a bit sneaky but it organises (.) it is like a journal (.) I do not tend to use diaries

The extract in Example 1 is taken from a study of the organisational use of e-mail (see Brown & Lightfoot, 2002; Brown, Middleton & Lightfoot, 2001). The subject of the interview – a middle manager in one of the organisations studied – invites the interviewer to look at the monitor of her desktop computer. On the monitor, a Windows-based system is running, with an e-mail management program (Microsoft Outlook™) already open. The manager gestures to the left-hand side of the screen where a 'tree' of folders is located: 'if you look down this side it has everything I am working on'. This tree is described by the manager as a 'filing cabinet' – a highly significant artefact for the structuring of her daily work practice.

As the manager's description progresses, the importance of the folder tree is worked up as a means by which a flow of information – the potential future relevance of which is unclear at the time of receipt – can be stored until such time as the relevance can either be established or discounted: 'everything is important as it could have something important in it.' To put matters in a slightly different way, what this manager is concerned to do is preserve the past in terms of maximum interpretative flexibility.

In this way, the e-mail tree – the mediating artefact by means of which the past is rendered fit for future remembrance – is compared by the manager to other kinds of tools, such as diaries and filing cabinets. All these tools allow for a cutting up and redistribution of the present moment as e-mails that drop into the manager's in box are moved into folders in much the same way that written memoranda might be placed into physical files or a personal diary might break a record of a day down into distinct activities and situations. This works to effect a kind of commemorative 'triage'. Everything that might possibly be relevant to each distinct project that the manager is engaged in ends up distributed into electronic storage in such a way that it may be recalled and acted on depending on future contingencies: 'you sent me an e-mail saying that you'll do this so (…)'.

In the last chapter, we were concerned with the manner in which objects mediate remembering. This led us to analyse how fluid social relationships become stabilised or 'slowed down' when they are translated by mediating artefacts. We were then able to show that artefacts provide a means for people to relate to the totality of their past, to turn around on their own duration, in a relatively bounded fashion. If, as Bergson claims, our past experience is not neatly divided in episodic terms, then mediating artefacts may provide a foothold on the past that allows for the necessary dissociation, the construction of boundaries and circumscribed 'events'. Objects lend something of their durability to how we relate to our 'unlimited experience'.

The gesture the manager in the example above makes towards the folder tree on her monitor may be interpreted as a similar use of mediational means to bound past experience. However, her gesture goes somewhat beyond this. What she indicates is, first of all, that she is *authorised* to treat communication with her colleagues in this way – although note the hint that keeping e-mails in this way might be problematic: 'it seems a bit sneaky but it organises.' This authority is, then, granted by her place in a network of responsibilities and chains of reporting. The network is, in turn, governed by rules of practice, including formal statements. Most importantly, this network is itself held in place by a myriad of standards – some purely technical, such as the general use of Microsoft Outlook™ in the organisation, some of a regulatory nature, such as the treatment of e-mails as semi-formal business records.

Remembering activities, such as the invocation of past promises, is, in this case, interwoven with the maintenance and reproduction of formal modes of organising. The past is continually distributed and reworked as part of a generalised programming of the future, be that the prediction of likely contingencies in the execution of a project, or the building up of formal and informal audit trails designed to bulwark the current organisational form against future uncertainties. There is, then, a tension between the desire to preserve the interpretative flexibility of both past and future (for instance, by leaving open potential nuances of an e-mail message, making recoverable information that at the time seemed barely relevant to matters in hand) and the equally strong desire to make both future and past appear entirely tractable and manageable. It is this tension relative to memory that exists at the heart of practices of formal organising that will be of concern in this chapter.

Consider, for instance, the extract in Example 2, taken from a study of teamwork in a neonatal intensive care unit (see: Brown & Middleton, 2005; Middleton & Curnock, 1995). Here, a group of junior and senior doctors working in the unit are discussing difficulties in ensuring that the new born babies are given prescribed doses of vitamin K (it is routine in the post-natal care of breast-fed babies in the UK to administer an oral preparation of vitamin K to protect them against a rare but fatal form of haemorrhagic disease).

Example 2

Senior registrar: (....) now the vitamin K comes up every week (.) I've thought about this and I think the system that might work (.) but in fact I think we need Dr Smith here (.) would be that where a baby is born in the labour suite we have a slip which has got a sticky back and one of the mother's stickers goes on that slip and that's either stamped or it's pre-printed with the vitamin K prescription (.) and most slips could go onto a clip on each post-natal ward so that when you come to the post-natal wards you're signing this slip you wouldn't be looking around for the notes (.) and then the ward clerk would put those signed slips in the notes (.) that would mean that babies didn't get missed (.) it would mean you didn't have to look for the notes and it wouldn't involve any extra work except for the ward receptionist who would already be putting results into notes (.) it would still mean that there was a problem in as much as you're only visiting each post-natal ward once a day (.) any advances on that system? (.) anybody got any problems with that system?

Junior Dr 1: why can't the obstetricians- I mean?

Senior Registrar: because we've already had that debate and they won't

Junior Dr 2: but Miss Jones's requested them to apparently

Senior Registrar:	well they won't (.) I mean that's already been explored I think by Dr Smith in depth and er they're prescriptions for babies and we're paediatricians that's the argument
Junior Dr 1:	but they're doing more to see every mother routinely without bias
Senior Registrar:	well if you want to pursue that argument I think it'll be much more tortuous and erm probably eventually unsuccessful because the babies because we're paediatricians
	(....)
Senior Registrar:	the reason for having a slip is to disassociate it from the notes which you've been telling me are difficult to get hold of (.) that you have problems getting hold of the mother's notes (.) so if the slip goes in the notes (.) it might as well be in the notes (.) the stamp might as well be in- there's no advance on the present system

The historical problem that the doctors are discussing is that, for medico-legal reasons, each oral administration of vitamin K requires a doctor's signature on the prescription. Under normal circumstances, such signatures are available during the daily paediatric post-natal ward rounds. However, a baby's post-natal condition might deteriorate, necessitating its transfer from one of the maternity wards of the hospital to the specialist care environment of the intensive care unit prior to them having received any vitamin K. In addition, immediate access to the mother's notes recording whether or not vitamin K had been administered could not be guaranteed. What the Senior Registrar suggests is a formal solution to the problem, involving a system of slips.

Individual doctors may 'forget' to ensure that vitamin K is given. What is proposed here is technical solution to the problem of such 'forgetting', which involves putting a system in place, such that the burden of 'remembering' is transferred to an artefact – in this case a slip that would be transferred between wards.

This is a routine instance of what Latour (1994) refers to as 'technical mediation'. The properties of 'remembering' and 'forgetting' are transferred to a mediating artefact, where they become matters of 'recording' cases and 'issuing' slips. This system, then, takes charge of remembering practices so that it no longer matters whether or not a given a doctor recollects if any particular baby transferred to the intensive care unit has or has not in fact received the vitamin K injection. The action has already been programmed in advance by way of the preprepared slip. Latour refers to this as an 'exchange of properties' between human doctor and non-human artefact, who are now entangled together in the translation of activities around the care of the premature baby.

In Latour's work, and more generally in ANT, the success of this form of mediation is considered secure when the activity becomes obligatory for all concerned. In other words, if all the medical staff involved in the care of a premature baby are obliged to attend to and act on the slip – for instance, if the slip is held at a central nurse station in the unit so that it enters into the formal distribution of duties to nursing staff – then the technical mediation will make the issuing of the vitamin K a near automatic event. However, in this particular case, we see that the junior doctors resist the proposed technical mediation. This is noteworthy, given that the system, as envisaged, would appear to effectively resolve a long-standing organisational difficulty. Instead, the junior doctors take the opportunity to 'do history' – in this case by rehearsing how the problem has been knocked back and forth between groups of medical practitioners.

In Examples 1 and 2, we see that the application of modes of formal organising and an accompanying reliance on technical mediation to 'take charge' of remembering activities does not necessarily deliver a clear management of the present concerns. Indeed, in Example 2, there appears to be a concern on the part of the junior doctors that the resolution of a technical issue of recollection renders invisible or leads to a forgetting of what is for them an important social division between obstetricians and paediatricians. Moreover, we see that the efficacy of technical procedures creates new dilemmas in the practice of remembering. For instance, in Example 1, the manager seems unable to simply delete any e-mail that she receives. *All* messages might be potentially relevant at some indeterminate point in the future, so she seems compelled to keep them all – a practice that requires some effort on her part. For this manager, we might say, the realisation that it is technically possible to preserve the past in a manageable form creates a situation where it became all but impossible to exercise discretion when deciding what aspects of the present ought to formally recorded – best just to keep everything!

Formalisation/standardisation

Our efforts in this book to outline a social psychology of experience in relation to remembering and forgetting have concentrated on the question of elucidating the relationship, set up by Bartlett, between experience and organised settings. Following Bergson, we have been treating experience in terms of duration – that is, as the 'unlimited' or 'virtual' intersection of numerous planes of experience in the continuous 'gnawing of the past in the present'. We initially saw how a turn towards discourse and communicative action provided an empirical means of understanding how the past is invoked and made relevant – that is, 'actualised' – in relation to current actions. We then expanded our approach to include reference to the discursive management of interdependencies in experience. However, in subsequent chapters, we have been turning more towards the features of organised settings themselves, initially in terms of how place is 'territorialised' within zones of personal relations, and then with regard to the use of mediating means, such that social relationships become entangled with artefacts and procedures.

We now wish to push this analysis forwards towards the study of 'formally organised settings', where remembering and forgetting are subject to technical or technological rationalisation. When occasions for remembering are structured in advance by a formal assembly of technical procedures, only that which is deemed fit for remembering by standardised methods is automatically admitted into the practice. We may see this as way of approaching questions of ideology, of analysing mechanisms that ensure formal control over the definition of the past in the present, but we would do well not to overstate the power of such formal organisation. In practice – as Examples 1 and 2 show – there is a tension between what is recalled and forgotten by technical mediation and the live concerns of members whose remembering practices are obliged to pass by way of such mediation.

Our project in this chapter, then, is to understand this tension and illustrate its practical management in formally organised settings using material drawn from the two studies previously introduced – the organisational use of e-mail and teamwork in neonatal intensive care.

Throughout this chapter, we will refer to formal assemblies of technical procedures as 'infrastructures'. Our use of this term follows Bowker and Star's (1999: 6) definition of infrastructure as a 'large-scale system of formal categories and standards'. The two elements of infrastructures – classification/categorisation and standardisation – are indissociable.

Classification requires the creation of a set of principles such that a coherent and comprehensive set of mutually exclusive categories can be put into play that can 'code' matters at hand as 'cases' – for instance, the naming of electronic folders as 'projects' into which all incoming e-mails in a manager's inbox can be redistributed.

Standards are 'agreed rules for the production of [textual or material] objects' (1999: 13). That is, methods for ensuring that objects are mutually compatible, such that they can fit and work together. Considerable labour goes into the production and enforcement of standards as by definition, the viability of a standard depends on its widespread adoption. For example, the slip proposed by the Senior Registrar will only ensure that vitamin K prescriptions are given if *all* the relevant medical staff in the hospital use the slip on *all* relevant occasions.

Bowker and Star (1999) argue that infrastructures do not by themselves determine activity. A given system of classification and a set of standards must be adopted and performed by members to have any kind of organisational efficacy. There are innumerable instances in the history of science and technology of infrastructures that 'did not take' in organisations because users failed to adopt the classificatory principles as indispensable tools for 'thinking' and 'acting'. Part of this adoption process is the tailoring of a given infrastructure to local contingencies. For example, Marc Berg's (1997) work on informatization in medical decision making displays how medical practitioners and administrators adapt formal standards and classifications in computer software to fit with existing practice. The implementation of a given infrastructure may well involve a subtle modification of the classificatory system as it is put to use – for instance, the leaving blank of certain data entry fields or the supplementation of electronic records with informal records.

Traditionally, this work of tailoring standards is referred to as 'workarounds' – that is, the informal negotiation of some inflexible element of an infrastructure by users in the form of ad hoc procedures. A more precise term often found in the literature on collaborative work practices is 'articulation work' (see Schmidt & Bannon, 1992; Star & Strauss, 1999; Suchman, 1993). It means the management of local contingencies by means of the rapid stitching together of whatever resources are at hand. Articulation work can be seen in the way that users employ infrastructures to non-standard ends. For example, in e-mail use, the manipulation of subject headings on mails and strategic use of markers of importance can be used as devices to outwit automatic filters placed on e-mail accounts (see Sproull & Kiesler, 1991). We can illustrate the utility of this term by applying it to the Example 3, which involves a number of neonatal medical practitioner (Middleton & Curnock, 1995).

Example 3

Key: S = sister; SN = senior nurse; C = consultant

S: (....) yeah sometimes (.) and I think it should say reserved cots and it should be indicating that they mean reserved cots in labour ward [yeah] because that's only the ones that we should be worried about is the ones that are round the corner [mm that's right] who are expected to deliver but I think (.) when you put reserved cots (.) I think that the interpretation could be different

SN: but p- people are always expanding that= if the= that they're always wanting one in brackets hydrop section tomorrow morning or that sort of thing

C: that's the problem (.) I mean a hydrops baby is at great risk (.) it's gonna need intensive care and he is gonna have a section (.) but he could actually be on the post-natal ward until they take them down to the section

S: but that= we would probably have that in the diary and we would know about it (.) [yes] what worries me is sometimes and quite often now and it's= it's quite a new thing at report you're actually hearing about what's lying upstairs=

C: yeah that's irrelevant it's nothing to do with-
S: I don't think we should bother about it=(&)[
C: [yeah we must dismiss that figure
S: & you know but now you're told there's 29 weekers (.) 27 weekers (.) 26 weekers (.) but you don't want to know until they're down the labour ward but I do want to know about the hydropic one and er [yeah mm] you know (....)

A continual concern in the unit is that of managing the demands of unpredictable workloads. Specifically, this concerns the range and extent to which the admissions policy should be tailored in relation to potential problems. This turns around the question of what classification system and accompanying criteria should be used for determining the density of workload and the capacity to admit within the finite resources of the unit.

One strategy is the reservation of space for upcoming deliveries of babies who may be in need of intensive care: 'I think it should say reserved cots and it should be indicating that they mean reserved cots in labour ward'. However, unless the delivery is earmarked as a Caesarean section, the actual timing of delivery for a baby who is likely to be born 'preterm' is uncertain. Indeed, prolonging the pregnancy usually increases the baby's viability and the quality of developmental outcomes. Reservation procedures are therefore problematic in a service that is set up to respond to emergencies. It is possible to end up in the situation where admissions are refused because the unit is theoretically at capacity when, in fact, a significant number of spaces are not currently occupied. Spaces are being reserved for babies whose mothers have preterm complications but who have not yet gone into labour. The issue, for staff in the unit, is how to adjust admissions criteria in such a way as to limit the expanding range of possible births for whom the unit may well have to cater.

This is indeed what use of the 'reserved cot' classification was meant to achieve, but staff in the unit believe that the classification has drifted or been expanded. In other words, staff outside the unit have performed their own articulation work by adjusting the classification as a device to ensure that particular cases are guaranteed space. This means that internal management by the unit of space and the leeway for decisions concerning admissions has spun out of control: 'when you put reserved cots (.) I think that the interpretation could be different', 'p- people are always expanding that= if the= that they're always wanting one in brackets hydrop section tomorrow morning or that sort of thing.'

Thus, the range and relevance of just what reservation of space entails is called into question. There are clear circumstances where reservation makes sense: 'that's the problem (.) I mean a hydrops baby is at great risk

(.) it's gonna need intensive care and he is gonna have a section.' However, what unfolds is the relationship between the place of the potential case – that is, where the mother is currently resting, on the post-natal or labour ward – and reservation of space. The post-natal ward is the place where mothers would be admitted to hospital for observation in advance of an impending section or delivery in a problematic pregnancy ('hydrops'). The labour ward is the place where birth occurs: 'that's the problem (.) I mean a hydrops baby is at great risk (.) it's gonna need intensive care and he is gonna have a section (.) but he could actually be on the post-natal ward until they take them down to the section.' Such babies are also recorded as potential cases by other means: 'but that- we would probably have that in the diary and we would know about it (.) [yes].'

The problem is that the use of reservation has extended to other cases who have been admitted to the post-natal ward: what worries me is sometimes and quite often now and it's- it's quite a new thing at report you're actually hearing about what's lying upstairs.' The unit is starting to have its workload determined by mothers who are on the post-natal ward with pregnancies at different gestational stages: 'you know but now you're told there's 29 weekers (.) 27 weekers (.) 26 weekers.'

The solution to this expanding range of potential cases and accountability for staff in the unit is to realign potential workload with those mothers who are actually on the labour ward, except for exceptional cases that have specified sections arranged. Those cases lying upstairs are dismissed: 'you don't want to know until they're down the labour ward.' It is the significance of being on the labour ward that redefines the way in which 'reserved cots' is interpreted in terms of space allocation. The articulation work, here, then involves respecifying 'reserved cots' in terms of the actual presence of the mothers on the labour ward. Note, that this form of articulation work also effects what Bowker and Star call 'selective forgetting'. Those mothers who are not present on the labour ward are not visible in terms of the unit's admissions procedure. This lack of visibility is not some oversight – they are not simply forgotten about due to inadequate information – but a strategic decision. The unit chooses not to attend to mothers before their arrival on the labour ward – 'you don't want to know' – excepting specific contingencies – 'I do want to know about the hydropic one.'

Selective forgetting is, then, a notable feature of the implementation and tailoring of an infrastructure to local contingencies. Forgetting, or rendering invisible under specific sets of conditions – is what has to happen to manage the application of the classification system. However, there is another, more radical, form of forgetting that Bowker and Star (1999) point out. 'Clearance' is the wholesale dismissal of cases that do not fit with a proposed set of classifications. Consider, for instance, the manager in Example 1, who has classified all of her categories for storing e-mails in terms of ongoing projects. What does she then do with e-mails that do not appear to be related to any project in particular? One option is to find some spurious reason to associate the e-mail with a project – perhaps on the basis that the sender is tangentially involved in the project in question. This would be a form of articulation work. However, a more likely option is that the manager would be forced to either create a new folder that is negatively defined in relation to project work – a 'rubbish' category called something like 'Everything not to do with projects' – or simply to delete the e-mail in question. This dilemma arises because the act of establishing 'projects' as the classificatory principle renders invisible everything that cannot, by means of articulation work, be made to fit with such categories.

Clearance is, then, also a condition of the implementation of infra-structures. In order to preserve a particular version of the past, everything that does not fit must be modified, systematically forgotten or rendered irreversibly invisible.

Zones of technical activity

Bowker and Star's work allows us to see that, for infrastructures to 'take charge' of remembering, a negotiation must take place between the generalised, impersonal set of categories and standards and the local contingencies that routinely occur in a given setting. Typically, this negotiation involves an active process of forgetting. The problem, then, is to understand how this negotiation is conducted.

Halbwachs provides further insight here. In Chapter 7, we discussed at length his notion of a zone of personal relations. For current purposes, we may take this to mean a collective that has 'inscribed' or 'implaced' its own identity and past in its immediate environment. Halbwachs contrasts this with what he calls a 'zone of technical activity'. By this he means formal procedures, abstract rules, technical decisions – 'knowing and ... applying the rules and precepts that in every period prescribe for the func-tionary the general terms of the actions, linguistic forms, and gestures of his (sic) function' (1992: 160). Such activity can so densely structure a practice that 'in their rigidity and generality [the rules and precepts] imi-tate the law and forces of matter' (1992: 161). Moreover, it is the general form that this activity takes, rather than its particular material realisation, that is critical. We take all this to be synonymous with infrastructure.

Halbwachs' concern is to display that zones of technical activity – despite their rigid and general appearance – are subsumed within zones of personal relations. He uses the example of the legal system. This appears to be an entirely impersonal set of rules and procedures that are used to adjudicate cases. The judge, for instance, is, in principle, required to leave to one side the forms of knowledge that are granted to him or her by virtue of the zones of personal relations he or she may routinely inhabit. However, in practice, the judge will routinely adjust technical decisions to fit with their personal, situated judgement, informed by reference to some ongoing zone of personal relations. The local and the particular then absorb and modify the general and the impersonal. For Halbwachs, this argument is part of his wider set of claims that collective remembering can be seen in operation in even the most apparently rarified and abstract domains of human activity.

However, Halbwachs does not explore the terms on which this negotiation takes place in any great detail. That is, the kind of alignment work that is required to adjust and tailor infrastructures to fit with the contingencies of local practice. Indeed, seen in Halbwachs' terms, there is something quite paradoxical about the very idea of this process, for is it not the case that infrastructure is what the collective *creates* in order to objectify or implace itself in such a way that it can withstand the mortality of any given member? Why, then, should it be necessary to continuously negotiate and readjust what infrastructure affords? Yet, Bowker and Star (1999) claim that there is an inevitable tension, or 'torque', between infrastructures and their users. Why should this be so?

In his essay 'Archive Fever', Jacques Derrida (1995) offers an illumination of this paradox. Derrida is concerned to describe the relationship between the 'archive' – that place where memory is formally recorded – and the living, spontaneous memory that requires this external preservation. Here, Derrida is thinking of both the technologies involved in formal organising and the kinds of psychological processes described by Freud. He notes the etymological roots of 'archive' in *arkhē* – a classical Greek term that means both 'commencement' and 'commandment'.

Commencement is the positing of origins, the establishing of the original, authoritative version of something. Commandment is the issuing of law, the practice of judgement. These two senses of *arkhē* are embodied, Derrida claims, by the figure of the *archon* – a magistrate who takes charge of the archive and is granted the power to practice law on the basis of the authoritative records that they alone are allowed to store, review and interpret. The archive is, then, not merely the place where the past is stored up but also where the present is judged. This immediately sets up the problem of how this judgement can authorise itself in relation to the past – that is, of the relationship between these two activities.

There is, then, a potential tension at the heart of the archive, but also between the archive and the living memory it seeks to preserve. As the archive must always be external to what it preserves, it is inevitable that there is some discontinuity between these two forms of memory. Moreover, the basis for archiving in the first place is that living memory fears its own dissolution, that it will be unable to adequately relate to its own past. Freud famously named the source of this anxiety as 'death drive' – the impulsion towards self-destruction, to literally erase oneself from memory. Put in more banal terms, we might say that we do not trust ourselves to remember and that organisations do not trust their members to remember properly. However, this anxiety is also productive as it feeds our desire to engage all the more enthusiastically with the work of archiving. Finally, as archiving is a kind of repetition – or remembering 'again' – it is, in some sense, corrosive of the living, creative movement of thought (Freud also saw repetition as of a piece with our death drive). This means that, in order to properly 'live', we must make some sort of break with the archive to avoid simply repeating again the past that it preserves. The consequence of all this, for Derrida, is that, at the very heart of the desire to archive – or archive drive – is the simultaneous desire to have done with the archive altogether – or archive fever.

If, as Michael Lynch (1999) suggests, we treat infrastructures as endowed with an archival role – he uses the phrase 'archontic infrastructure' – we may see how these tensions at the heart of the desire to preserve the past in formal terms are played out. For example, in Lynch and Bogen's (1996) work on the 'Irangate' hearings, the relationship between Oliver North and the public documents he claimed to have shredded raises the question, how an authoritative version of the past can be reconstructed when the archive has been systematically corrupted by the very individual – 'the archon' – charged with its safekeeping?

If we place these concerns in the context of the study of the organisational use of e-mail, we are able to gain additional purchase on the issue that emerged (see Brown & Lightfoot, 2002). This is the practice of routinely archiving e-mail messages and the use of such archives. The scope and extent of this practice is vividly illustrated by Example 4, taken from an interview with one of the senior managers in one of the two organisations studied (see Brown, Middleton & Lightfoot, 2001 for further details).

Example 4

ReadyAds Managing Director: I am the worst I am afraid (.) I am probably the last person you should ask because I am probably the most hated in IT because my e-mail (.) my e-mail erm file is bigger than probably the rest of the company ((laughter)) I wish I was joking it is huge (.) I never delete anything (.) I am afraid I keep (.) I get regularly

> erm nice messages from IT saying 'can you please
> take your file to less than ten gigabytes' ((laughter))
> which is just obscene and I go through trying to rifle
> out crap but I do find that my housekeeping is very
> poor with e-mail and that is part of the problem (…)
> I mean if I show you my e-mail trees erm there is my
> basic list of e-mail folders ((laughter)) OK (.) and then
> I can show you each element just for the purpose of
> the tape recorder enn Geoffrey is now looking at a tree
> which is about erm shall we say you can see ((laughter))
> we are looking at a tree of e-mails of maybe 50 folders
> deep?

Here, a manager describes his practice of storing huge amounts of e-mails – a practice that is clearly perceived as problematic in some quarters of the organization: 'I am probably the most hated in IT'. The speaker provides a great deal of detail (some of which is clearly meant to be heard as over-stated, as indicated by the laughter) in order to emphasise the peculiarity of what he routinely does in this massive archival effort. By underscoring the effort involved, the speaker hints at the scale of the potential benefit, that massive effort here implies substantial reward. However, what is important in this example is the way in which the manager makes his personal rela-tionship to the archive and archival labour central to his representation of his place in the organisation. He presents his *attachment* (in Gomart & Hennion's, 1999, sense) to the archive as critical to his ongoing organisa-tional position and 'power', but this clearly comes at some cost.

The manager might be described as being caught up in the logic of con-tinuously maintaining and updating 'archontic infrastructure'. He is car-ried along by the 'archive drive'. We might ask who is working whom? Is the informal archive that this manager maintains simply a useful supple-ment to his own activities or does the ever escalating commitment to archival labour mean that formal practices of remembering become ends in themselves?

Overcoming infrastructure

In exploring how practices of remembering and forgetting operate in formally organised settings, we have arrived at a question of what happens when 'archontic infrastructures' take charge of the preservation of the past. How can members of an organisation relate to this demand to incessantly record and archive? To put it slightly differently, how do they experience their attachment to the archive? In Example 5 (Brown, Middleton & Lightfoot, 2001) the same manager offers a slightly different rationale for his storing of e-mail messages.

Example 5

> *ReadyAds Managing Director:* (....) and the other side of it is that I like to keep prompts for myself because we are actually talking about minutes at the end of the day- that is what we are talking about (.) erm I do keep prompts of the discussions that have taken place so that I can go back to them and refresh enn you know my memory as to what I said or what action points were agreed and follow them up.

The manager here describes how records and minutes stored in the form of e-mails can support his own personal attempts to avoid forgetting: 'refresh enn you know my memory'. What he does here is to invoke the classic concern with memory as an incidental activity that we discussed in Chapter 6. His recollection of what was said in a meeting is thereby purged of any strategic motive. His memory cannot then be said to be biased as what he recalls is an incidental feature of browsing the archive. Indeed, in the final part of Example 5, memory recall is placed on an even more neutral footing when the manager invokes the necessity of keeping to prior obligations as a good reason for retaining old messages. The archive is then positioned as a neutral source of information, the role of which is to enable managers to maintain their obligations by standing in for their own 'faulty' memories. By emphasising his 'passive' attachment to the archive, which is represented as a simple prosthesis designed to correct natural human failings, the manager is able to publicly disavow his strategic motives in archiving the e-mail messages. A similar description of the nature of e-mail archiving is provided in Example 6 with another manager (Brown, Middleton & Lightfoot, 2001).

Example 6

> *ReadyAds New Media Manager:* yes I think it is useful as a reference (.) it is very useful as a reference and if you are talking to (.) if I am discussing something with a member of my team I could discuss for 20 minutes what they need to do and I do follow it up with an e-mail as I know that he will forget the essential parts of it (.) because he's so busy (.) and a lot of people think 'God what is the point (.) why don't you just send an email in the first place or why do you have to follow it up' (.) that is just the way they work in that way and I just want things to work (.) whether or not they are in a sensible way or not or immediate way as long as you get results (.) that is what I feel is very important

Note that there is a similar appeal to faulty memory in this extract, but here the problem lies not with the speaker, it lies with a member of her team: 'he's so busy'. The archive is presented as a kind of common memory that is shared by the manager and her team and fills in for any problems that may have occurred in other forms of communication. As the speaker is keen to stress, these problems occur simply in the usual course of events, it is the way business is conducted in the team: 'that is just the way they work around here'. There is some indication from this and what follows that the manager herself is not necessarily to be included in the category 'they'. The manager also attends to the problem that routine use of the archive may be seen as unnecessary or a potential threat to good working relationships by appealing to pure pragmatics: 'I just want things to work (.) whether or not they are in a sensible way'. In this extract, the attachment of managers to the archive is again represented in passive terms, as a simple necessity in the routine way of conducting business.

We may see the previous examples as illustrating what Halbwachs has to say about 'zones of technical activities'. E-mail archives – part of the 'archontic infrastructure' of these two organisations – are held to be value-free spaces where formal procedures are applied to preserve the past in such a way that the organisation may carry out its routine functions effectively. The value of investing this massive effort in the recording and preservation of the past – in effect, the 'remembering again' that Derrida describes – is that it overcomes the frailty and intrinsic unreliability of organisational members. The passive attachment of members to the archive is, then, an absolute necessity. However, following Halbwachs, we may come to suspect that this neutral representation of archiving does not adequately reflect practice.

Example 7 (Brown, Middleton & Lightfoot, 2001) from the organisation Oilsite occurred during a discussion with a manager in which he describes a particular technique that he has evolved for making what he sees to be the best use of the e-mails he archives.

Example 7

Interviewer:	right (.) what about generally with e-mails (.) do you tend to archive a lot of them?
Oilsite Manager Design Engineering:	I archive all of them erm all of them (.) 90 per cent of them (.) I mean obviously if I see there are 5 or 15 different messages about a meeting then I will try and bin those erm (.) first of all I started by trying to archive them by project and that lasted about a week and I now archive by month and I keep 12 months so at the end of the month I throw them into an archive

Interviewer:	right (.) do you go back to revisit them once they are in the archive?
Oilsite Manager Design Engineering:	oh yes (.) given the nature of our work it is absolutely invaluable to me (.) this will search and find a document on here ((typing, showing example)) so you can actually see my archives (.) here in fact I have got just over 12 months but I just archive by year and month and then this year I have started to also archive my out-going messages by month and then I just click on this search and find and away I go (.) I mean it can take 2 to 3 minutes because there are 5 or 6000 messages in that archive (.) I guess that I average about 500 messages a month at the moment but in particular with commercial matters on projects and where I need to track progress (.) it is invaluable and I do go back through the archives.
Interviewer:	so when you are tracking progress through the archives do people write you e-mails saying that they have got to this stage or I am going to do this and you can go back and say 'well have you done that?' (.) is that the kind if thing that you mean?
Oilsite Manager Design Engineering:	yes (.) or I have got a contractor who will turn around and say 'well you did not give me access to that site until erm April and then I was held up for six weeks because::' I mean now I can electronically check that very quickly and erm before I mean we had this kind of system (.) it was just a pain to get into (.) so it has made traceability much easier

The extract begins with the manager expressing a concern with the system. He has difficulty keeping up with the amount of messages he receives, which impels him to use various methods of archiving. We can read this as a concern to retain the past in the most useful way, to view the past as a resource that ought to be stored in such a way that it can be realised to maximum effect in the present. The archive is, then, presented as a value-free 'zone of technical activity'.

Although the extract begins with a problem that emerges as a result of the way in which the system is ordered, it rapidly becomes apparent that this problem of ordering the system is really about ordering people – that is, of managing a zone of personal relations. The issue that this manager returns to is how to tie messages to people and people to deadlines. What really matters for this manager is having a means of enforcing obligations. The way that this is formulated is not as a matter of issuing direct commands, but, rather, as a result of establishing order in the archive. The archive, then, makes it possible to exercise action at a distance – that is, bind people into a social order represented by the archive. Ordering the elements in the archive becomes the way of making sure that contractors – who may be on the other side of the globe – are tied into project deadlines. The ordering of the system, then, becomes, for this manager, literally a way of ordering the world.

Here we see Derrida's analysis of the archive vividly illustrated. When properly ordered, the archive provides for a clear and accurate recording of the past. It is then, peculiarly enough, the past as it ought to be when it is dissociated from the strategic concerns of the present, such as contractors who appear to confabulate prior access agreements. In this sense, the archive, which is meant to be a supplement, a mere aid, ends up becoming *more* accurate and, ultimately, *more* 'real' than the world it was meant to represent. It is on this basis that the archive can then be seen to authorise judgement. The manager can make business decisions effectively because he can now 'electronically check that very quickly' and is able to claim that the archive makes 'traceability much easier'. His power, then, comes from his active attachment to the archive, which then grants him the role of 'archon' – both archivist and judge.

Cooper (1992, 1993) has eloquently described how information communication technologies enable remote control by 'setting up' a greatly reduced or abbreviated model of the world that legislates for various kinds of action. A spreadsheet, for example, can act as a means for summating and comparing a vast range of activities within an organisation. If what one contributes to the organisation is not visible on the spreadsheet, then one may be excluded from future planning and strategy (see Munro, 1998). In Example 7, the ordering of the e-mail archive becomes a way of creating an abbreviated version of Oilsite that is used to order the future in advance – the future becomes 'antecedent to itself', in Whitehead's terms. The manager orders relationships between contractors and staff by ordering the e-mails within the archive. What is recorded in those e-mails is treated as the 'true' version of the past, to which the authors of the messages then become committed in advance of any subsequent version they might offer. In this way, the archive programmes the future and calculates in advance what is to be done.

The idea that social order is secured by offering up an abbreviated version of the world in advance, whether in the form of a diagram, a map, a table, a system of records or an e-mail archive, is also discussed widely in ANT (see Latour, 1987; Callon, 1991). Indeed, ANT holds that one of the principal aims of technical mediation is precisely to secure this translation of broader social relationships in a form that is tractable and calculable.

The spreadsheet or the 'league table' is a very potent symbol of the aspirations of modern formal organisation – namely, to be able to hold all that is deemed relevant about the world on a single sheet of paper. Matsuda (1996) refers to the technique of producing detailed archives (such as forensic records, mnemotechnical systems, anatomical maps) as a form of 'memory' being peculiar to modernity. However, what is critical here is not only control over the past, but the 'in advance' effect of being able to programme the future. It is this effect in particular that concerns Derrida in his discussion of archives as it underpins the 'archive drive'. In order to programme the future, it is necessary to expand the reach of the archive as far as possible, to be able to continuously record ever more of the past in ever greater detail.

In the examples that we have discussed, managers experience their attachment to e-mail archives, to 'archontic infrastructure', in two ways. To the extent that they see their strategies and ability to exercise control 'in advance' and 'remotely, they describe themselves as *actively* attached. However, as this is granted on the condition that there is ongoing and, to some extent, ever more rapacious activity concerning storing and organising e-mail messages, managers also describe themselves as *passively* attached. The two forms of attachment are, then, the basis on which these managers negotiate their relationship to the formal organisation of remembering.

There is, though, also a third sort of relationship that emerges. Some senior managers in both organisations no longer use e-mail. What is more, many of their key meetings are not formally recorded (see Brown & Lightfoot, 2002). Why should this be? We would argue that the reason is to be found in one of the implications of Derrida's analysis of archives. When the future is already programmed 'in advance', our ability to respond freely in the present is severely circumscribed. The 'dead hand' of the past weighs all too heavily in the here and now. This, then, gives rise to the desire to have done with the archive altogether, to break with both past and future as they are mapped out, to escape the continuous and deadening recording of the present.

This, as we have already mentioned, is what Derrida terms 'archive fever'. In the case of e-mail archives, it gives rise to managers *detaching* themselves altogether by refusing, with certain limits, to engage with archiveable forms of communication. In so doing, they grant themselves the ability to act without reference to the past as preserved and the future as programmed in advance.

The critical point that Derrida makes is that this detachment, which is, in effect, a decision to radically 'forget' or 'clear' the past as it is formally recorded, is not some aberration. Rather, it is part of the very logic of the archive itself. Archive fever – the overcoming of the archive – is there all along, haunting the archive drive.

Summary

In this chapter, we have explored how 'formally organised settings' may 'take charge' of remembering. We have discussed this in terms of formal assemblies of technical procedures – or 'archontic infrastructures'. Such infrastructure is produced by technical mediation, the embedding of social practices of remembering in formal classifications and standards. When this occurs, individual acts of remembering or forgetting are obliged to locate themselves in relation to what is granted by the infrastructure. However, as we have seen in the case of work in the neonatal intensive care unit, in practice, members engage in articulation work in order to respecify classifications and find 'workarounds' for standards. This can involve some form of selective forgetting. Halbwachs notes as much in his own description of the way in which zones of personal relations envelop and restructure zones of technical activity.

We then moved to focus on the study of the archiving of e-mails in organisations. We took Derrida's discussion of the archive as the basis for exploring the kinds of relationships managers have with the vast e-mail archives that they become obliged to maintain. Two forms of attachment – active and passive – were read from the examples. E-mail archives can be seen to extend managers' powers to act by virtue of the preservation of the past and the programming 'in advance' of the future. However, these archives also enrol managers into the demands of continuous maintenance.

Drawing on both ANT and Derrida, we considered the peculiar status archives acquire when they come to appear more 'real' than the organisational activities that they are meant to represent in a simplified form. The detachment of some managers from archontic infrastructure could, then, be read as directly produced by the tensions that make archiving possible in the first place.

Our discussion of formally organised settings has revealed a general problem with how past experience is mobilised in the present. When the past is systematically preserved or objectified in a process that subjects it to continuous calculation, then 'living' becomes no more than enacting a future that has already been programmed in advance.

We may, then, note the relevance to an understanding of the social psychology of experience of two phenomena that are often thought of as peculiarly modern. The first is the premium that is placed on a detailed knowledge of one's own past. To be a self-aware, in, for example, most forms of therapeutic practice, is to be able to offer rich accounts of the relationships between the most 'private' aspects of one's experience and one's current character and conduct (see Rose, 1996). This is further supported by the vast range of technologies, from photography to websites, that allow people to continuously record and display their own past, often in minute detail.

The second, is the tendency to conceive of change in radical terms, as constituted by a wholesale 'break' with the past. This rhetoric of 'revolution' stretches from modern understandings of politics to science and even to how knowledge itself is conceived (see Bachelard, 1968; Foucault, 1972).

In some sense, this second tendency is conditioned by the first, in that, if the present is determined by the past, then change can only be seen to occur via wholesale revolution. What, then, is the impact of understanding 'remembering' and 'forgetting' in terms of the past as directly constituting the present and the future as realised by a radical break? How have these modern tendencies shaped the psychology of memory? To what extent is it possible to offer an alternative conception of experience? It is to this that we now turn in the remaining chapters.

TEN

Collecting and dispersing experience: spatialising the individual in the mass

In the last chapter, we concluded our exploration of 'organised settings' by analysing what happens when remembering becomes embedded in 'archontic infrastructure', or, formally organised settings. We established that what is at stake here is the relationship between the individual and the past that is formally amassed in such a way as to render the future programmed 'in advance'.

In this chapter, we will now tack in the opposite direction to explore this general problem of how individual experience is managed in relation to the 'burden' of the past. This problem may be seen as emblematic of modern cultural discourses concerning memory (see Matsuda, 1996; Klein, 2000). In particular, it is critical to understanding how identity and change are negotiated, and the way in which significance is accorded to the details of our past experience.

To address this further, we will return in particular to Bergson's conception of unfolding experience as 'duration'. One of the obstacles to appreciating Bergson's work on duration and memory is the position he adopts, as a process philosopher, on 'change'. In Chapter 4, we outlined how process philosophy tries to avoid the language of substance by emphasising action and events over 'things'. Indeed, for process philosophers such as Bergson, what we call 'things' are, in reality, only transitory forms that subsist in the continuous ongoing flow of change. A form is a 'snapshot' made by our senses, a 'partial view' that is 'cut out' from the 'undivided flux' of the real by virtue of the 'gap' we, as living beings, are able to open up between action and reaction. Our perception of form is, then, essentially a 'reflection of our possible action' on the world.

For Bergson, change is primary. Reality itself is a 'fluid continuity' that does not admit to natural breaks. To experience reality as such is, then, to live out this movement of constant change, akin to an endless melody that never repeats itself at any point. Now it should be readily apparent that this notion of experience is radically at odds with how we usually consider our personal history. We typically consider our past to be made up of discrete moments and events, punctuated with phases and distinct periods. It is the function of memory to draw together these various parts and assemble them in such a way that we can reflect on past experience and thereby assess how it has shaped our present life. This way of approaching memory is indelibly associated with the notion that people are self-constituted individual entities more or less internally consistent over time. As we indicated in Chapter 1, John Locke (1690/1975) famously referred to this as a 'forensic' concept of self. On this account, to be a person is to be endowed with a chain of successive memories that map out what we have seen, what we have done, what we are. We are, then, defined by our memory. Individuality consists of a lengthy chain of memories, like so many beads on a string, the unique ordering of which expresses our personal identity.

This 'forensic' notion of identity is retained, in essence, by the modern psychology of memory. Consider the following statement by Elizabeth Loftus (1994: 18) on the fundamental importance of memory for psychological functioning:

> life would consist of momentary experiences that [would] have little relation to one another. Without memory we could not communicate with other people for we could not remember the ideas we wished to express. Without memory, we would not have the sense of continuity even to know who we are.

The endowment of a chain of successive memories is, Loftus claims, what makes it possible for ideas to take hold. The automatic formation of a sequence of past instants makes it possible for us to have and express ideas that would otherwise be fleeting sensations that would disappear without trace. Moreover, without this successive accretion of the past, we would have no sense of ourselves as a continuous, relatively stable entity that passes through time, much as an arrow passes over a series of points in space.

We see in this passage an expression of the modern tendency to think of memory in terms of continuity structured by virtue of 'forensic' links that stands as the ultimate guarantee of personal identity. It follows, then, that 'change' must be seen as some kind of break, followed by a reforging of the links in a new continuity assembled from the same elements. However, throughout this book we have made very different assumptions – drawing variously on Bergson, Halbwachs and Bartlett – about the relationship between memory and identity. We have approached remembering as a discontinuous process, where aspects of the past are *dissociated* as they are brought forth to serve the needs of the present. Where continuity appears, we have treated this as an achievement that is produced by communicative pragmatics or the management of inderdepencies in experience or by virtue of incorporation or mediational means or in relation to formal technical procedures.

However, irrespective of the potential merits of the approach we have been taking, we clearly have to explain why there is such apparent divergence between our commonsense modern experience of remembering and the alternative assumptions that we have been making. The answer lies in Bergson's claim that duration encompasses multiple intersecting planes of experience and, moreover, that we impose order on these 'virtually coexisting' forms of experience by projecting the logic of spatial relationships. This is what Bergson calls the 'cinematographical mechanism of thought'. In this chapter, we will briefly discuss this mechanism and the way in which past experience becomes 'spatialised'. We will then illustrate this process by analysing how family websites function as the mediational means for constructing a spatialised or 'cinematographical' version of family history in the present.

The cinematographical mechanism of thought

Bergson's (1992: 31) conception of 'duration' is an attempt to 'recapture reality in the very mobility which is its essence'. In order to think of time in this way, it is necessary to make a clear separation from space.

Throughout his writing, Bergson continuously admonished all attempts to reduce time to space, including, notoriously, Einstein's Special Theory of Relativity. For Bergson, time must be thought of as movement, as change, entirely without reference to 'the thing which changes'. This means that Bergson rejects any conception of time that is framed in terms of a series of instants. Understood in this way, our lives constitute a finite series of discontinuous moments. The role of psychological processes must then be, as Loftus claims, to restore a kind of continuity by preserving each passing instant in such a way that they can be threaded together with the present moment. Can continuity really be constructed in this fashion, though?

Bergson argues that the artificial division of duration into instants inadequately grasps the nature of change that is proper to time. The problem arises, Bergson claims, because of the great difficulty involved in perceiving change for what it is, as an indivisible movement. Bergson's (1992: 142–5) favoured example of this is the act of watching a hand passing before one's eyes. We see the hand begin moving from point A and coming to rest at point B. Between A and B, movement occurs, but what is the character of this movement, of this change?

Our tendency is to consider that we might precisely calculate the movement that occurs in the interval AB by breaking down the trajectory of the moving hand as a series of points through which the hand passes in succession. What this amounts to is a dividing up of the space between point A and point B and then fitting the movement of the hand on to this space. However, this operation leads to a paradox (1992: 143):

> How could the movement be applied upon the space it traverses? How can something moving coincide with something immobile? How could the moving object be in a point of its trajectory passage? It passes through, or in other terms, it could be there. It would be there if it stopped; but if it should stop there, it would no longer be the same movement we were dealing with. It is always by a single bound that a passage is completed.

The moving hand does not actually come to rest at any of the points we could estimate for the interval AB. Were it to do so, the movement would be complete, to be followed be a new movement. The best that we can say is that the movement itself is indivisible – it has no real constituent parts. After the movement has been completed, however, we can estimate, with varying degrees of precision, points where it may have concluded, but then these points are not part of the movement itself. They are merely 'virtual' points that enable us to make calculations and predictions.

Bergson (1998: 272–316) refers to this tendency to conceive of time and movement in terms of its precise opposites – the timeless and the immobile – as the 'cinematographical mechanism of thought'. In essence, this is the view that we have of the passage of time – as the unfolding of a series of moments – that emerges when we seek to reconstruct duration on the basis of the 'snapshots' our perception takes of passing reality. This is akin to the way that a cartoon or moving picture is traditionally generated by the rapid succession of still images. To think in this way is to 'set going a kind of cinematograph inside us' (1998: 306).

Yet, to understand time, to understand change, to understand reality itself in this way, is, Bergson (1992: 13) argues, to eliminate 'what one feels and lives'. Our lives are not 'unrolled' from the past like the frames of a film, nor are they 'unfurled' like the opening of a closed fan. Were this to be so, then time and change would be nothing, they would 'serve no purpose', as each successive instant of our life would be, in some sense, predictable from the previous one, being nothing more than a linear series of 'virtual halts'. Common sense tells us that this view inadequately grasps the nature of change (Bergson, 1998: 316):

> there is *more* in a movement than in the successive positions attributed to the moving object, *more* in a becoming than in the forms passed through in turn, *more* in the evolution of form than the forms assumed after one another … becoming exists: it is a fact.

Put simply, change happens. We are always involved in a process of becoming something different to that which we are right now. This process is neither reducible to a series of discontinuous instants nor to a set of discrete forms without some considerable cost. For, if we reduce time in this way to a series of instants, we will find that, no matter how small we make the distance between the instants, the change between them will continue to elude us (this is reflected in the philosophical example known as 'Zeno's paradox'). We will, then, 'always experience the disappointment of the child who tries by clapping his hands together to crush the smoke' (1998: 308).

Note that Bergson (2001: 117) is not arguing that time *cannot* be treated in this way as clearly it can, this being precisely what is done in mathematical treatments of time as a variable, as in the following:

> when the astronomer predicts, e.g. an eclipse, he does something of this kind: he shortens infinitely the intervals of duration, as these do not count for science, and thus perceives in a very short time – a few seconds at most – a succession of simultaneities which may take up several centuries for the concrete consciousness, compelled to live through the intervals instead of merely counting the extremities.

The astronomer is in the business of making predictions and, as a consequence requires that time be treated as a clear metric that will enable otherwise remote temporal occurrences to be brought together in the same calculation. Bergson's concern is that the intervals between these mathematically established points, which the astronomer can so readily dismiss, are precisely what we, as living beings, are 'compelled to live through'. The time of the astronomer, then, is fundamentally 'inhuman', it is a 'pulverised time' that cannot instruct us as to the real, qualitative experience of enduring as a living, acting being.

The cinematographical mechanism of thought has a practical value in our everyday affairs. If a person wishes to act on something – perhaps grab a moving hand before it smacks his or her cheek – then obviously the ability to anticipate a given point in space, the 'virtual halts' where the movement might be arrested, is essential. The cinematographical method of understanding time is then, the 'only practical method' as it 'consists in making the character of knowledge form itself on that of action' (1998: 306–7).

To the extent that our knowledge is premised on spatial reasoning, we may say that our intellect is fashioned on a 'logic of solids' (1998: ix). So, while our experience of duration is that of an indivisible continuity, our tendency is to attempt to render this experience in spatial terms, to transform change into permanency, mobility into immobility. This ongoing 'spatialisation of experience' contracts duration into the appearance of stability. It condenses 'into perception, the oscillations of matter, and into concepts, the constant flow of things' (1992: 89). However, this condensation does not of itself arrest movement, but merely creates the illusion of immobility (1992: 143–4):

> Movement is reality itself, and what we call immobility is a certain state of things analogous to that produced when two trains move at the same speed, in the same direction, on parallel tracks: each of the two trains is then immovable to the travellers seated in the other. But a situation of this kind, which after all, is exceptional, seems to us to be the regular and normal situation, because it is what permits us to act upon things and also permits things to act upon us: the travellers in the two trains can hold out their hands to one another through the door and talk to one another only if they are 'immobile', that is to say, if they are going in the same direction at the same speed. 'Immobility' being the prerequisite for our action, we set it up as a reality, we make of it an absolute, and we see in movement something which is superimposed.

Stability is, then, a product of our efforts to act on the world, but it does not actually halt or erase movement. In this sense, the stability we produce is a complicated coordination of movements, a hooking together of the unfolding pattern of our own actions with those of another.

In summary, Bergson argues for the primacy of movement and change. He displays that, without according change primacy, one attempts to reconstruct on the basis of immobility, on what does not change. All such attempts are inevitably doomed and give rise to paradoxes such as Zeno's well-known puzzles (Achilles and the tortoise, for example). Moreover, if duration – as the indivisible experience of change – is reduced to a series of instants, we will be led to understand the future as merely the unrolling of a set of possibilities that are given in advance. This is precisely the kind of problem that we identified, with Derrida, in the last chapter in relation to the translation of remembering by formally organised settings. However, the 'cinematographical method' is eminently well adapted to serve the needs of immediate action. Ultimately, the problem lies with the secondary projection of this method, this 'logic of solids', on to the totality of our past experience.

Family websites

We will now try to illustrate how the 'spatialisation of experience' operates by demonstrating how it is performed within family websites. These particular websites are interesting for a number of reasons. First of all, these are public arenas where memory is explicitly at issue. Most websites of this kind are dedicated to making visible the identity of the family as a discrete group. This typically involves 'doing history' in such a way that casual visitors to the website can grasp the elementary details and significance of the narratives that are offered.

Second, as the Internet is the homogenous space par excellence – that is, a seemingly endless succession of interlinked pages that can be traversed and searched in a non-linear fashion – the presentation of family history in the medium is necessarily 'spatialised'. The details of the way this spatialisation proceeds, then, provides an instructive case.

Third, as web pages are an asynchronous medium (that is, reader and writer are not co-present in the interaction), these sites visibly deploy a range of devices designed to create a sense of 'shared presence'. We may understand this shared presence as something like what Bergson describes as the illusion of immobility produced by the coordination of movement.

Family websites serve multiple purposes. They serve as a forum for communication between extended family members who are not in close geographical proximity and within a more diffuse group of 'friends' ('family' and 'friends' being two common categories used to divide material on websites). The sites also serve to make visible and continuous the identity of the family itself – or at least an identity framed by those family members (typically parents) charged with the upkeep of the site. The maintenance of identity obviously involves commemorative practices, such as noting significant events, birthdays, marriages and so on. Finally, the websites also act as a means by which independent activities of the family can be tied together in one location and made to appear coherent. For instance, hobbies may be displayed alongside professional activities or children's interests may be made visible alongside structured accounts of their ongoing development.

The spatialisation of experience

Tying together the multiple purposes served on the typical family website requires that the ongoing experiences of family members be rendered visible and communicable. As a consequence, such ongoing experience is necessarily spatialised – that is, divided up in such a way that it can be described, viewed or calculated by the visitor to the site. For example, on the index page of the site dedicated to the Orvin family, there is a box marked 'Announcements' that is continuously updated. Recent contents include (www.orvin.net/Home.html):

> *June/July:* The family went home to Norway for my Dad's funeral. These are some of the *happy moments* from an otherwise sad trip.
>
> *May 1st:* Took the kids to San Diego *Wild Animal Park* (click on link for pictures).
>
> *February 5th:* Celebrated my 40th on a sailboat with a couple of friends. *See Pictures from the trip here.*

The structure of the announcements acts to cut the ongoing experience of the Orvin family into an ongoing set of significant events, which are then rendered visible in the form of a photographic record that is hyperlinked to the underlined text. It is notable that the announcements contain minimal evaluation or reflection. The experience is not framed to any great degree in advance, the viewer being invited to 'see for themselves' what happened.

This way of structuring experience is followed through in the section marked 'Adventures'. A hyperlink leads to an animation of a set of revolving images taken from various trips made by some or all of the family. Putting the images in motion – that is, reconstituting movement from what is static – constructs an internal dynamism to the 'adventures', that they are both interrelated and part of an ongoing stream of activities that is outside routine family structures. However, this also suggests a tension between the desire to communicate the qualitative nature of the experience (what it felt like, how it unfolded) and what can be actually be seen in a photographic record.

For instance, clicking on an image of a sailboat captioned 'Bahamas July 97' leads to a page of images with the text: 'Islands of Abaco in the Bahamas – We rented a 46-foot sailboat, and sailed around the Island of Abacos for 10 days. A beautiful 10 days with plenty of R&R'. This minimal description is substantiated by photographs of the adult Orvins with two other couples (Allison and Neil, Suzie and Dan) posing on the sailboat, smiling to camera. Large hardback books and beer bottles appear in the foreground and a scanned image of a label emblazoned 'Kalik – Beer of the Bahamas' appears below the main text. What this collection of images confirms is that, for the casual viewer, there is actually very little to see. The experience, presented on a single page, is stripped of any form of intensity. It is left to the viewer to reconstruct what it must be like to have the time to read a substantial book lying under the blazing Bahama's sun or imagine the pleasure of sipping the just opened Kalik beer (visibly frothing in the bottle neck) in the shade of the boat's wheelhouse as the boat nudges out into vivid blue waters surrounding the Abacos. The tone of the experience can only be implied from the spatial composition of the images. It cannot, of itself, be made visible.

A different means by which the intensity of everyday experience can be rendered fit for consumption by others is seen in the 'Juvin' family site. A section marked 'chaotic neutral' features an ongoing 'weblog' or 'blog' written by Julie, the mother of Alex. 'Blogging' – an Internet activity that has grown in prominence in the past few years – usually takes the form of an ongoing record of comments on everyday life by the author. Blogs are somewhere between a diary and a newspaper column, depending on the given blogger's preferred style, and are typically updated on a daily or near daily basis. A recent entry by Julie records a notable event (www.juvin.com/julie):

October 04, 2003

We were witness to an amazing event last night. People had camped out overnight to get tickets and then again to get decent seats. Those who couldn't get tickets thronged outside the entrance anyway, hoping for no-shows. Fans came bearing flowers and goodness knows what else. We didn't have tickets, but a buddy hustled us through the back door and seated us within spitting distance of the one and only, Stephen Hawking.

For those who don't know, Professor Hawking, or Stephen, as all the Nobel Prize winners in the audience seemed to call him, is a British physicist, best known as the author of *A Brief History of Time* and *The Universe in a Nutshell*. He lives in Oxford, England, 11/12 of the year and in Pasadena the other 1/12 as a permanent guest researcher at Cal Tech, giving maybe one talk in the US a year, so we felt very fortunate for the opportunity to hear him speak.

Last night Stephen lectured on the topic of Godel and M Theory. Having been wheelchair-bound since the 80s by Lou Gehrig's disease, he 'spoke' through a special computer with a synthesized American accent, which everybody found funny. A lot of the actual lecture flew right over my head, with me feeling very much the underprepared student, but the rest was conversational and hilarious. The man has a wacky sense of humor. He chose six questions from a pool presubmitted by Cal Tech students to answer at the end of the lecture, and four were totally tongue in cheek, such as 'If there was a death match between you and Dr Baltimore [President of Cal Tech], who would win?' and 'What would be your campaign slogan if you were running for governor of California?'

In the end, what truly stood out for me were his conclusions about ongoing developments in physics, which really jived with my personal philosophy: while we may never know the secrets of the universe, what really matters is the journey of discovery.

Posted at 09:24 pm

As a record of the event, the entry moves between two registers. It is in part a journalistic account of the lecture, making much of the inferred character of Stephen Hawking and the contrast between the technical content and the jovial questions, but it also takes the form of a reflective diary entry, with the concluding reference to Julie's 'personal philosophy' framing the piece: 'In the end, what truly stood out for me'. The described events are then ultimately presented to the reader as exemplifying a personal commitment to a 'journey of discovery', which is not in itself observable in the same way. Ongoing matters of substance – the personal philosophy – are then articulated by arranging the account in such a way that they appear to emerge naturally from the event. To put it slightly differently, the commentary is arranged in such a way that everything points towards inner experience, in a manner akin to the way in which the arrangement of forms in perspectival painting creates an implied vanishing point. However, contrast this with part of the entry from the following day:

October 05, 2003

So, I'm coming clean with my new addiction: I'm totally obsessed with any and all products that come on a wipe. It began innocently enough with baby wipes, specifically the unscented aloe-infused variety. Then it was the Clorox and Lysol wipes, which come in regular fresh scent and lemon scent. (Yes, I've tried both.) Then it was the Oil of Olay Daily Facial wipes. My latest acquisitions are Windex and Glass Plus wipes and Fantastic wipes with Orange Action. After trying all the above, I no longer have any desire to use the bottled stuff. Wipes just *rock*. Next on the agenda: Pledge furniture wipes.

Posted at 01:14 pm

This entry is clearly not meant to be read as a significant event, despite the use of the terminology of 'addiction' and 'obsession'. Indeed, it may be the very insignificance of what is described that is central to the extract. By listing the range of wipes in such minute detail, Julie articulates a form of experience that involves a curiosity with mundane products. This might be said to be easily recognisable modern Western experience – to be a consumer confronted with a dazzling and confusing range of choice and change in goods available for purchase. However, in making this mundane experience a matter of 'obsession', Julie renders it into an opportunity to render her life distinctive. Cleaning wipes can become a source of interest, of pleasure, when one approaches them with a spirit of curiosity. She makes of the mundane a further means for disclosing character and, if we consider the two entries sequentially, what is being done is to efface the differences between what constitutes newsworthiness and what does not. The lecture and the cleaning wipes have an equivalent place in the daily activities of Julie's life; they are part of the same texture. The obvious spatial juxtaposition serves to construct something of the changing rhythms of everyday life in Julie's family.

What we begin to see, then, is that spatialisation of experience does not necessarily result in the kind of disruption or misapprehension that we might take Bergson to be suggesting. Rather, spatialisation is a dynamic process, where the cutting up and arranging of experience can be done by means of the adoption of a range of styles that make it possible for something of the movement of duration to be reconstituted. This may, admittedly, often be faux movement of the cinematographic kind that Bergson describes, but, as we have seen, with the arrangement of objects in the Orvin's photographs and the juxtaposition of entries in the Juvin Chronicles, it allows for something of duration to re-emerge.

This is also the case with those aspects of websites where experience is thoroughly frozen. The inevitable need to constitute the family for the casual viewer in such a way that it can be surveyed 'at a glance' creates problems. Which image will capture what it means to be a member of this family? How are complicated relationships to be demonstrated? The Neale family's (at www.neale.co.uk) site has a novel resolution to such questions in the form of the cartoon image that adorns its home page – shown in Figure 2.

Figure 2   A cartoon introduces the Neale family

Here, everything is given 'at a glance'. We see something akin to a classic nuclear family of two adults and three children, accompanied by two domestic pets. The viewer is also able to read off something of the family structure, with the adult posed behind the children, the father standing furthest back, with the adult arms encircling the children, who are ordered by age in the same positions adopted by Olympic medallists. Furthermore, gender distinctions are also present – the camouflage outfit of the son contrasting with the pink heart worn by the younger daughter, the father's shaved hair juxtaposed with the mother's long locks, which seem to cascade downwards into the same colour hair of the older daughter, illustrating family lineage. However, this immediate constitution of the family is also undone at the same moment. The cartoon depiction effectively ironises the image of a nuclear family. For instance, the drawing of the father's glasses leaves him with bulging eyes, which appear to be almost crossed. His mouth is set in a tiny frown framed by his beard and moustache. The son is also refusing to smile, his expression taking on the rictus of the terrified or the terminally bored. The sun, personified in a slightly disturbing way, with eyes screwed tightly shut around a mouth of uneven tombstone-like teeth, neatly sets off the whole scene as one that is impossible, that plays with other kinds of realities.

A similar kind of compression is achieved on the Maltezo family's website. Here, the author – youngest son, McDeceno – has included a 'dedication to every single person that makes up my family' in the form of a photograph and a small description of the current circumstances. His own dedication reads (www.geocities.com/maltezo/home.html):

at the age of 18, I am attending Porteville College. I am currently studying to be a licensed vocational nurse. Maybe later in life I will become a doctor. For now, I am just enjoying my time living in California.

This dedication not only performs a *spatial* compression, by reducing McDeceno's life to a few lines of text, but also enacts a *temporal* compression by reducing the future to a single line of aspiration. However, this contrasting of present with future is more complicated than it appears at first glance. The aspiration 'Maybe later in life' to become a doctor contrasts with Mc Deceno's current studies to become a 'licensed vocational nurse'. As the two professions are not equivalent in status, it would appear that the author is flagging his current studies as being a matter of choice rather than ability. He could 'later in life' train for a more prestigious career, but right now there are other concerns. There is also the implication that his time in California is bounded in some way (the distribution of the family between California, Hawai and the Philippines is a concern all through the material on the site). Temporal compression, then, does not necessarily result in clarity, but, rather, creates a kind of structural ambiguity in the family profiles.

The construction of shared presence

As we discussed earlier, one of Bergson's central claims is that the notion of people inhabiting the same temporal framework is illusory, akin to that of two trains momentarily finding themselves travelling at the same speed. The question, then, is how this appearance of a shared temporal framework is constituted. Across the websites we see a range of techniques whereby this is achieved. The Orvin's site, for instance, uses the familiar device of the calendar to spatially organise significant events. We can see January in Figure 3.

The events that are brought together here are mostly birthdays, excepting the commemoration of the first date of the Orvin adults on the 10 January. However, some of these birthdays are more significant than others – notably those of Toby and Tess, the family's two children. The choice of pictures representing the birthdays is also of interest. Finn – the father – is represented by a childhood photograph, whilst Kirsten (Finn's aunt) and Morsan (Finn's mother) are given presumably contemporaneous images.

Now, given that the function of a calendar is to subject the unfolding of time to a common, socially constituted, chronographical framework that standardises events, this lack of a common standard in the nature of the photographs depicting birthdays sits somewhat uneasily. It suggests that what is relevant, in a temporal sense, about each birthday is different in each case. For the Orvin's children, birthdays are markers of ongoing development, hence the need for a recent image. For the elder family members, birthdays are opportunities for commemoration, hence the indeterminate

Figure 3   The Orvin family's calendar for January 2003

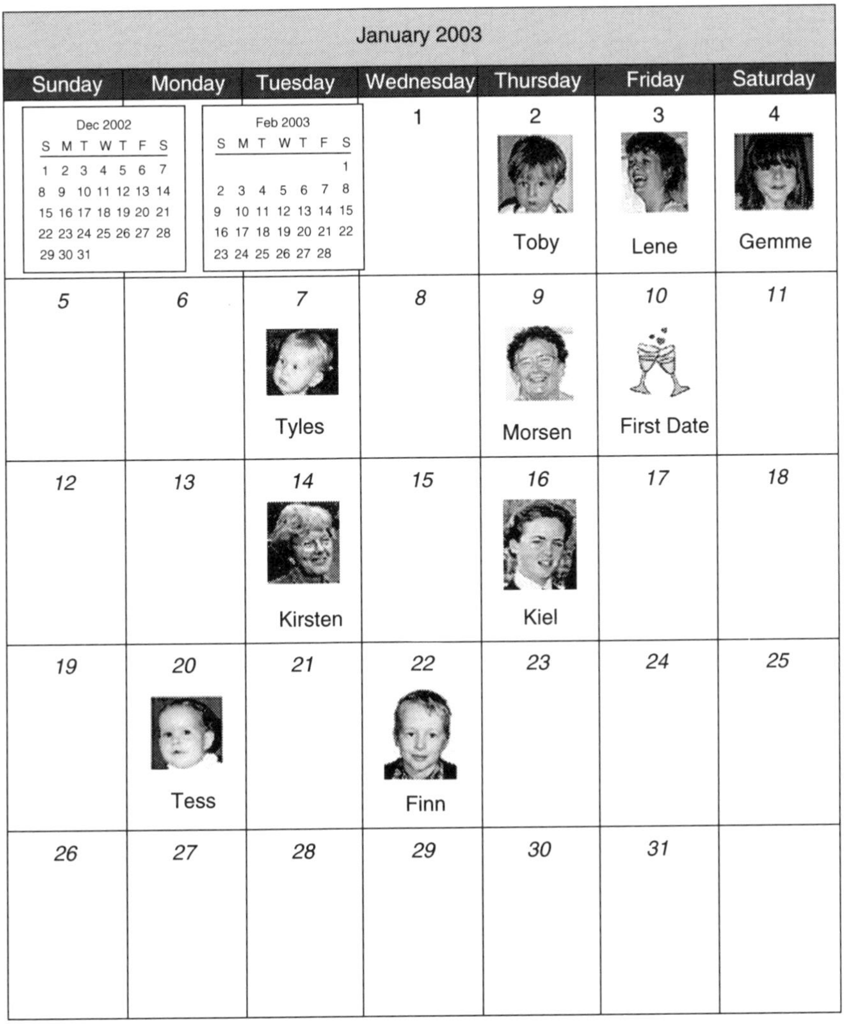

January 2003						
Sunday	Monday	Tuesday	Wednesday	Thursday	Friday	Saturday
Dec 2002 / Feb 2003			1	2 Toby	3 Lene	4 Gemme
5	6	7 Tyles	8	9 Morsen	10 First Date	11
12	13	14 Kirsten	15	16 Kiel	17	18
19	20 Tess	21	22 Finn	23	24	25
26	27	28	29	30	31	

images to denote the status of a senior without establishing a precise age. For Finn himself, birthdays constitute moments for ironic self-reflection, hence the childhood photograph, along with the animated clock counting down the days, hours, minutes and seconds until his next (forty-first) birthday – 96 days 8 hours 14 minutes 12 seconds at the precise time of writing.

The shared presence that is created by the calendar is then rendered ambiguous as the viewer cannot be clear about precisely what kind of event is being commemorated. This is particularly the case with the 29 June birthday. The family member here is Trond, Finn's brother, who, tragically, died during childhood. This poignant calendar entry is different again to the range of January's entries. Overall, the entries do not sit together as a standardised set of events in a manner that might be expected.

The FamTeam website, which publicises the broad range of activities of the Arndt family, takes an even more direct approach to constituting shared presence. The Arndt family comprises 14 children, plus parents Rick and Cathy. Their family is described as being modelled on a traditional Christian institution, where the role of the father is to act as 'spiritual head of the home and as protector of women and children'. Together, the family participates in a 'family-based Christian outreach effort' built around 'twice-a-week meetings at THE FATHER'S HOUSE CHRISTIAN COMMUNITY', a series of media productions, such as the 'Safe at Home' cable television show, and a family softball team.

The vast family website includes a range of features, such as downloadable games and family videos, some of which are available on a subscription basis. Rick Arndt posts a daily spoken message entitled 'Dad's fireside chat'. The page on which the sound files are posted depicts Rick leaning against a wooden bureau, microphone in hand. The effect is that of the visitor entering his personal study.

The following are extracts from the 'fireside chat' of 16 October 2003. The nine-minute chat describes events of that day, such as the illness of one of the youngest Arndt children and an unexpected visit from an old neighbour, along with progress reports on the website and a new house that the family is constructing by themselves. The following extract features the references throughout the chat to David Paul (www.famteam. com/firesidechat.htm):

well (.) I'm in the attic again once again with the baby (.) it worked out that he's next to me (.) well actually about six feet away (.) little David Paul even though he's been having a fever lately he seems to be in pretty good spirits (.) he threw up a bit here tonight (.) Cathy and I came up here for a little over an hour after a very busy day (.) I'm praying right now that God will just heal little David Paul (.) healing him completely (.) I'm glad that he's had a good attitude and been very (.) you know (.) relatively restful except for throwing up a few times but he's been in good spirits but I can tell he's not quite himself (.) Cathy toward the end of the evening was starting to cough and is run down so Lord just help her too (.) I'm surprised with me now speaking for several minutes that little David Paul hasn't (.) stirred too much (.) now of course around here when you talk a lot (.) that may seem so normal (.) so comforting to him (.) that the babies like him (.) he and other babies simply think subconsciously oh good (.) there's a familiar voice and go to sleep

There are numerous dietic features of this talk – 'I came up here', 'I'm praying right now', 'around here when you talk a lot' – that are precisely designed to establish a sense of time and place. It is around these features that Rick hangs details of the day's ongoing events in the Arndt household. The minute detail in which the events relating to the care of the sick infant David Paul are reported – such as the number of times he has been sick, the 'little over an hour' his parents spent watching over him, Cathy's coughing – create a rich temporal and spatial framework within which the listener is invited to vicariously experience life among the Arndts. This experience is structured in advance by Rick's orientation to a taken-for-granted account of family life, indicated in descriptions such as that of the baby's response to be surrounded by the continuous talking of its siblings.

Celia Lury (1997) terms this induction into the everyday experiences of others 'interiority without intimacy'. What she identifies is the tension between the making visible of daily life in minute detail with the simultaneous estrangement from potential matters of real substance. For instance, Rick's fireside chats do not typically dwell on the nature of his particular Christian beliefs or explicate the basis for his values and personal commitments (although these kinds of issues are raised elsewhere on the website). It would seem that this kind of reflection is disruptive of the attempt to create shared presence. To put it more crudely, the more deeply one is drawn in to life with the Arndts, the less able one is to question or evaluate that life. A form of closeness is available at the cost of simultaneous distancing.

Narratives of the possible

We may reformulate Lury's 'interiority without intimacy' in line with Bergson's distinctions between quality and quantity and virtual with actual. To see the details of a person's everyday family life is to be exposed to their life in its actuality – this many children, this kind of home, this type of job, this many hours spent at work and so on. These are all what Bergson would call quantitative matters, designations of people, things and events in terms of clearly calculable judgements.

We can extend these judgements almost infinitely. There are always potentially more and more things to notice about the family and their activities. Indeed, we might say that the ultimate family website might be one in which each family member would be continuously tracked and profiled in the manner of contestants on reality television programmes, such as *Big Brother* or the central character in the film *The Truman Show*. This would be a completed spatialised form of experience – everything is there to see, the smallest details, every aspect of daily life rendered utterly and relentlessly visible.

Bergson's point would be that this quantitative rendering of life does not exhaust experience. Far from it. Our experience flows, it is a matter of constant change as qualities blend into one another. This 'virtual experience' of continuous potential, of the mixing of purely qualitative distinctions, underpins the actual. This experience cannot be given 'at a glance' as it is not a spatial matter. It is, rather, the texture of life in the time of its being lived.

In Chapter 4, we described why Bergson adopts the language of 'actu-alisation' in favour of 'possibility' – because it avoids the paradox of assuming that the future already exists in some latent sense prior to its unfolding. However, as Bergson makes clear, as we must necessarily spa-tialise experience to serve the needs of action, the tendency is to confuse the virtual with the actual and real, qualitative change with quantitative possibility. For example, many websites feature narratives that recount the history of the family by projecting current states of affairs backwards to putative causes. The following narrative is offered as part of a descrip-tion of the youngest son on the Bayou Spirit website (http://members. tripod.com/bayouspirit/index.htm):

> Then there is the youngest son. The day before my Grandma passed away, she looked at me and said, 'You have four beautiful boys.' I said, 'Grandma, I have three beautiful boys.' She said, 'No, you have four beautiful boys, and the next one is going to be very special.' Our youngest son was born ten months later in the same zodiac sign as Grandma. He is the one that we threw out most of the rules for and just enjoyed. By the time you go through this three times, number four was just instinct, no Dr Spock or any-thing. He was nine years younger than his oldest brother but I don't think he was ever a baby. When he was only three, he had quite a collection of Matchbox and Hot Wheels cars which are not even recommended for children that young. But he just blended right in. Once when I was pregnant for him we stopped and bought snow balls (a Southern summer treat (.) My husband, without thinking, bought six, including one for his son who was not yet born! He was hard to wake in the morning, so I would start at his toes and sing 'Itsy bitsy spider' as I worked up his little body. Now he has an incredible fear of spiders! Some things even a mother can screw up.

The start and end of this narrative consist of stories where the place of a further child in the family is created in advance of his birth. In Grandma's prediction and the husband's absent-mindedness, a fourth son is consti-tuted and treated as an actuality.

The slippage between possible and real involved here is one that Bergson identifies as being a common tendency. Once some event has come to pass – such as the presence of four boys within the family – the tendency is to see the event as always having been possible. However, to do so is to suggest that the event was in some sense there already, awaiting reali-sation. For instance, the claim that 'He is the one that we threw out most of the rules for and just enjoyed' is a retrospective evaluation. No doubt it came to pass that rules slipped, that in the accommodation of the family to the new child, previous anxieties about parenting disappeared. This seems more likely than a conscious, planned throwing out of the rules. Similarly, the attribution of the son's spider phobia to the affectionate toe tickling constructs a line of causality between past possibility and current reality that makes it 'the mirage of the present in the past' (Bergson, 1992: 101).

The tendency to project possibility into the past results in the construction of clear causality and influence – that is, 'forensic' links – where it may instead be more appropriate to think in terms of contingency and change. Furthermore, this slippage in thought is itself necessary rather than erroneous. In order to spatialise experience, one is more or less compelled to fashion acts of remembering in causal terms. The past must be 'tamed' to fit into the shape of the present.

We might, then, say that, just as the construction of shared presence involves a simultaneous proximity and remoteness, so, in the act of remembering, there is in the same gesture a *collection* and *dispersal* of past experience (see Cooper, 2001, for further discussion of these terms). Only some selected aspects of the past are admitted into the present, and only then on the condition that they are transformed into a clearly defined form. This acts to efface or foreclose on a myriad of other 'virtual' relationships and potentials that may have been bound to the same recollections. Yet, this actualisation of the past – dividing it up and fashioning it for the needs of the present – does not exhaust these potentials. This is why, ultimately, Bergson insists on distinguishing the virtual from the possible – the present is not put together from possibility as a model is assembled from a kit, but is, instead, a movement of creation in relation to a 'virtual' past that is never exhausted and is infinitely renewable.

The tension between the spatialisation of experience and virtual potential can also be seen in attempts to make visible the experiences of others that are unable to report them. On the Orvin's website, a section dedicated to the two young children of the family contains the following (www.orvin.net/Babyy.html):

> I was born on Sunday January 2nd year 2000 at 2:28pm. It sure was a rough day, but when I met my mommy and daddy I forgot all about the hard work. I was 7 pound 5 ounces and 20 inches, I don't know why that matters but everybody asks me those stats. If I must say, I do think I look handsome, so you fathers with young daughters: LOOK OUT. I hope you enjoy the web pages that I created, it took nine months of planning, creating and hard work. Actually entering it was the first thing I did when I came home. Look around but please understand that I need a little more time to complete some of the pages. I *am* tired after making my way in to everybody's life.

This text attempts to resolve the difficulty involved in making the experiences of young family members visible by attributing words to three-year-old Toby himself. As the words so clearly do not originate from Toby, this sets up a problem for the reader, who is left unclear as to the level of irony involved in the text. However, this irony also serves a purpose as it allows for some of the ambiguities about commemorating the birth of a child to be addressed. For example, the bare facts of the newly born – 'those stats' – are recorded, but ironised in the next sentence – 'I don't know why that matters'. This reflection is only possible from the position of the newly born himself, who can safely be assumed to be indifferent to such normative measures.

Writing in the child's 'voice', then, allows something of the complex experience of the relationship between new borns and parents – which cannot be reduced to the at-a-glance 'stats' – to be articulated, notably in the description of 'meeting' – 'when I met my mommy and daddy' – and 'joining' – 'I *am* tired after making my way in to everybody's life.'

Such descriptions also serve to project possible futures – notably in the warning to 'fathers with young daughters'. However, in so doing, there is risk of rendering Toby's experience as a mere reflection of his parents' aspirations and concerns – again, the 'possible' as the projection of the 'real'. Contingency and potential are to some extent foreclosed.

The autonomy of the past

For Bergson, the actual represents only the 'leading edge' of the unfolding of duration, understood as the totality of 'virtual experience'. This is not to say that the virtual is 'disorderly' but, rather, that it is 'simply the order we are not looking for' (Bergson, 1992: 98). In our acts of remembering, we make the past fit into the shape of the present. In so doing, we seek forms of order that are coherent, predictable and familiar and, moreover, seek to suppress that which does not line up in such a way.

The virtual, then, might be simply glossed as the range of alternative modes of ordering a given recollection that are granted by our experience – the possible orderings that we 'are not looking for'. Understood in this way, the virtual has a kind of autonomy of its own that resists our attempts to settle, in any lasting way, the nature of the past. Alternative orderings of a given recollection can 'bleed' into remembering. For example, on the Maltezo site, McDeceno reflects on the ambiguous status of his knowledge about his childhood in the Philippines (www.geocities.com/maltezo/home.html):

> Though I can't remember my past in the Philippines, I still can listen to stories about the Philippines told by my family. I don't know if the stories that they tell me are true because they like to have a little fun with me by telling me stories that sound so unreal. Like how the Philippines is a very haunted place. My favorite story has to be the one that explains why I didn't have teeth on my upper jaw. When I was little I didn't have

much teeth, so I looked kind of funny. My family said that when I was in the Philippines I bit this boy named Binbin. I guess his mom (I think) did some kind of voodoo on me to make my teeth fall off. This story is stupid, I can't believe they actually made me believe this when I was little.

McDeceno wrestles with the desire to connect with his heritage and the unreliable nature of the accounts of his childhood provided by his family that 'sound so unreal'. Indeed, the discovery of this unreliability is in itself central to his dilemma. However, we might say that this 'unreality' is precisely what deepens his relationship to the Philippines. What makes the story of the missing teeth so appealing is its 'fantastic' quality, the sense that what is being told beggars belief. If a completely veridical account of the incident were available, that would serve to destroy those elements that give the story its charm.

There is, then, often something at stake in keeping the relationship with the past as it is recollected open and, to some degree, fluid. The Philippines as it exists for McDeceno in the unreliable accounts of others is, in all likelihood, a more potent resource around which to constitute his identity than the Philippines as it might be narrated in, say, a modern history textbook. The autonomy of the past – that is, the resistance of the past to be absorbed entirely into a given framework – is, then, of a piece with an openness towards the future. If the past is not simply a range of given possibilities, then the future is not already determined in some fashion. Rather, time is precisely the elaboration and refashioning of the given or, as Bergson (1992: 93) puts it 'the living being essentially has duration; it has duration precisely because it is continuously elaborating what is new and because there is no elaboration without searching, no searching without groping. Time is this very hesitation, or it is nothing'.

By way of illustration of what Bergson means by 'elaboration' and 'hesitation', consider the sections of the Orvin's website that commemorate the life of Finn's brother, Trond, who, tragically, died during childhood. The page begins with an animation displaying Trond's full name and a photograph of 'a young Trond'. Text then gradually appears, as though it is being typed, followed by a series of further photographs. These images are named and dated – 'Probably the last picture taken of the whole family: Jon, me, Trond, Ole, Dad and Mom. Taken in Oslo at Aunt Else in the summer of 72'. They also feature records of commemorative activities: 'On every December 23rd the family goes to the cemetery where Trond rests and lights three candles for each of the remaining brothers. This picture is from 1995: in the back, left to right, is Victoria, Siri, Christine, Mom and Donna. In front, we have Alex, Ole, Jon and me'. In the background, as the images move in and out of view, a version of the song 'Candle in the wind' plays.

This combination of animation, images and sound is a 'solution' to the problem involved in commemorating Trond, but what kind of problem? In effect, it is the problem of premature closure, having said all that needs to be said and having put an end to the matter. The relatively sparse text on the page indicates that this is not the case, that the memory of Trond remains active. Although the images are named and dated, they do not fix the past, they do not exhaust the range of emotions or experiences that are involved in this commemorative work. Hence, by literally putting the images and text into movement, the page creates its own form of openness to the past. There is, then, a kind of hesitation expressed here. Not everything can be given at once. Moreover, a sense that the fragmentary series of photographs of Trond presented are not a replacement for the work of commemoration itself, but, rather, a means of renewing and elaborating that work (hence the doubled effect of displaying the commemorative act of the annual visit within a second, electronic commemorative act).

Elaboration and hesitation are, then, the characteristics by which something of the virtual remains exposed in the ongoing spatialisation of experience that marks our actual existence. To put it another way, if spatialisation is one part of a circuit that runs from virtual to actual – that is, 'actualisation' – then hesitation and elaboration are the return part of that circuit – that is, 'virtualisation'. In one direction, the past is subject to dissociation, as it is projected and inserted into the present. In the other direction, the resulting version of the past is re-exposed to duration, opened up to an ongoing work of expansion and elaboration.

Summary

We began this chapter with the acknowledgement that our commonsense modern understanding of remembering is cast in 'forensic' terms. Understood in this way, the past is seen to be a continuous thread of moments that directly condition the present. Change, when it occurs, takes the form of a 'break' in this continuity and succession. Following Bergson, we can now see that the 'forensic self', which informs the current psychology of memory, is a most peculiar conceptual arrangement. It assumes a form of 'pulverised' time, where movement is reduced to immobility and real change becomes a series of jumps between static points. Small wonder that, to reconstruct the continuity of ordinary experience, it becomes necessary to conceive of a complicated system that can organise and synthesise these 'instants' into something that resembles time as it is lived.

The alternative that Bergson (1992: 179) presents – that of duration as real, qualitative change – leads us to think of selfhood not as a machine for synthesising experience, but, rather, as 'the continuous life of a memory which prolongs the past into the present'. Selfhood is, then, a movement in relation to the mass of the past. It is a way of managing and focusing this mass in relation to the needs and demands of the present. In order to think of selfhood in this way, it becomes necessary to reconsider the relationship between perception and memory as that between the 'actual' spatialised form our experience takes and the 'virtual' qualitative forms of experience that make up the totality of our past.

Recollection, then, can be understood as a circuit that moves from the virtual, from the relatively undifferentiated potency of the past, to the differentiated, spatialised actual. This phase of the circuit – actualisation – involves *dissociation* instead of association. Recollection, here, is a part of 'cutting out' of experience to fit the cloth of present action.

What of the return part of the circuit? We have illustrated how the turning back from the actual to the virtual – virtualisation – involves what Bergson refers to as 'hesitation' and 'elaboration' – that is, an openness to the past, a turning away from a spatialised form of experience towards duration itself.

Such a form of recollection seems entirely alien to the kinds of tasks and activities typically studied by psychologists, which treat the retrieval of memories as more or less clearly defined data for the cognitive system. What kind of 'data' would be produced by duration itself? How would remembering proceed on this basis? What kind of experience would be involved? How might we conceptualise such self-knowledge? It is to these questions that we will turn in our final study.

ELEVEN

Cutting experience: intersecting durations in making lives matter

In the last two chapters, we have described experience in relation to organised settings in terms of the 'burden' of the past on the individual. In Chapter 9, we looked at how the past becomes stored up in 'archontic infrastructure' and the types of workarounds and forms of attachment that users of such an infrastructure adopt. In Chapter 10, we turned from space to time and explored how experience becomes 'spatialised' within family websites in order to make it available 'at a glance'. However, in both chapters it became apparent that, while the spatialisation of experience – or conversion of the past into a readily available form – is required in order to serve the needs of action, the accompanying 'forensic' conception of self is not a good basis on which to ground a social psychology of experience.

The problem is that, once the objectification of time as a series of instants is understood as given in the natural order of things, then we are robbed of the means to understand how movement and change occur in our unfolding experience. Moreover, we are led to erroneously assume that the order we impose on the past, in our efforts to 'turn around' on our experience, is in some way final and determinate. To put it another way, that we can have done with the past, exhaust its possibilities and come to a lasting understanding of precisely how it conditions the present moment. As we noted in Chapter 9, this is a peculiarly modern approach to memory.

In Chapter 10, we concluded by noting that there are good reasons for refusing to settle the past in this way, that, instead, commemoration may be best achieved by leaving open and unspecified our relationship to the past. By way of a further example, consider the 'monument against fascism, war and violence' constructed by Jochen and Esther Gerz in the Harburg district of Hamburg. This monument consists of a hollow aluminium

12-meter pillar coated in soft lead, which visitors were invited to mark or deface with a steel nibbed pen. The pillar was then gradually lowered into the ground at the rate of 1.5 metres, until it eventually 'disappeared' altogether (see Young 1993: 28–36 for further details). In this way, the record contained on the pillar is erased – the burden of remembering is transferred back from the monument to the visitors.

Now, the particular character of the Gerz's monument is bound up with the problem of preserving the memory of the Shoa. As Young (1993) describes, attempts to preserve this most unthinkable event in recent European history, have often taken the form of 'counter-monuments', such as Gerz's disappearing pillar, that reference the systematic attempt to erase the Jewish people. These are monuments designed to provoke a work of remembering by withdrawing the supports and material resources on which collective memory typically depends. Yet, these counter-monuments, or self-erasing infrastructures, display that memory need not depend on the spatial organisation and recording of the past that make it available 'at a glance'.

Similarly, Argenti (1999) describes a range of ethnographic examples of 'disposal monuments'. These are commemorative objects that, although fashioned with great care and precision, are only used as part of a single commemorative event. After the event has concluded, the object is discarded (or sold on to tourists).

The purpose, then, of these objects is not to store up the past in a spatial location, but, rather, to make it possible for the present to be turned back on or opened up towards the past in a commemorative event. Having made this 'untimely' event possible, the object itself is of no further use.

In Chapter 8, we discussed the mediation of remembering by artefacts in a slightly different way. There, we described how artefacts lend something of their stability to memory, how they act as markers of past social relationships. The displacement of artefacts across time could, then, serve as potent reminders of both the form past experiences took and what has now been lost. The Gerz's monument and the disposal monuments described by Argenti appear to function in a slightly different way. Rather than lend their stability to the past, they appear to do the exact opposite by first lending then withdrawing their support from the past, thus rendering the past itself unstable and problematic. However, is this not precisely the kind of relationship to past experience that Bergson invokes in his description of 'elaboration' and 'hesitation' that we engage in when confronting the past as an indeterminate mass of 'virtually coexisting' memories?

In this chapter, we will explore this 'indeterminate' relationship to past experience. We will argue that, rather than undermining memory, such a relationship may actually serve to afford a cohesive and productive way of turning around on past experience. Moreover, we will show that, in Bergson's terms, 'hesitation' or 'openness' to the burden of the past is part of what it means to 'think in duration'.

In Chapter 4, we described how this deceptively simple injunction forms the basis for what Bergson calls 'intuition'. In this chapter, we hope to go some way towards recovering this term as a way of referring to a non-subjective form of knowledge, orientated towards change, that is best characterised as an 'event' rather than a capacity.

One obstacle to realising this ambition is the apparently subjective use that Bergson makes of 'duration'. For Bergson, duration – as it is the endurance of a living being in time – must necessarily be individual. Each being has its 'rhythm of living', its own way of experiencing movement and change. One upshot of this argument is that, as Mullarkey (1999a) describes, it is no longer possible for any one temporal perspective to be represented totally by another. Now, this position brings Bergson's approach up against some serious objections.

As we discussed in Chapter 3, Halbwachs (1980) argues that, if this is so, then it is not possible for any kind of communication to occur. Sociality is impossible if we all exist in our own 'private' streams of consciousness and becoming. However, Halbwachs' objection is misplaced. Bergson is *not* arguing that it is impossible to experience anything of another's duration. Obviously we can and this is precisely what is accomplished by the spatialisation of our experience. We coordinate our mutual durations in such a way that we are not even aware of their difference, just as the two travellers on trains running alongside one another become unaware that they are actually moving. In this way, we see that the use we have made of Halbwachs' work in Chapters 7 and 8 to understand how people become 'incorporated' or 'translated' into a form of common experience, actually illustrates the process of coordination that Bergson describes in the 'two trains' example.

However, to understand the full implication of this example, we must acknowledge that what Bergson argues against is the idea that we could ever *entirely* grasp the duration of another. In order to do so, it would be necessary for our own rhythm of living to take on the pulses and contours of the other's in such a way that there would no longer be any difference between us. We would, in effect, become the other.

As this is clearly some kind of fantasy, Bergson insists on the difference. However there is another reason for Bergson wanting to make duration a singular experience. One of Bergson's long-running concerns, visible from his earliest work, is that if we try to understand the totality of our past experience in spatial terms – that is, project the 'logic of solids' on to memory – we will be led to think of our past as something that could be abstracted, that we could 'protract or contract' our lived experience as we see fit.

For example, in *Duration and Simultaneity*, Bergson (1999) takes issue with Einstein's Special Theory of Relativity because it suggests, he claims, that lived experience is reducible to a mathematically derived conception of space–time.

Now, Bergson does not in any way doubt that relativity theory, in general, constitutes a productive advance in human thought (1999: 154). He does, however, take issue with the idea that it is possible for the experimenter, as an observer, to place herself or himself at will in different frames of reference. This occurs in the infamous 'twins paradox'. This is a thought experiment where Paul dispatches his twin brother Peter in a rocket that travels away from the Earth for a year at slightly less than the speed of light before making the opposite journey back. When Peter returns, Paul has aged 200 years.

Bergson argues that the interpretation of this paradox by Einstein depends on an analytical sleight of hand, where the position from which it is possible to describe the duration of both Peter and Paul is not itself 'relativised'. In other words, the analyst/experimenter is granted not merely the power to access the duration of both brothers, but also his or her or 'its' (as the experimenter may be replaced by a mechanical recording device) own duration is seen as entirely without consequence for the procedure. For Bergson, the real duration of the experimenter can neither be dismissed nor reduced to a mechanical measure of duration (such as by a clock) without creating an entirely 'inhuman' vision of experience that singularly fails to map on to the world of our everyday affairs. It is all very well and good for the theoretical physicist to imagine one twin bidding farewell to his brother, who is blasted into space and will not return for another 200 years, but this interval of 200 years is precisely what the earthbound twin is 'compelled to live through' – the real qualitative experience of living, acting and ageing. It is the dismissing of this experience as without consequence for relativity theory that Bergson objects to and this is the basis of his attempt to propose duration as a corrective to an entirely scientific conception of time (see Callon, 1999).

What Bergson proposes instead is that, although the duration of each living being is irreducible to that of another, our respective durations may 'envelop' one another. This is the meaning of the sugared water example we discussed in Chapter 4. When our duration becomes enveloped by that of another, something of the qualitative character of our lived experience is exposed to us. In being made to wait, we are forced to confront the indeterminate character of our unfolding experience. The implication of all this is that, although the duration of each living being is irreducible to that of another, the mutual enveloping of durations results in a fundamental interdependency. Our lived experience, then, includes – and is included in – the durations of others. In this chapter, we will argue that this mutual dependency of durations is central to a social psychology of experience.

Setting for the study: reconciliation and remembering

The material that will serve as the basis for our discussion is drawn from Kyoko Murakami's (2001a, 2001b) work concerning the post-war consequences of being a prisoner of war. Murakami gathered a corpus of interviews with British Second World War veterans who were prisoners of war in the Far East. During their period of captivity, the interviewees worked to build the Thai–Burma Railway before being transferred to a copper mine in Japan. Some 50 years later, in 1992, 28 former British POWs returned to a memorial site in the vicinity of the mine. This visit was part of a whole series of events that were organised as a result of the grass roots rather than state-initiated efforts of Japanese nationals living in the UK, veterans' associations and people in the locality of the memorial to promote reconciliation. The memorial site and the circumstances of its creation and maintenance became the focus of efforts to organise the reconciliation visit for the surviving POWs.

'Reconciliation' is a fraught issue here. The severe experiences of POWs in South East Asia and Japan during the Second World War are well known and have been dramatised in popular Western films, such as 'Bridge over the River Kwai' and 'Merry Christmas Mr Lawrence'. Many surviving former POWs still hold the view that inadequate reparation has been made by Japan, as a nation, for their treatment. In more recent years, this has turned on the question of whether or not a formal apology – that is, 'saying sorry' – can be identified in statements made by figures such as the Japanese Prime Minister and Emperor Akihito. However, what concerns us here is the interplay between practices of remembering and those of reconciliation. How and in what ways are the post-war lives and wartime experiences of these veterans gathered up in the emergent collectivity of such practices? How do these practices emerge and sustain themselves? In what ways does 'reconciliation' turn on the mutual envelopment of individual durations?

Practices of remembering and reconciliation

There are initially two approaches that we might be tempted to make to understand reconciliation as a social practice. One is to begin from historical givens and then explore how individuals contextualise their own 'memories' in relation to some 'grand narrative' of events, such that they can construct plausible personal identities and biographies (see, for example, Neisser, 1982). This requires the study of how the patterning of history can be taken as some global benchmark and context for an individual's memory and identity. Such work explores how autobiographical memory and identity is patterned in relation to significant events, such as declarations of war, assassinations, centenaries, national commemorations and celebrations and so on (see Conway, 1997).

In this sense, history would serve as the ultimate reference point around which individual lives, individual durations, might be organised. However, as Halbwachs shows, the formal accounts of history are rarely stable enough to serve as clear grounds. History is refracted by the collective frameworks that define membership in such a way that it is not clear what a given event means, not even that it has significance as an 'event' for everyone (indeed, punctualising some matter to constitute an event can be part of what sustains a collective, as we saw in Chapter 6). For example, the death of Princess Diana in Paris in 1997 is a classic instance of what might be seen as a 'global benchmark', defined as an event that individuals are able to spontaneously and vividly recollect. However, barely six years later, this event seems curiously dated, to have lost some if its holding power, overtaken perhaps in Western Europe by the complexities of September 11th 2001 and the subsequent conflicts and controversies in Afghanistan and Iraq. Maybe this is an instance of a memory 'crisis' in modernity (or postmodernity) – events decline at a far greater rate than they previously did in European and North American historical consciousness. It is more likely, though, that the global political framework in which something like the Kennedy assassination or the coronation of Queen Elizabeth II made sense is now far more complex, or the representation of such events in social scientific research assumed a misplaced homogeneity (see, for example, Michael Schudson's 1990 analysis of a similar process at work in the Washington press corps' recollection of the popularity of Ronald Reagan).

In any case, we cannot assume that a 'global benchmark' or a 'grand narrative' is as singular and coherent as it may appear at first glance. The alternative is to begin from the other direction, by localising experience within lived interaction and examining how the past – as both an individual and collective concern – is made relevant within the local pragmatics of communicative action (see, for example, Billig, 1999; Edwards & Potter, 1992; Middleton & Edwards, 1990a). This is broadly the approach that we have taken in Chapters 5 and 6. However, the risk is that, in approaching events such as Bill Clinton's grand jury testimony (Locke &

Edwards, 2003) or the media coverage of Diana's death (MacMillan & Edwards, 1999) as specific, local interactional accomplishments, the broader forms of experience that are involved in such interactions are rendered invisible. We are tempted to see our relationship to the past as worked out, moment by moment, via the pragmatics of communicative action.

If we apply these two approaches to reconciliation, their mutual inadequacies become readily apparent. Beginning with the global, we necessarily turn away from the actual experiences of former POWs and towards the range of grand narratives to be found in various historical records and popular films. However, these narratives do not always sit easily alongside one another. For example, the narrative of the atonement of the Japanese people, and the return of Japan to the 'high table' of nations following demilitarisation, is precisely one that former POWs would seek to dispute. We cannot, then, use historical time as a clear benchmark for individual lives. Also, working from the other direction, we find rapidly that if we stay with the narration of experiences and the reconstruction of the past to fit the interactional demands of the present moment, something of the very essence of reconciliation appears to elude us. This is because it is surely in the nature of reconciliation that there is some greater substantive matter in place, always already 'there', as the grounds on which interaction occurs – that is, a relationship to the broader experience always precedes the locally occasioned pragmatics of its telling.

Mediating between times

One solution to the problem of understanding the relationship between personal experience and the broader historical narratives that inform such experience is to focus on the mediational means via which these two ways of relating to the past are connected together. James Wertsch's (2002) work on collective remembering in the former Soviet Union illustrates this well.

Wertsch is concerned, among other things, with the nature of generational differences. He argues that the continuity in the accounts of the past produced by the generation who grew up in post Second World War Soviet Russia can be directly indexed to a massive state control of history education in terms of curriculum content and timetabling. Control over mediational resources was a means of ensuring that what can be collectively remembered is shaped to fit official, state-sponsored versions of the past.

Most Soviet citizens, however, felt an all-pervading sense of distrust of the narratives and resources provided by the state. This cynicism with regard to official narratives reflects what Wertsch terms a more general 'tension' between individuals and the mediational tools that resource human activity. Wertsch argues that, although we may be familiar with some narrative and draw on it as the mediational means with which to explicate some aspect of our experience, we do not necessarily 'appropriate' it entirely – that is, in some sense we refuse to commit ourselves, we withhold our belief.

What Wertsch offers is an innovative way of analysing the relationship between individual lived experience and historical time as defined by the state-sanctioned 'grand narratives' of Soviet history. Soviet citizens necessarily drew on such mediational means and, as a consequence, patterned their experience in part around these narratives, but, at the same time, avoided subsuming their individual biographies. There is, however, more that we can say about the resulting 'irreducible tension'. The widespread sense among Soviet citizens that counternarratives could not be publicly voiced was founded on the operation of a massive system of monitoring, recording, reporting and archiving information on individuals that was formalised in a party administrative apparatus. This colossal system of surveillance acted as an 'archontic infrastructure'. To be a Soviet citizen was, then, to be 'attached' (in the sense described in Chapters 8 and 9) to this infrastructure.

What is at stake, then, is not simply control over what can be said or done, but also the ordering of the past in such a way as to programme the future 'in advance'. To the extent that citizens were necessarily attached to Soviet archontic infrastructure (by means of, for example, the minute control over education in state-sponsored history that Wertsch describes), their own individual durations became collected into this programming, this rendering of the future as 'antecedent to itself'.

This shift towards mediation, attachment and infrastructure provides us with the basis on which to reformulate our concern with the relationship between individual experience and history. Rather than see this relationship as the patterning of two versions of the past or, indeed, as mediated by a third intermediate cultural tool, we may instead assume a chain of translation in which a series of durations are progressively collected up and dispersed.

At every point in this chain, there is something like what Latour (1996) calls an 'exchange of properties'. For Latour, this is a matter of the mediating artefact taking on or being delegated some aspect of human activity. The classic example Latour (1992) uses is how the hotel delegates the work of reminding guests to return their keys to the key itself by enlarging the fob in such a way that guests can no longer fit it in their pocket, obliging them to remember that they have to return it to reception.

However, if we begin instead with the notion of collecting together durations, we may interpret this example in a slightly different way. What the heavy key fob does is oblige guests to structure their time in relation to the working hours of reception. They are obliged to wait. In the same way, Halbwachs (1980) describes how the buyer and seller are obliged, by the very immobility of the goods, to wait for one another, at least for the duration of the sale. This collecting together of durations is made possible by the material intransigence of the mediating artefact – the key fob, the goods for sale.

If we follow ANT by analysing each link in these chains of translation, we will then gain some sense of how people become tied together by these artefacts. However, unlike ANT, what we consider to be tied together is not the spatially defined properties of people and artefact who become entangled, but, rather, the respective (and irreducible) durations of each 'actor'.

For example, Marcel's leap into the past begins by supping the hot tea from a teaspoon. The time it takes for the madeleine to dissolve and the tea to cool, such that it is necessary to drink it using a spoon, are bound to Marcel's duration. It is the coming together of these different unfolding temporal patterns – Marcel's 'dreary morning', the madeleine becoming dissolved in the cup, the tea cooling – into a very particular configuration that opens up the 'dark region' of the past. In other words, it is because Marcel is forced to wait for the cooling tea, in the same way that Bergson describes waiting for the sugared water, that these very different durations become mutually enveloped. As a consequence, Marcel discovers that this envelopment discloses to him something of his duration. He is able to turn around on his own experience by virtue of being tied into that of another, of being made to wait.

We can analyse the circulation and dispersal of mediating artefacts as they produce chains or networks of translations, but with the proviso that what is thereby tied together is not merely the capacity to act, but also the respective durations of people and artefacts. Consider again the Gerzs' monument. This acts as a point around which a diverse collection of local inhabitants of Hamburg and visitors may participate in a work of remembering. However, that work – which may for each individual last a matter of minutes as they etch a few words on to the pillar – is bounded in that the inscriptions are destined to disappear into the ground. The time taken for the pillar to disappear then unites these portions of individual durations and binds them to the temporal fate of the disappearing monument. Networks of translation are, then, not simply spatial arrangements of people and things, but also knots that tie together different durations.

Enveloping durations in networks of reconciliation and remembering – circulating reference

Can we apply these insights to the experiences of the former POWs? Take the image in Figure 4, published as the front page of *The Independent* on 28 May 1998.

Figure 4 POW protests at Emperor Akihito's state visit reported in *The Independent*

The accompanying article refers to the official state visit made by Emperor Akihito to London in 1998. The visit became a focal point for protests by former veteran POWs. This culminated in a demonstration by veterans, performed at the roadside of the official procession of the Emperor to Buckingham Palace. Most veterans expressed their protest by symbolically turning their back to the procession as the Emperor's car approached. However, the picture that accompanies this headline – widely broadcast at the time and still available on the BBC's web archive (see http://news.bbc.co.uk/1/hi/uk/100502.stm) – shows one former POW veteran setting fire to the Japanese national flag.

In what way does this image and headline represent 'reconciliation' or, apparently, a 'lack' of reconciliation? We might be tempted to see it as representing a 'feeling', an 'attitude' or a 'state of mind' on the part of these particular former POWs, which is 'expressed' in turning their backs on the Emperor and burning flags. However, Latour (1999) helpfully points out that if we approach human action in this way, we will remain locked in the impasse of explaining how the 'inner world' of cognition or emotion pours itself out into the 'outer world' of things. This is not to say that 'feelings' or even 'states of mind' are unimportant, merely that the phenomenon that concerns us – that is, reconciliation – ought not to be localised in any one point of the chain of translations that make it what it is – that it, instead, 'circulates all along the reversible chain of transformation' (Latour, 1999: 71).

If we follow this approach, then what we may say is something like the following. What this newspaper front page depicts is a former POW who has a particular orientation towards his past experience. His duration is 'marked out' for him by that portion spent as a POW. Subsequently, he feels aggrieved that his particular duration – and those of fellow veteran POWs – has not been adequately included in the historical narrative that the Japanese nation offers up about its own past. In what sense, though, is this a 'lack of reconciliation'? We would argue that it is by actively attaching himself to the burning flag that the individual depicted begins to construct himself as a subject who is 'not reconciled'. Moreover, that this construction, this way of turning around on his own duration, depends on the former POW taking up the time of the Japanese Emperor. That is, in the moments of the flag's burning, the duration of the Emperor is enveloped by, becomes tied to, that of the former POW.

The work of constructing a subject who is 'not reconciled' does not end when the embers of the flag fall away, but is, rather, sustained and reiterated in the taking of the photograph, the subsequent publication in the national newspaper (along with other associated media events) and its website archiving. These subsequent translations of the event – the flag burning – act to 'amplify' it still further and, to the extent that it is 'amplified' in this way, the phenomenon of 'irreconciliation' becomes more durable (see Latour, 1999). However, what 'durability' means here is that flag burning envelopes more durations because, as an event, it recruits the time of others to it. It ties together a whole series of durations in such a way that, ultimately, a certain portion of the historical relationship between Britain and Japan become marked in terms of the protests.

Now, the point is that none of this is reducible to the 'emotions' or 'state of mind' of a given individual. 'Irreconciliation' as a phenomenon and the production of the veteran POWs as subjects who are 'not reconciled' is an outcome of a chain of translations that amplify the events – what Latour calls 'circulating reference' – and a tying together of durations that is thereby achieved.

Let us now return to the particular group of former POWs who took part in Kyoko Murakami's (2001a) research. Figure 5 shows a photograph of a commemorative grave site in Japan that became a point of passage in the veterans' participation in their post-war 'reconciliation visit' to Japan. The following details are also drawn from Murakami's research.

Figure 5   Commemorative grave site for POWs who died in Japan

© Kyoko Murakami

The grave site is a commemorative site in a Japanese village where 300 British prisoners of war worked in a copper mine from 1942 until the end of the war. A memorial site was intentionally created by local Japanese people. Initially, it was a small grave with a wooden cross and a commemorative plaque recording 16 soldiers who had lost their lives. This site was built by the surviving British POWs before they left for Britain in 1945.

After the war, the site, known as *gaijin-bochi* – 'a grave for foreigners' – continued to be maintained as part of the activities of a senior citizen's group. The group provided voluntary routine care of the grave, including weeding and the maintenance of floral tributes.

In 1990, former student workers, who worked with British POWs in the mine, held a memorial as part of their high school reunion. This was to commemorate the relocation and refurbishment of the grave and memorial to a new site some 100 metres away. The whole memorial was redesigned and refurbished, with a new copper cross and stone memorial plaques being placed to the left and right of the cross. To the right of the grave, a replica of the original roll of honour of the names of those soldiers who had died was reinstated (this can be seen in Figure 5). Also of significance, was that, to the left of the cross, a further plaque was installed, inscribed in Japanese, giving a brief history of the grave, marking the wartime presence of the British soldiers who worked at the copper mine. These soldiers became known among themselves, and to others, as the 'Iruka Boys'.

This grave was virtually unknown to the outside community, let alone to the British until two people who had associations with Britain 'discovered' it . Taken by his colleague, Father Murphy, a Catholic priest, visited the grave. He wrote an article about this visit for a religious newspaper, which is reprinted in *A Little Britain* (Former FEPOWs & Holmes, 1991). This article was brought to the attention of one of the Iruka Boys, who contacted the Catholic priest and they began corresponding. In addition, Keiko Holmes, who was originally from this community, now residing in the UK, learned on one of her visits home that the grave had been refurbished. A copy of the correspondence between the Catholic priest and the Iruka veteran, was sent to Keiko Holmes in London. She established contact with the surviving Iruka veterans, visiting them in various parts of England.

The visits led to the publication of *A Little Britain,* which notes the special significance of a memorial that has been maintained by the former adversaries of those commemorated. This is a collection of memoirs of the Iruka camp, correspondence between Japanese and British people about the discovery of the grave and accounts recorded by Keiko Holmes after visiting some of the Iruka Boys.

Keiko Holmes was a key figure in contacting surviving Iruka Boys, organising the first reconciliation visit to Japan in 1992 and in sustaining further such activities (see www.agape-reconciliation.org/ for further details). It was as a result of these contacts that the post-war veneration by, and significance of the site to, the local Japanese population came to the attention of Iruka veterans back in the UK. A total of 28 surviving Iruka Boys and their spouses, accompanied by Japanese nationals residing in the UK, subsequently went to Japan for a joint memorial service to commemorate the dead POWs. Before and during the trip, there was a significant amount of publicity in Japan about this visit. The general public made monetary contributions and wrote letters of support to the reconciliation trip committees. One of the former POWs wrote and published a personal memoir of camp life in Burma and Japan (Walker, 1997).

There are several ways in which we can think about the process of remembering and reconciliation as it occurs within this network. We can consider the grave as a commemorative site, a privileged space, that gathers around it a heterogeneous collective of local villagers, former POWs and other tourists. We might then say that the very bringing together of this unlikely collective is, in itself, evidence of 'reconciliation' – that is, the memorial mediates a collective activity that constitutes the work of reconciliation. We can also see that the memorial passes through a variety of transformations – a 'discovery' by tourists, a place of pilgrimage by former POWs, an object of newspaper and media reports and, of course, physically by being moved and refurbished by villagers. Each transformation translates the memorial into a new set of relationships and concerns.

The identity of the memorial – what it is, the work it does – is, then, subject to a process of circulating reference. The memorial is translated in the social practices and mediated actions of organising and taking part in reconciliation trips, doing research on the experience of reconciliation and talking about the memorial service and the veterans' war-time experiences and so on. It is translated into textual resources of discursive remembrance, such as reunion and reminiscence, visual images, newspaper articles and personal memories and letters. What the memorial is, as a phenomenon, cannot be localised in any one of these chains of translations, but is, rather, the emergent effect of these circulating references. Even the memorial site literally moved in one of the transformations that form part of this network of reconciliation and remembering!

Considering the memorial as either a privileged space of commemoration or a phenomenon distributed into a set of circulating reference means treating it in spatial terms. Certainly the memorial is a spatial entity – and it does link together other spatial locations and people, but it is also an entity with its own distinct form of duration. For example, the growth of the vegetation around the original cross established the rhythm and routine of tidying and repair by the citizens of the village. The discovery of the refurbished memorial by the 'tourists', coupled their own durations to that of the village and the grave site, which led, in turn, to the association of the durations of the former POWs. The memorial does not, then, merely associate spatial elements but also gathers together or envelops temporal relationships. It makes different rhythms of living beat together without reducing any one of them to another. For instance, the revelation that villagers in Japan had been tending the memorial over the years allowed the former POWs to turn around on their own previous experiences in a different way, resulting, in one case, in the publication of those recollections.

How, though, does the Iruka memorial grave site achieve this coupling of spatial relationships and juxtaposition of durations? Is it because of its particular material features (as with the disappearing pillar of the Gerzs' monument)? Not in this case, as what matters is how the memorial is constituted by the circulating references. As an artefact, the memorial is then defined by the kinds of translations it undergoes and the effects it produces in the people who become attached to it. Indeed, we might say that the former POWs who returned became passively attached to the memorial.

That is, they chose to submit themselves to a relationship with the memorial site that would mean coupling their own particular concerns and experiences to those of the local Japanese community.

Perhaps, then, we ought to consider the memorial as a kind of subject in itself? That is not quite right, through, because the memorial is, rather, the basis on which the veterans are able to construct a form of subjectivity by means of passive attachment – that is, a subjectivity that is 'on the way to reconciliation'. The memorial is the medium for establishing fragile relationships of reconciliation and the very presupposition of its significance makes these relationships possible.

The memorial site is, then, ultimately, neither a simple object like any other nor properly a subject in its own right. It is both. It is a kind of third party beyond any immediate context of communication – a common medium to which all parties can appeal. It is both object – the entity that circulates and is dispersed – and subject – the recipient of attention as the point of passage that collects together the durations of reconciliation and remembering.

Collection and dispersion

So far, we have argued that reconciliation is distributed throughout a chain of translations that 'amplify' it as a phenomenon by increasing its 'circulating reference'. That is to say, reconciliation is not to be found 'within' either the former POWs or the villagers, but, rather, is what emerges from the complex relationships that they enter into. The memorial is an object that mediates these relationships, but is a most peculiar object. It is more than simply a point in geographical space. It can be positioned in all sort of ways – as a local place, perhaps, a forgotten place of burial for fallen comrades, a local place that translates enmity into respect, as extended into networks that gather up the distal concerns of families and friends, a centre of coordination for reconciliation.

The memorial site, then, gathers up relationships. It brings together different local concerns and, in this sense, it might be said to collect together 'differences' – in experience, recollection, culture, history – while refusing synthesis. Cooper's (2001) description of collection and dispersion as a provisional movement that generates the appearance of cohesion while preserving difference has some purchase here. In particular, what is gathered together but simultaneously preserved are different durations. The cycles of tending and care lived out by the village elders become joined to the rhythms of ageing and commemoration endured by the former POWs. The durations come to mutually envelop one another via the mediation of the memorial site. This is, then – as Bergson would suggest – a matter of juxtaposition rather than synthesis as there is no common reference between them.

Yet, the more the memorial site performs this work of gathering, the more the site itself appears to disperse into the network and, consequently, the more ambiguous it becomes. The memorial site becomes an indeterminate object that weaves the emergent collectivity of remembering and reconciliation. Kevin Hetherington (1997) calls this kind of indeterminism 'functional blankness', after the work of Michel Serres (1991). In an analysis of the dilemmas surrounding the incorporation of a material artefact – a piece of pottery called 'Ozzie the Owl' – into a museum display, Hetherington argues that this blankness is highly potent as it calls into question the forms of ordering into which it is subsumed and allows them to be reformulated. It does this by means of its constitutional indifference to existing order, meaning that it can take up multiple sets of positions. It is an element that potentially fits anywhere – at least, in this case, within the restricted confines of a pottery display.

'Constitutional indifference' is worth dwelling on. Hetherington and Lee (2000) offer the useful example of a set of dominos. All domino tiles have two parts, each with a number of spots. A given domino, then, has two properties – meaning that, as the game progresses, there are two different ways in which it might be played. However, there is one tile that is different. This tile has no spots at all – it is blank on both parts. The blank domino can be played at any moment in the game. It fits anywhere, at any time. This makes it the most useful of all the tiles as, constitutionally, it is absolutely indifferent to what is happening at any point in the game.

A 'functionally blank' object that is 'constitutionally indifferent' to existing order is, then, the mediator par excellence. Blankness is not lack. The blank tile does not have fewer properties than the other domino tiles – it has more. In fact, it has *all* of the properties. This is what we have argued in the case of the memorial. It gathers up all the properties of the network. It is a project for village elders *and* a discovery by accidental tourists *and* the place of the reconciliation trip *and* a media 'event' *and* the subject of a piece of research *and* many other things besides.

In the previous chapter we returned to Bergson's opposition between 'virtualisation' and 'actualisation'. Bergson (1992) argues that, to understand creation and change, we must not think of 'possibility' as something that pre-exists the coming to pass of some event. If reconciliation could be said to be what emerges from the network of translations that has grown around the memorial, then this reconciliation was not a 'possibility' that awaited the memorial's accidental discovery or the arrival of the aeroplane full of former POWs. Rather, a collective phenomenon of reconciliation was created as something novel via the mediation of the memorial site. The memorial is, then, the means by which the 'virtual' unlimited experiences of the villagers, former POWs, visitors and researchers become gathered together around an 'actual' spatial location. However, this gathering together does not exhaust experience. There is much that is not said, not recorded, not expressed, not made visible in the coming together at the memorial. In the same way, the trip does not reconcile *all* parties, such that they have 'left behind' the past or seek to live together in a 'harmonious' and 'reconciled' future. Rather, the gathering together allows each party to turn around on their own duration as it is enveloped by and juxtaposed with the duration of the other and it is the mediation of the memorial as blank object that makes this possible.

Redemption accounting

Although we cannot ever fully grasp the duration of another, we can partake of something of it when it is directly juxtaposed to our own. This juxtaposition, or mutual envelopment, does not require a common frame of reference, but, instead, the mediation of a blank object (such as the memorial). The peculiarity of this object is that, while it appears to have no properties in particular, it is capable of summing up or enumerating all of the properties of the relationships that are gathered around it. It can, then, take on the appearance of a common ground or that of another subject in the relationship (see also Marilyn Strathern, 1996, on 'hybrid objects' and the enumeration of networks), but, properly speaking, it is neither of these things. We should think of it as a provocation or catalyst for complexification of relationships (this is Michel Serres' formulation – see Serres, 1982b; Brown, 2002, 2003, 2004).

We have stated that reconciliation is a collective matter that is not 'within' an individual. Nevertheless, as a social act, reconciliation clearly involves the individual being able to articulate a changing relationship to his or her own past. We might describe this as being able to 'open up' that past in a different way, to refuse or suspend the existing ordering of the past. This would, then, be the kind of 'hesitation' and 'elaboration' that Bergson claims characterises the movement of virtualisation. It is also the kind of knowledge practice that he elliptically terms 'intuition'. We illustrate this point with reference to Example 1, taken from an interview in 1999 in Murakami (2001a). The participants in the interview were two ex-POWs, a spouse, a Japanese contact and the interviewer – the researcher.

Example 1

Key:
F = ex-POW
M = Japanese contact
Int. = Interviewer

F: I was in Battersea Par:k some years ago (.) after the war (.) ten years after the war (.) ten years after the war (1.0) and I'm sitting out in the open air a with cup of tea at the table and two little (0.8) children running around in front of me (2.0) and I said to myself, 'oh my god >is that Japanese<' because they could be Chinese or (0.8) [Thai (.) it at [any=

Int.:   [humm   [humm

F: >you know what I mean< but to me they were Japanese (1.0) I thought (0.8) I didn't have to wonder very long because just behind me (there's) somebody calling out '*Oi, koi*' right? 'come here' or

Int.: humm

F: yes? I thought I know that= that means 'come here' or means 'come back' (.) I half reluctantly turned around and (at) the next table behind me was a Japanese man and woman (.) they all got up and they went down (.) stood by the lake (.) and this is the story (.) he took a picture of his wife and two children (.) she came and took a picture of him and the two children (.) and me being= I don't use the camera and all that (.) but what I would normally do in a case like that (.) and I have done it many times I would go out and say and 'Excuse me (.) do you mind if- would you like me to take a photograph of all of you?'

Int.: yes

F: I half got up and I thought 'no why should I?' and I regretted that (.) I regretted it (.) but some years later (.) when I was over at Keiko's place in Croydon (.) a Japanese man (.) lady (.) doctor?

M: Hiro?

F: and the two children they came and they stood on the stairs by Keiko's room there and I took a photograph with my camera then (.) I thought perhaps I've been redeemed at last (.) ha ha ha (.) you know that's a little thing

Int.: yes

This sequence occurred following a request by the researcher for the interviewees to reflect on and illustrate the consequences for them of participating in the return visit to Japan in 1992. This particular story was told after the speaker shared with the rest of the participants an episode of a 'little reunion' with his 'old mates' at Heathrow airport on the day of their departure for Japan on the reconciliation trip. He said 'that this reunion put him on the road to reconciliation' after having experienced the camaraderie of seeing them at the airport.

The story, then, does a work of summation. It gathers up a series of events that are crafted together as 'redeemed at last'. At the same time, it performs a work of dispersion in that wartime experiences are pushed outside the narrative – they are not directly articulated here. We can identify the moment of collection and dispersion in the interaction itself from the way in which the relationship between the speaker and the hearer/present others are interactionally making sense of the narrative. This sense-making is a kind of a settlement, in terms of establishing a shared sense of the past and the significance and upshot of the current interaction. We can see that there is a symmetry of action between the speaker's photo-taking experiences on the two different occasions – before and after the recon-ciliation trip. This story invokes a notion of change and presents a basis for evaluating that change. It summates the way in which the speaker, Fred, has changed due to participation in the trip. The story marks the speaker's change in attitude towards the Japanese and delineates the new perspec-tive that Fred now possesses. This change is presented by him as a possible redemption: 'I thought perhaps I've been re<u>deem</u>ed at <u>last</u>', even though 'you know that's a little thing'. The first 'story' does not stand alone. Immediately, the speaker produces the second story as a way of establishing his entitlement to being a changed person (see also Sacks, 1992). There is a sense, then, in the discursive organisation of these accounts, of the ways in which local (subjective dispositions, for example) and historical issues (such as collective identities – the Japanese) are made to intersect.

What we see in this intersection is precisely the kind of 'hesitation' and 'elaboration' that Bergson describes. Fred is disturbed by the call '*Oi koi*'. As we discussed in Chapter 7, this phrase acts as an 'order word' or 'pre-cept' that immediately incorporates the hearer into a recollected zone of personal relations. To hear 'come here' spoken in Japanese is to 'feel' the visceral force of the recollection. However, in what follows next, Fred describes how he also felt compelled by the norms of politeness that cor-respond to the usual social relationships he inhabits. He is, in a sense, between two zones of personal relations. The tension between them is dramatised by the half getting up, that there is a hesitation, a pause. What happens in this pause? That is precisely what is at issue in the narrative. Fred is confronted with the unexpected ambiguity of seeing Japanese people play out a pleasant family scene before him. His cup of tea in Battersea Park has become something else entirely.

Bergson claims that our perception 'cuts out' forms in the real and does so with a view to action. However, in the extent to which we are able to delay that action and wait, we are able to allow our perception to unfold in a wider duration. We may live what we see at 'a slower rhythm' and, hence, allow differences to re-emerge in our perception. Now the hesitation on Fred's part results in precisely this experience of 'waiting'. For as long as Fred waits, his own duration is enveloped by that of the other – the family members who take turns to line up, smiling, in front of the camera. This juxtaposition, then, allows for an ambiguity, a possible 'elaboration', as something of Fred's unfolding duration – a former POW, someone who would otherwise like to help, enjoying a cup of tea in the open air in the park – is disclosed to him. What Fred then experiences is close to what Bergson would call 'intuition' – that is, the suspension of ready-made categories in favour of a direct experience of change, of ambivalence. Then the event passes, Fred sits down and returns to his cup of tea.

The second event that Fred describes does not involve the same kind of interruption or pause. There is no break in the flow of activities as Fred snaps a picture of the two Japanese children on the stairs. Instead, the hesitation is between the two events as Fred subsequently contrasts the routine flow of the latter event with the interrupted activity of the former. In gathering up these two events together, Fred discovers a way of 'slowing down' and turning around on his own duration, refusing the order that has been put on the past. This results in the elaboration or reconstruction of himself as 'redeemed at last'.

As with the example of the memorial grave site, it is the juxtaposition of durations that allows for the 'slowing down' and 'hesitation'. However, in this second example, the mediating objects are discursive – an over-heard utterance – '*Oi koi*' – and Fred's occasioned narrative that allows for the two events to be gathered up together. Nevertheless, the effect is the same – it affords a work of collection and dispersion, whose potency is that it provides the basis for calling into question the ordering of lived experience into which Fred is subsumed and allows it to be reformulated. The utterances, no less than the memorial, 'contain' the difference that makes the difference.

We want to conclude this analysis with a few brief remarks about self-hood and agency. Bergson describes selfhood – the continuity that we see as defining our unfolding experience over time – as consisting of multiple, intersecting 'virtual' planes of experience. It is the differences between those planes, between the way that they intersect in the 'cutting out' of our present actions, that has concerned us in this chapter. Indeed, those moments when we have some sense of the differences are at the very heart of the practices of remembering and reconciliation that we have discussed.

Now, typically, we might conclude that 'agency' is reflected in the ability to manage and stabilise those differences to produce a coherent account of the past. However, with Bergson, we want to argue the contrary. Agency is what emerges from the gaps, the discontinuities between durations – the 'zones of indeterminism' as Bergson calls them.

Fred's agency is most explicit in the moments of hesitation and elaboration as he rises from his teacup in a Battersea Park that are now distributed somewhere between two different worlds. The kind of practical knowledge that arises in those moments is 'intuitive' – it is an appreciation or a 'sympathy' relating to the difference between and within the two durations that are momentarily mutually enveloped. Similarly, the agency of all the former POWs is at its most profound when their own 'rhythms of living' stand juxtaposed to those of the Japanese villagers, via the mediation of the memorial.

Agency is, then, a kind of ambiguity, a break with what we expect. The exercise of agency is a break, a rendering of oneself as other than was previously understood to be the case. It is the experience of difference – between and within durations – that makes the difference.

Summary

Our concern here has been with unfinished business – unfinished business consequent on having lived through and experienced the privations of wartime incarceration and forced labour as prisoners of war. Such experiences and events remain live concerns for first-hand participants in their relationships with others, the patterning of their lives and the ways in which they participate in highly mediated sets of relationships.

We do not treat the dynamic of reconciliation as one of settlement, resolution, the 'conversion of experience into finished products' as our sense of identity, of selfhood, is itself always 'unfinished business' (see Holland, Lachicotte, Jr, Skinner & Cain, 1998). Instead, we have analysed reconciliation in terms of the attachment of people to broader networks of relationships that amplify and translate their own particular concerns. We did this not to discount personal passions or entitlements, but, rather, to show how a phenomenon such as 'reconciliation' is produced by the mutual enveloping of individual experience with that of the durations of others.

In this chapter, then, several lines of argument that have stretched throughout the book have come together. We have treated practices of remembering as collective rather than individual phenomena. We have also seen how they occur within networks of relationships mediated by objects. More importantly, though, we have seen how these relationships join together time as well as space or, to put it slightly differently, have arrived at the point where Bergson's account of memory as the 'past gnawing into the present' within irreducible durations runs into Halbwachs' account of memory as distributed across intersecting collective frameworks. We have formulated this in terms of 'collection' and 'dispersion' of durations. In particular, we have argued, following Bergson, that what is important is how these mutually enveloping durations disclose differences between and within one another while remaining 'irreducible'. To think of remembering and forgetting in this way is, then, to attempt to 'think in duration'.

Finally, we hope to have displayed that it is unnecessary to invoke a 'forensic' conception of self to understand how we make use of our own 'unlimited experience' in the routine (and not so routine) business of living. If the unfolding of our personal experience is, as Bergson insists, not simply the realisation of a future that is already programmed in advance, then remembering and forgetting cannot simply be the retrieval or not of the already known, the restoration of the prior links in the chain of past moments that supposedly make us what we are. Rather, we must think of remembering and forgetting as a creative process that is entirely coextensive with the novelty and change of our unfolding durations. As Bergson (1992: 93) observes, 'the living being essentially has duration; it has duration precisely because it is continuously elaborating what is new and because there is no elaboration without searching, no searching without groping. Time is this very hesitation, or it is nothing'.

In this chapter we have sought to show that 'hesitation' and 'elaboration' are not exceptions to, but the very ground on which our agency is exercised. With this in mind, we will now take on the question of what a social psychology of experience might look like.

TWELVE

Unlimiting experience: dynamics of remembering and forgetting

We speak of change, but we do not think about it. We say that change exists, that everything changes, that change is the very law of things: yes we say it and we repeat it; but those are only words and we reason and philosophise as though it did not exist. (Bergson, 1992: 131)

A few years ago, we both attended a workshop in Manchester where we presented some work on practices of remembering in organisations. The presentation went well, we thought. We had made our points about remembering as a collective activity built around communicative action. Everybody in the room – mainly sociologists, anthropologists and organisation theorists – had nodded sagely in what we took to be agreement.

Afterwards, over coffee, we chatted with a social anthropologist. She casually enquired about how we theorised subjectivity. Suppressing the urge to choke on the coffee, we smiled wryly at one another and began the usual explanation of how those kinds of questions were not really of interest to us, how the kind of psychology we practise looks to the collective as the unit of analysis and so on. 'Yes', she interrupted, 'I understand all that. What you are describing is exactly what I would do, as a social anthropologist, but you are psychologists. You must have some notion of interiority, mustn't you?' In the moments of stunned silence that followed, the lumps of dissolved biscuit in our coffee cups became suddenly and curiously interesting.

This book has been a long time in the making. Its current form owes its shape partly to that workshop and the subsequent conversation. For some time now, psychology has stood apart from the other social sciences. There are many reasons for this isolation – not least, the drive to establish psychology as something like a 'natural science'. However, in recent years, work in social and in cultural psychology has sought to reopen a dialogue. The fact that we, as psychologists, can sustain a conversation with sociologists or historians is an achievement, a change. That achievement, that change has been brought about by the opening up of the discipline to broader currents of thought, along with the simultaneous rediscovery of thinkers who have operated within psychology, such as Bartlett, Vygotsky or James. However, there is a danger that this opening up is something of a one-way street. Psychology imports concepts and methods from the social sciences and, in so doing, makes itself over in their image. What we learnt in Manchester is that, if psychology wishes to reclaim its place within social science, something more will need to happen.

Our social anthropologist friend suggested that what this would involve is theorising what goes on 'inside' the individual. Now surely this is precisely what we – and many others within the discipline – have tried to resist! When psychological phenomena are located within people, rather than as part of the broader sets of relationships people share, then all manner of empirical and logical puzzles follow.

Wittgenstein, notably in his *Philosophical Investigations*, displayed the insoluble nature of such puzzles. His answer – that psychological phenomena should be seen as problems of language, matters of description, rather than substantive issues involving 'minds' and 'bodies' – is a good one and psychologists and philosophers such as Mick Billig, Derek Edwards Rom Harré, John Shotter, Jonathan Potter and Margie Wetherell have all shown how psychology might be reconstructed on this 'discursive' basis. However, that is not really what the social anthropologist was getting at. What she was pointing to was something subtler.

It is well recognised across the social sciences that the 'Cartesian' model of the subject – where mind, or cognition, is treated as something distinct from embodiment (usually with the promise that 'one day' it will be possible to rejoin these separated twins) – is unsustainable and unworkable. No one knows this better than social anthropologists, who have been exposed to cultural systems of thought that not only refuse to make this kind of separation between cognition and embodiment, but would regard Cartesianism as an exotic, mystical and thoroughly peculiar way of understanding selfhood. However, social anthropologists – notably Clifford Geertz (1983) – have also noted that there are no cultures that do not have something like a conception of self that is applied to people as distinct from, say, rocks and trees. We take it that what is meant by this is a notion that implies a continuity of being or a sense of identity throughout time. Memory is undeniably critical to such a notion.

So, the question that must be central to psychology is something like what form does this continuity of being take? Throughout this book we have been using the word 'experience' to denote this continuity. This, we want to argue, ought to be the pivotal concern of psychologists. One might argue that this is precisely what psychologists have traditionally studied. The experimental study of memory, for instance, locates 'experience' in the inherent power of the cognitive architecture of our brains to store and retrieve and, thus, synthesise moments of perception in such a fashion that we can catch hold of our own thoughts and their relationship to what happens around us.

However, what we see here is a *spatialised* conception of experience. Our experience of time is treated as a matter of passing moments or the shift between predefined stages. As Bergson argues at length, this notion of time as a series of 'instants' presents an impoverished view of psychological life. Our continuity as beings comes from the undivided way in which we endure through time. Our thoughts and feelings do not fade as fleeting moments because time does not, for us, break into tiny segments. Our duration is a continuous 'gnawing of the past into the present', where the present is infused with the burden of a past that does not pass, does not ever escape us. Bergson's view of duration as 'unlimited experience' is, then, the basis for the way we understand not just memory, but all psychological phenomenon.

Nevertheless, the spatialised view of experience – which is, as Bergson states, a necessary part of our powers to act – captures something of what it means to be a person. Indeed, we often do tend to think of ourselves in spatial terms, as 'containers' of our own experience. However, we only do so by transposing the spatial terms in which we understand action to our understanding of change and time. What Bergson calls the 'cinematographical mechanism of thought' is critical to our ability to live and act. We could not survive without it, but it does not allow us to adequately think about the kind of movement and change that are proper to our experience of enduring as living beings.

There is, then, a tension between the spatialised forms our experience takes and those intersecting 'virtual' forms of experience that constitute us as dynamic, living, temporal beings. The problem is that psychology has not been sensitive to this tension because it has ceaselessly attempted to grasp change by means of its precise opposite. Memory has then been theorised as though it were necessary to 'preserve' or 'store up' the past in some vessel. The past, as Bergson shows, cannot be thought of in this way because it is not wholly reducible to space. Neither, then, is memory.

A 'social psychology of experience' would set itself the task of understanding the relationship between our 'spatialised' forms of experience and our 'unlimited' forms of experience or, to put it another way, between our powers to act and the 'virtual' aspects of our being. This very broadly maps on to Bartlett's concern with how experience is afforded within organised settings, which has provided a guiding thread throughout this book. We see such a project as building on work in sociocultural and discursive psychology.

Sociocultural work has placed mediation at the centre of human relationships and promotes a form of non-reductive materialism – that is, it allows for discussion of the grounding of our lives in a material world of objects without reducing psychological phenomena to the properties of one particular object – namely, the brain. In Chapter 8, we argued that the turn to mediation shows that our social relationships are forged from our relationships to objects.

Discursive psychology has demonstrated that thought is best approached as a public, action-orientated process, which can be studied empirically in the rhetorical and interactional organisation of everyday affairs. This insight is pivotal to the whole empirical basis of this book – in particular, the studies in Chapters 6 and 7.

Yet, a turn to 'experience' presents difficulties for both these approaches. For sociocultural work, experience would need to be located in the relationship between the distinction that Gee (1999) makes between 'mind stuff' and 'social stuff'. Gee (1999: 310) defines the sociocultural approach as the study of the development of mind along the pathways opened up by culture such that 'patterns of socioculturally specific and ideologically laden practices, activities and institutions reflect and are reflected by the patterns in our mind'. Experience is, presumably, the dialectic of mutual reciprocity between mind becoming social and sociality affording mind. However, we see this as a relationship between two forms of spatiality.

As we have shown, it is of course critical to grasp the manner in which an individual's actions are orientated towards broader frameworks, such as the infrastructural arrangements we studied in Chapter 9. However, the division between 'mind stuff' and 'social stuff' does not hold when the turn is made from spatiality towards duration. In Chapter 11, we showed how, in the case of reconciliation, the relationship between the 'individual' and 'collective', the 'personal' and the 'historical', depended on the encounter between different durations. Thus, the socialising of mind needs to be seen in relation to the spatialisation of duration and the broader opposition between the *actualisation* and *virtualisation* of spatial relationships.

Similarly, the notion of experience is troublesome for discursive psychology. This latter approach might be characterised as a 'war' on interiority, where any form of 'inner' or 'private' experience is viewed with extreme suspicion. Discursive psychology adopts a position of radical empiricism – only those aspects of psychological phenomena that are publicly available for study are worth pursuing. We also pursue this strategy to some extent. In Chapter 5, for example, we argued for memory as a form of communicative action where remembering – as an activity, a verb – replaced memory – as a thing, a noun – as the central object of study.

However, we also recognise the limits of this form of empiricism. Bergson (1992: 211) considered himself to be a radical empiricist of sorts, yet he defines the term – which he attributes to William James – in a very different way:

> Antiquity had imagined a world shut off, arrested, finite: it is a hypothesis which answers certain demands of our reason. The moderns think rather of the infinite: it is another hypothesis which satisfies other needs of our reason. From the point of view taken by James, which is that of pure experience or of 'radical empiricism', reality no longer appears as finite or as infinite, but simply as indefinite. It flows without our being able to say whether it is in a single direction, or even whether it is always and throughout the same river flowing.

Species of empiricism differ with respect to the fundamental characteristics of the world that they confront. Either the world is finite and, hence, in principle, knowable in its entirety or else it is infinite, such that human knowledge must seek to confine itself within its own limits. Although Bergson sees these options as belonging to different periods, we may see a tension between them as being at the very core of modern science, including psychology. Radical empiricism, then, is a refusal of these two alternatives. It proceeds from the claim – derived from process philosophy – that the world itself is subject to perpetual change – it is 'indefinite', it 'flows' without our being able to say to what end or in what direction or, indeed, whether or not that flow ever has a kind of identity. This is not to say that there is neither stability nor identity to things, but merely that such 'immobility' is exceptional, a special case.

If this is so, then not only is our knowledge in general destined to be incomplete and partial, but, moreover, it, too, must enter into the dynamic of perpetual change. So, for Bergson (1992: 11), a 'radical' empiricism is one that is able to fashion concepts that, as far as possible, are 'cut to the measure of the reality in which we live'. In other words, such concepts are sensitive to change and duration, as well as the spatial forms our experience necessarily takes.

Our argument is for a further 'radicalisation' of the radical empiricism of discursive psychology. In practice, we see this as being achieved by treating the interactional organisation of psychological phenomena as standing in relation to a wider experience of enduring in time. For example, in Chapter 6, we acknowledged that the past may be 'inbuilt' within a given interaction in ways that are not immediately visible. We tried to articulate something of this by pointing to how issues of 'succession' and 'change' become concerns for participants and how experience is itself constructed via various interdependencies, such as between the incidental and the intentional and as both individually and collectively relevant. However, it was only by Chapter 11 that we were able to demonstrate that these relevancies arise in a turning around on duration – that there is a time at work – a 'hesitancy' and 'elaboration' – that is different to that established by the more or less orderly sequence of turns that unfold in a given interaction.

What we are proposing, then, is not a return to interiority, nor a move away from empiricism and towards the theoretical. Rather, it is an attempt to get closer still to practice, to life as it is lived, which means recognising that an actual piece of interaction coexists with a virtual, unlimited set of experiences. Once again, we take this ambition to be patterned on Bartlett's definition of schemas as 'organised settings'.

We have been able to move beyond our starting points in sociocultural and discursive psychology by turning away from Bartlett and towards two other central figures – Maurice Halbwachs and Henri Bergson. These two are odd bedfellows, admittedly, and they are often seen as incompatible, but this supposed tension between their approaches becomes less marked when we consider their work from the perspective of a psychology of experience. Halbwachs and Bergson are united in their joint opposition to an experimental psychology of memory. Both argue that psychology requires profound reorientation in order to gain any purchase on remembering.

In relation to *individuality*, this means recognising that our sense of ourselves as individuals is, as Halbwachs argues, based on a prior sociality. We are always already social beings who 'create' ourselves as individuals. This is achieved partly by virtue of the distinctive position we occupy in relation to several collective frameworks at once. This spatial juxtaposition has a profound effect on 'the succession of our remembrances' and, consequently, on the kind of continuity we are able to construct for our lives. What Bergson adds to this is that spatial juxtaposition also involves the mutual envelopment of durations. As we endure in time, our rhythm of living is slowed or quickened in relation to the durations of others. We might say that the time of our own life includes within it others' interdependent durations through and with which we endure.

Remembering, then, involves a turning around on these 'virtually coexisting' durations. This is the wider import of the following notorious passage from Halbwachs (1980: 44):

> Often we deem ourselves the originators of thoughts and ideas, feelings and passions, actually inspired by the group. Our agreement with those about us is so complete that we vibrate in unison, ignorant of the real source of the vibrations.

To be a part of a collective is to find one's own duration coupled to those of others. The unwinding of our lives proceeds in tandem, as with the passengers on the two trains described by Bergson. Indeed, so close is this coupling that it scarcely seems like there is any movement at all. This is why Halbwachs emphasises that a collective may often consider itself to be existing in a timeless state. Yet, this timelessness is actually a complex juxaposition of durations – a 'vibration in unison'. So 'complete' is the resulting illusion of immobility, that it is scarcely surprising that we tend to see ourselves as authors of ideas and actions that are actually afforded by the relationships within the collective. We may be tempted to consider our recollections as uniquely personal thoughts without realising our dependency on the collective frameworks in which they are articulated.

In relation to **models of memory**, Halbwachs and Bergson offer a range of tools for seeing remembering as an active process that is orientated towards the demands of the present. Bergson's approach to memory is built around distinctions between 'habit memory' and 'recollection memory', and between 'virtualisation' and 'actualisation'. We could make a potential correspondence between habit memory and procedural memory, and between recollection memory and declarative memory. That is certainly possible, but we must be careful not to commit Bergson to a form of reductionism. Habit memory, for instance, is certainly automatic and involves little by way of cognitive resources, but we would be in error to see it as located entirely within the body. Habit memory is, instead, the incorporation of the individual into a wider set of relationships, as we demonstrated with the material in Chapter 7. When we learn our way around a building where we have begun to work, for example, our learning constitutes an answer or a solution to the problem created by the collective organisation of the workplace, of which our bodies are but one constituent part. That answer is usually already prescribed in some sense by the infrastructure we are compelled to interact with. Our studies in Chapter 9 displayed the dilemmas that can result from such incorporation. We also showed how managing an attachment to an 'archontic infrastructure' becomes a way of dealing with the 'in advance' programming of the future that occurs when remembering is subject to formal rationalisation.

Habit memory interacts with recollection memory. Bergson describes this in two ways. It may be that recollection memory is engaged when habit memory fails to adequately inform action, which, indeed, is the preferred reading of the relationship by Bergson scholars such as Mullarkey (1999a, 1999b). However, it may also be the case that recollection and habit memory are artful devices that in some sense 'complement' and 'correct' one another. For example, in Chapters 5 and 7, we discussed the same piece of data twice – a sequence involving an extended narrative concerning drinking alcohol by an older woman, Sue. The first time we discussed Sue's narrative, we were concerned with recollection memory. We pointed out how Sue works up her account by using detail and how the contribution of her interlocutors renders the eventual recollection a collective accomplishment. Our second discussion concentrated on how certain kinds of speech acts are precisely designed to incorporate the recipient by provoking habit memory, encouraging a 'feeling' for place that is difficult to resist. The crucial point is that, in both cases, 'memory' is an activity performed by and within the collective.

Seen in this way, habit remembering and recollection remembering can be studied as two ways of constituting a compelling relationship with the past and committing others to that relationship. Chapter 5, then, was mostly concerned with recollection remembering, understood as a discursive activity. By Chapter 7, we were able to show how this stands alongside habit remembering, which, although also partly discursive, involved the recruitment of the body.

What Halbwachs adds is that these two forms of remembering correspond to two aspects of a collective framework. Recollection memory creates a set of discursive resources – images and ideas – that define the group. However, habit memory gives rise to a physiognomic system, where meaning and value are inscribed into the very contours of the material environment. Now the point is that both activities involve the effort of an artful reconstruction of the past as it is prolonged into the concerns of the present. Both activities are also spatial, in as much as they involve a clearly differentiated 'cutting out' of the past as it becomes actualised.

Bergson's second distinction – between actualisation and virtualisation – needs to be understood in relation to his definition of duration as the 'past gnawing into the present', as an indivisible unfolding of experience that is entirely distinct from both perception and spatial relationships. To think memory from the perspective of duration is to consider memory not as a capacity that is switched on and off as we need to store and retrieve past experience, but, rather, as the totality of our past experience, as the burden of the past 'pressing against the portals of consciousness'. In this sense, memory is 'always on'. We do not need to question how the past is preserved, but, rather, how it is held back, how it is 'forgotten'. Memory in its 'pure state' is, then, synonymous with 'unlimited' forms of experience – that is, experience that goes beyond the narrow confines of immediate action. It is these forms of experience that are, we feel, at the very core of psychological life, yet are almost entirely absent from the psychology of memory.

The problem that Bergson grapples with at length in *Matter and Memory* is the relationship between action and the 'virtually coexisting' planes of past experience. His description of 'actualisation' – the way in which recollection becomes concentrated in such a way as to be reinserted into our ongoing actions – emphasises that remembering is always conducted with a purpose, it is never 'speculative'. In later works, however,

Bergson also illustrates how we engage with 'virtualisation' by turning around on our own duration. Bergson's enigmatic description of 'waiting' for the sugar to dissolve in hot water, for example, allows us to see that, when our duration becomes mutually enveloped by that of another, something of our 'unlimited experience' is disclosed to us. The sugared water makes us wait and, in the resulting impatience and uncertainty, the hesitation and elaboration, our past becomes a source of novelty and change.

Now, this coupling together of durations provides a very subtle answer to Halbwachs' accusation that Bergson is unable to describe how a singular, individual 'flow' of experience could ever gauge itself (and hence communicate with) that of another. However, it is Halbwachs who provides the key to understanding how that juxtaposition might actually occur. In his description of the role objects play in mediating remembering practices, Halbwachs is able to demonstrate that the coupling together of durations is never direct – it requires the intervention of some third element. These elements act to 'slow down' and 'stabilise' the relationships between individuals. The shopkeeper and the customer must both orientate themselves towards the goods. The older people we met in Chapter 8 must coordinate their mutual recollections via the sack aprons. Marcel requires the madeleine-infused spoon of tea to make his own 'leap' into the dark region of the past.

In Chapter 11, we saw how this entanglement of people with the mediational means via which they remember – which was already prefigured in our discussions of Halbwachs' notion of 'physiognomy' in Chapter 7 and in the treatment of 'organised settings' at varying degree of scale in Chapters 8 and 9 – takes on its full meaning when viewed from the perspective of duration. We have sometimes referred to this entanglement – using notions derived from Michel Serres, Bruno Latour and ANT – as chains of translations or networks of relations between people and things. At other times, we have suggested an equivalence with Bartlett's notions of 'schemas' – that is, organised settings. In both cases, though, what we want to suggest is that it is important to think of such sets of relationships as standing in an ambiguous relationship to space. This was apparent in the family websites described in Chapter 10, where the spatial organisation of memory seems to be continuously undermined by a relationship to time. It is when we approach networks or organised settings as the coupling together of durations that we understand why this ambivalence appears so strongly, because the juxtaposition of durations does not map clearly or cleanly on to space.

It is at this point that Bergson's opposition between 'virtualisation' and 'actualisation' proves most useful. If we wish to compare durations – understood as irreducible patterns of movement and change – then we can only do so qualitatively. If we wish to further grasp how those durations might be collectively described, without seeking to impose some spatial order, then we can do so only by characterising them as 'potentials' – that is, as 'virtual'. Nevertheless, this qualitative difference between durations is not entirely indeterminate. It is neither vague nor mystical. As we saw in Chapter 11, the envelope of one duration by another creates very real, very tangible forms of experience. It is this 'sympathy', grounded in the movement of the real itself, that Bergson calls 'intuition.

We could go so far as to say that selfhood is itself an aspect of experience that arises, in part, from just such processes of interruption and elaboration. Our own duration is continually being incorporated, enveloped by the durations of others. At the same time, we are ourselves enveloping others in our particular duration. This process, or play, of mutual envelopment – so well described by Halbwachs in *The Collective Memory* – is a better conception of the role that memory plays in the sustaining of our personal identities than the 'forensic' notion of self. To be a self is to be caught up in, defined by, entangled with, this virtual play of mutually enveloping durations. Selfhood, then, is not a 'thing' that flows in duration, but the name we give to the shifting intersection of experiences, of which our present consciousness is only the 'leading edge'.

Our selves are not entirely 'virtual'. The final point of contact between Halbwachs and Bergson is around 'dispersion' or 'forgetting'. For the experimental psychology of memory, forgetting can only be a species of error. That error is always instructive in some way – indicating perhaps some malfunction in a particular cognitive process or, instead, some overall limitation to the shape of our cognitive architecture. However, it remains the 'opposite' of remembering.

For both Halbwachs and Bergson, forgetting is a necessary aspect of remembering. From the perspective of Halbwachs' collective frameworks, forgetting is a work of calling time on the past or allowing its selective prolonging into the present in order to shore up the structure of a given framework. A given act of remembering, then, necessarily implies a simultaneous act of forgetting, in the same way that the coronation of a new monarch is premised on a mourning of the deceased one. Thus, remembering can only occur as a result of an accompanying act of clearance or the preclusion of 'this' over 'that'. We saw this particularly exemplified in Chapter 9 in the case of 'archontic infrastructures', where forgetting, in various forms, is intrinsic to the way in which 'archives' are structured and users become 'attached' to them.

Bergson extends these insights into the nature of forgetting by inverting the relationship between dispersion and remembering. To remember is precisely to 'hold back' the burden of the past. Remembering is, then, an act of 'dissociation', a cutting out of some aspect of the past to fit the cloth of the present. This inversion reveals something of the otherwise hidden ethical basis of the psychology of memory. Forgetting is, typically, seen as unproductive, reflecting a limit or weakness. The more clear-cut the memory – the more accurately it is mapped on to some standard of truth and adequacy – the better. Here, sociological accounts of memory are in accordance. To remember is the valued process, not, to forget.

What Bergson offers is something different. Here, remembering and forgetting are caught up in an endless dynamic of the spatialisation of experience, the actualisation of the virtual. It makes no sense, then, to choose between these terms – they are necessary partners. In the same way, we might say, it makes no sense to choose 'memory' and 'history' or 'individual' and 'collective'. These, too, are terms that do not mark out opposing forces or represent mutually exclusive entities. Rather, they are moments in a process of movement and change becoming provisionally halted in such a way that that movement is renewed and takes on new direction. Remembering is this infinite renewal of a past that does not pass, in the same way that forgetting is a return of the given to a process of re-elaboration. It is this dynamic that a psychology of unlimited experience should seek to articulate.

As we envisage it, a social psychology of experience follows Bartlett by renewing the engagement of psychology with the broader social sciences – in particular, social anthropology, sociology and history. The contribution it would seek to make is by means of an analysis of how personal experience becomes afforded by and recruited to organised settings. At the same time, however, there is also a dialogue to be had with the experimental psychology of memory and cognitive neuroscience. At no point have we denied the clear and obvious role of neurological substrates in remembering – indeed, following Bergson, we would enthusiastically greet a comprehensive description of certain sorts of habitual activities and how the insertion of recollection in action occurs in terms of brain processes. What we have been at pains to emphasise, though, is that – to the extent that remembering is a spatially located activity – the greater part of that activity occurs collectively, in the engagement of people with their material environments. However, more importantly, memory, and experience itself, is fundamentally a matter of time, of duration. As such, it is not located anywhere at all, so to search for a way to catch hold of memories themselves within the brain is, as Bergson puts it, to risk tiring one's hand in the attempt to crush smoke.

We have returned now to where we started this book. To get to Parker's 'Cold Dark Matter: An Exploded View' in its current display at the Tate Modern, one must first pass through a room filled with what used to be rather quaintly called 'kinetic art'. These are works that artfully attempt to create the illusion of movement by combining materials that play with surface and depth. This kinetic art is no less worthy than Parker's piece. They each have their own value. At the Tate Modern, at least, one is not obliged to choose. That is what we must aim for in the psychology of memory.

References

Ansell Pearson, K. (2002). *Philosophy and the adventure of the virtual: Bergson and the time of life.* London: Routledge.

Ansell Pearson, K., & Mullarkey, J. (2002). Introduction. In K. Ansell Pearson & J. Mullarkey (Eds), *Henri Bergson: Key Writings* (pp. 141–156). London: Continuum.

Antze, P., & Lambek, M. (Eds) (1996). *Tense past: Cultural essays in trauma and memory.* New York; London: Routledge.

Argenti, N. (1999). Ephemeral monuments, memory and royal sempiternity. In Grassfield Kingdom. In Adrian Forty & Susanne Küchler (Eds), *The art of forgetting* (pp. 21–52). Oxford: Berg.

Ashmore, M., MacMillan, K., & Brown, S. D. (2004). It's a scream: Professional hearing and tape fetishism. *Journal of Pragmatics, 36,* 349–374.

Atkinson, R. C., & Schiffrin, R. M. (1968). Human memory: A proposed system and its control processes. In K. Spence & J. Spence (Eds), *The psychology of learning and motivation,* Vol. 2. New York: Academic Press.

Bachelard, G. (1968). *The philosophy of no: A philosophy of the new scientific mind.* New York: Orion Press.`

Baddeley, A. D. (1976). *The psychology of memory.* London: Harper & Row.

Baddeley, A. D. (1982). Domains of recollection. *Psychological Review, 89,* 708–729.

Baddeley, A. (1986). *Working memory.* Oxford: Clarendon Press.

Bakhurst, D. (1990). Social memory in Soviet thought. In D. Middleton & D. Edwards, (Eds), *Collective remembering* (pp. 203–226). London: Sage.

Bakhtin, M. M. (edited by M. Holquist; translated by C. Emerson & M. Holquist). (1981). *The dialogic imagination: Four essays by M. M. Bakhtin.* Austin, Texas: University of Texas Press.

Bangerter, A. (2000). Identifying individual and collective acts of remembering in task-related communication. *Discourse Processes, 30,* 237–264.

Bangerter, A. (2002). Maintaining task continuity: The role of collective memory processes in redistributing information. *Group Processes and Intergroup Relations, 5,* 203–219.

Barclay, C. R. (1994). Collective remembering. *Semiotica, 101*(3/4), 323–330.

Bartlett, F. C. (1925). Feeling, imaging and thinking. *British Journal of Psychology, 16,* 16–28.

Bartlett, F. C. (1932). *Remembering: A study in experimental and social psychology.* Cambridge: Cambridge University Press.

Bartlett, F. C. (1958). *Thinking: An experimental and social study.* London: George Allen & Unwin.

Bauman, Z. (1998). Pariah and parvenu. In J. Good & I. Velody (Eds), *The politics of post-modernity.* London: Sage.

Bellah, R. N., Madsen, R., Sullivan, W. M., Swidler, A., & Tipton, S. M. (1985). *Habits of the heart: Individualism and commitment in American life.* Berkeley: University of California Press.

Berg, M. (1997). *Rationalizing medical work: Decision-support technologies and medical practice*. Cambridge, Massachusetts: MIT Press.

Bergson, H. (translated by N. M. Paul & W. S. Palmer) (1908/1991). *Matter and memory*. New York: Zone.

Bergson, H. (translated by Mabelle L. Andison) (1946/1992). *The creative mind: An introduction to metaphysics*. New York: Citadel.

Bergson, H. (translated by Arthur Mitchell) (1911/1998). *Creative evolution*. Mineola, New York: Dover.

Bergson, H. (edited by Robin Durie) (1922/1999). *Duration and simultaneity*. Manchester: Clinamen.

Bergson, H. (translated by F. L. Pogson) (1913/2001). *Time and free will: An essay on the immediate data of consciousness*. Mineola, New York: Dover.

Bergson, H. (1919/2002). Memory of the present and false recognition. In K. Ansell Pearson & J. Mullarkey (Eds), *Henri Bergson: Key writings* (pp. 141–156). London: Continuum.

Billig, M. G. (1990). Collective memory, ideology and the British royal family. In D. Middleton & D. Edwards (Eds), *Collective remembering* (pp. 60–80). London: Sage.

Billig, M. G. (1996). *Arguing and thinking: A rhetorical approach to social psychology* (2nd Ed.). Cambridge: Cambridge University Press.

Billig, M. G. (1999). *Freudian repression: Conversation creating the unconscious*. Cambridge: Cambridge University Press.

Billig, M. G. (in press). *Laughter and ridicule*. London: Sage.

Birth, K. (2003). Past times: Temporal structuring of history and memory. Paper presented at the Society for Psychological Anthropology Bienniel Conference, San Diego, April 2003.

Blight, D. W. (1997). Quarrel forgotten or revolution remembered: Race and reunion in the memory of the Civil War, 1875–1913. In David W. Blight & Brooks D. Simpson (Eds), *Union and emancipation: Essays on politics and race in the Civil War era* (pp. 151–179). Ohio: Kent State University Press.

Bloch, M. E. (1998). *How we think they think: Anthropological approaches to cognition, memory and literacy*. Boulder, Colorado: Westview Press.

Bornat, J. (Ed.) (1994). *Reminiscence reviewed: Perspectives, evaluations, achievements*. Buckingham: Open University Press.

Bourdieu, P. (translated by R. Nice) (1986). *Distinction: A social critique of the judgement of taste*. London: Routledge.

Bowker, G., & Star, S. L. (1999). *Sorting things out: Classification and its consequences*. Cambridge, Massachusetts: MIT Press.

Brockmeier, J. (2002). Remembering and forgetting: Narrative as cultural memory. *Culture and Psychology*, *8*(1), 15–43.

Brown, S. D. (2001). Psychology and the art of living. *Theory & Psychology*, *11*(2), 171–192.

Brown, S. D. (2002). Michel Serres: Science, translation and the logic of the parasite. *Theory, Culture & Society*, *19*(3), 1–27.

Brown, S. D. (2003). Natural writing: The case of Serres. *Interdisciplinary Science Reviews*, *28*(3), 184–192.

Brown, S. D. (2004). Parasite logic. *Journal of Occupational Change Management*, *17*(4), 383–395.

Brown, S. D., & Lightfoot, G. (2002). Presence, absence, and accountability: Email and the mediation of organizational memory. In Steve Woolgar (Ed.), *Virtual society? Technology, cyberole, reality*. Oxford: Oxford University Press.

Brown, S. D., & Lunt, P. (2002). A genealogy of the social identity tradition: Deleuze and Guattari and Social Psychology. *British Journal of Social Psychology*, *41*, 1–23.

Brown, S. D., & Middleton, D. (2005). The baby as virtual object: Agency and difference in a neonatal intensive care unit. *Environment and Planning D: Society and Space*. In press.

Brown, S. D., Middleton, D., & Lightfoot, G. (2001). Performing the past in electronic archives: Interdepencies in the discursive and non-discursive organisation of institutional rememberings. *Culture & Psychology, 7*(2), 123–144.

Bruner, J. S. (1957). On perceptual readiness. *Psychological Review, 64*, 123–152.

Bruner, J. S. and Feldman, C. (1996). Group narrative as a cultural context of autobiography. In D. Rubin (Ed.), *Remembering our past: Studies in autobiographical memory*, Cambridge: Cambridge University Press.

Buchanan, K. (1993). Reminiscence and the social relations of ageing. PhD thesis. Loughborough University, UK.

Buchanan, K. (1997). Reminiscence and social exclusion. *Reminiscence, 15*(August), 3–5.

Buchanan, K., & Middleton, D. J. (1995). Voices of experience: Talk, identity and membership in reminiscence groups for older people. *Ageing and Society, 15*, 457–491.

Callon, M. (1980). Struggles and negotiations to define what is problemmatic and what is not: The socio-logic of translation. In K. D. Knorr, R. Krohn and R. Whitley (Eds), *The social process of scientific investigation: Sociology of sciences*, Vol. IV. Dorderecht: D. Reidel.

Callon, M. (1986). Some elements of a sociology of translation: Domestification of the scallops and fishermen of St Brieuc bay. In J. Law (Ed.), *Power, action, belief: A new sociology of knowledge?* London: Routledge & Kegan Paul.

Callon, M. (1991). Techno-economic networks and irreversibility. In J. Law (Ed.), *A sociology of monsters: Essays on power, technology and domination*. London: Routledge.

Callon, M. (1999). Whose imposture? Physicists at war with the third person. *Social Studies of Science, 29*(2), 261–286.

Casey, E. S. (1987). *Remembering: A phenomenological study*. Bloomington & Indianapolis: Indiana University Press.

Clark, E. C., Hyde, M. J., & McMahon, E. M. (1980). Communication in the oral history interview: Investigating problems of interpreting oral data. *International Journal of Oral History, 1*(February), 28–40.

Clark, N. K., Stephenson, G. M., & Kniveton, B. H. (1990). Social remembering: Quantitative aspects of individual and collaborative remembering by police officers and students. *British Journal of Psychology, 81*(1), 73–94.

Cohen, G. (1990). *Memory and the real world*. London: Lawrence Erlbaum Associates.

Cole, J. (1998). The work of memory in Madagascar. *American Ethnologist, 25*(4), 610–633.

Cole, J. (2001). *Forget colonialism? Sacrifice and the art of memory in Madagascar*. Berkeley: University of California Press.

Cole, M. (1991). Remembering the future. Paper presented at a seminar honouring George A. Miller, Princeton University, New Jersey, 2–4 October. San Diego: LCHC.

Cole, M. (1996). *Cultural psychology: A once and future discipline*. Cambridge, Massachusetts: The Belknap Press of the Harvard University Press.

Casey, E. S. (1987). *Remembering: A phenomenological study*. Bloomington: Indiana University Press.

Connerton, P. (1989). *How societies remember*. Cambridge: Cambridge University Press.

Conway, M. A. (1990). *Autobiographical memory*. Buckingham: Open University Press.

Conway, M. A. (1992). In defense of everyday memory. *American Psychologist, 46*, 19–26.

Conway, M. A. (1997). The inventing of experience: memory and identity. In James W. Pennebaker, Dario Paez & Bernard Rimé (Eds), *Collective memory and political events:*

Social psychological perspectives. Mahwah, New Jersey: Lawrence Erlbaum Associates.

Conway, M. A. (2003). The grounded self: How autobiographical memory limits what the self can be. Keynote address, International Conference of Critical Psychology, Bath, August.

Conway, M. A. & Pleydell-Pearce, C. W. (2000). The construction of autobiographical memories in the self-memory system. *Psychological Review*, *107*(2), 261–288.

Cooper, R. (1992). Formal organization as representation: Remote control, displacement and abbreviation. In M. Reed & M. Hughes (Eds), *Rethinking organization: New directions in organization theory and analysis*. London: Sage.

Cooper, R. (1993). Technologies of representation. In P. Ahonen (Ed.), *Tracing the semiotic boundaries of politics*. Berlin: Mouton de Gruyter.

Cooper, R. (2001). Interpreting mass: Collection/dispersion. In N. Lee & R. Munro (Eds), *The consumption of mass*. Oxford: Blackwell.

Cooper, T. (1999). Forgetting Rome and the voice of Piranesi's 'Speaking Ruins'. In Adrian Forty & Susanne Küchler (Eds), *The art of forgetting* (pp. 107–125). Oxford: Berg.

Curt, B. C. (1994). *Textuality and tectonics: Troubling social and psychological science*. Buckingham: Open University Press.

Dalrymple, J. (1999). Lead Article. *The Independent*, Thursday 12 August, 2.

Daniels, H. (1996). *An introduction to Vygotsky*. London: Routledge.

Daniels, H. (2001). *Vygotsky and pedagogy*. London: Routledge.

Danziger, K. (2002). How old is psychology, particularly concepts of memory. *History and Philosophy of Psychology*, *4*(1), 1–12.

Deleuze (translated by Hugh Tomlinson & Barbara Habberjam) (1966/1991). *Bergsonism*. New York: Zone.

Deleuze (translated by Richard Howard) (1972/2000). *Proust and signs* (complete text). London: Continuum.

Deleuze, G., & Guattari, F. (1988). *A thousand plateaus: Capitalism and schizophrenia*. London: Athlone Press.

Derrida, J. (translated by Eric Prenowitz) (1995). *Archive fever: A Freudian impression*. Chicago: University of Chicago Press.

Douglas, M. (1980). Introduction: Maurice Halbwachs (1877–1945). In M. Halbwachs, *The collective memory*. New York: Harper & Row.

Douglas, M. (1986). *How institutions think* (Chapters 6 & 7, pp. 69–90). London: Routledge & Kegan Paul.

Douglas, M. (1992). The person in an enterprise culture. In S. H. Heap & A. Ross (Eds), *Understanding the enterprise culture: Themes in the work of Mary Douglas* (pp. 41–62). Edinburgh: Edinburgh University Press.

Draaisma, D. (2000). *Metaphors of memory: A history of ideas about the mind*. Cambridge: Cambridge University Press.

Dreier, O. (1997). *Subjectivity and social practice*. Aarhus, Denmark: Centre for Health, Humanity and Culture, Department of Philosophy, University of Aarhus.

Dreier, O. (1999). Personal trajectories of participation across contexts of social practice. *Outlines*, *1*(1), 5–32.

Drew, P. (1992). Contested evidence in courtroom cross-examination: the case of a trial for rape. In P. Drew & J. Heritage (Eds), *Talk at work: Interaction in institutional settings* (pp. 470–520). Cambridge: Cambridge University Press.

Durie, R. (1999). Introduction. In *Duration and simultaneity*. Manchester: Clinamen Press.

Ebbinghaus, H. (1885/1964). *Memory: A contribution to experimental psychology.* New York: Dover.

Edwards, D. (1987). Educational knowledge and collective memory. *Quarterly Newsletter of the Laboratory of Comparative Human Cognition, 9*(1), 38–48.

Edwards, D. (1997). *Discourse and cognition.* London: Sage.

Edwards, D., & Mercer, N. (1987). *Common knowledge.* London: Methuen/Routledge.

Edwards, D., & Middleton, D. (1986a). Joint remembering: Constructing an account of shared experience through conversational discourse, *Discourse Processes, 9*, 423–459.

Edwards, D., & Middleton, D. (1986b). Text for memory: Joint recall with a scribe, *Human Learning, 5*, 125–138.

Edwards, D., & Middleton, D. (1988). Conversational remembering and family relationships: How children learn to remember, *Journal of Social and Personal Relationships, 5*, 3–25.

Edwards, D., & Potter, J. (1992). *Discursive psychology.* London: Sage.

Edwards, D., Middleton, D., & Potter, J. (1992). Towards a discursive psychology of remembering. *Psychologist, 5*, 56–60.

Edwards, D., Middleton, D., & Potter, J. (1992). Discursive remembering: A rejoinder, *The Psychologist*, October, 453–456.

Eisenberg, A. (1985). Learning to describe past experiences in conversation. *Discourse Processes, 8*, 177–204.

Engel, S. (2000). *Context is everything: The nature of memory.* New York: W. H. Freeman.

Engestrom, Y. (1987). *Learning by expanding.* Helsinki: Orienta-Konsultit Oy.

Fentress, J., & Wickham, C. (1992). *Social memory.* Oxford: Basil Blackwell.

Fivush, R. (1994). Constructing narrative, emotion and self in parent–child conversations about the past. In U. Neisser & R. Fivush (Eds), *The remembering self: Accuracy and construction in the life narrative* (pp. 136–157). Cambridge: Cambridge University Press.

Flavell, J. H., & Wellman, H. M. (1977). Meta-memory. In R. V. Kail & J. W. Hagen (Eds), *Memory in cognitive development.* Hillsdale, New Jersey: Lawrence Erlbaum.

Freud, S. (1960). *The psychopathology of everyday life.* London: Ernest Benn.

Former FEPOWs, & Holmes, K. (1991). *Little Britain.* Mimeo.

Foucault, M. (1972). *The archaeology of knowledge.* New York: Pantheon.

Gee, J. P. (1999). Comment: Mind and society: A response to Derek Edwards' 'Emotion Discourse'. *Culture and Psychology, 5*(3), 305–312.

Gergen, K. J. (1985). The social constructionist movement in modern psychology. *American Psychologist, 40*(3), 266–275.

Gergen, K. J. (1999). *An invitation to social construction.* London: Sage.

Geertz, C. (1973). *The interpretation of cultures.* New York: Basic Books.

Geertz, C. (1983). *Local knowledge: Further essays in interpretative anthropology.* New York: Basic Books.

Geertz, C. (1984). From the native's point of view: On the nature of anthropological understanding. In R. A. Shweder & R. A. Levine (Eds), *Culture theory: Essays on mind, self, and emotion* (pp. 123–136). Cambridge: Cambridge University Press.

Gibson, F. (1989). *Using reminiscence.* London: Help the Aged.

Gibson, J. J. (1966). *The senses considered as perceptual systems.* Boston: Houghton Mifflin.

Gibson, J. J. (1979). *The ecological approach to visual perception.* Hillsdale, New Jersey: Lawrence Erlbaum Associates.

Giddens, A. (1981). *A contemporary critique of historical materialism.* Berkeley: University of California Press.

Gomart, E., & Hennion, A. (1999). A sociology of attachment: Music amateurs, drug users. In J. Law & L. Hassard (Eds), *Actor Network Theory and after*. Oxford: Blackwell.

Goodwin, C. (1987). Forgetfulness as an interactive resource. *Social Psychology Quarterly, 50*, 115–30.

Goodwin, C. (2000). Action and embodiment within situated human interaction. *Journal of pragmatics, 32*, 1489–1522.

Gross, P. R., & Levitt, N. (1997). *Higher superstition: The academic left and its quarrels with science*. Baltimore, Maryland: Johns Hopkins.

Gupta, S. (1996). Memory and the role of remembering in ongoing thought processes. 2nd Conference for sociocultural research, Geneva, Switzerland.

Hacking, I. (1995). *Rewriting the soul: Multiple personality and the sciences of memory*. Princeton, New Jersey: Princeton University Press.

Halbwachs, M. (translated by Francis J. Didder, Jr, & Vida Yazdi Ditter, Introduction by Mary Douglas) (1950/1980). *The collective memory*. New York: Harper & Row.

Halbwachs, M. (edited, translated and with Introduction by Lewis A. Coser) (1925/1992). *On collective memory*. Chicago, Illinois: University of Chicago Press.

Harré, R., & Gillet, G. (1994). *The discursive mind*. Thousand Oaks, California: Sage.

Hebb, D. O. (1949). *The organization of behaviour*. New York: Wiley.

Heritage. J. (1984). *Garfinkel and ethnomethodology*. Cambridge: Polity Press.

Hetherington, K. (1997). Museum topology and the will to connect. *Journal of Material Culture, 2*(2), 199–220.

Hetherington, K., & Lee, N. (2000). Social order and the blank figure. *Environment and Planning D: Society and Space*. Vol. 18, 169–184.

Hewitt, H. L. (1997). Identities in transition: Formulating care for people with profound learning difficulties. PhD thesis, Loughborough University, UK.

Hewitt, H. L. (2005). *Using life story with the learning disabled*. Kidderminster: Bild Publications.

Hirst, W., & Manier, D. (1996). Opening vistas for cognitive psychology. In L. Martin, B. Rogoff, K. Nelson & E. Tolbach (Eds), *Sociocultural Psychology* (pp. 89–124). Cambridge: Cambridge University Press.

Holland, D., Lachicotte, Jr, W., Skinner, D., & Cain, C. (1998). *Identity and agency in cultural worlds*. Cambridge, Massachusetts: Harvard University Press.

Irwin-Zarecka, I. (1993). *Frames of remembrance: social and cultural dynamics of collective memory*. New Brunswick, New Jersey: Transaction.

James, W. (1890/1950). *The principles of psychology*. New York: Dover.

Kashima, Y. (2000). Recovering Bartlett's social psychology of cultural dynamics. *European Journal of Social Psychology, 30*, 383–403.

Klein, K. L. (2000). On the emergence of memory in historical discourse. *Representations, 69* (Winter), 127–150.

Kolers, P. A. (1975). Specificity of operations in sentence recognition. *Cognitive Psychology, 7*, 289–306.

Korolija, N. (1998). *Episodes in talk: Constructing coherence in multi-party conversation*. Linköping, Sweden: Linköping University Press.

Kroeber, A. (1923/1963). *Cultural patterns and processes*. New York: Harcourt, Brace & World.

Lansdale, M. (2005). When nothing is 'off the record': Exploring the theoretical implications of the recording of continuous memory. *Memory , 13*(1), 31–50.

Lashley, L. S. (1950). In search of the engram. *Symposia of the Society for Experimental Biology, 4*, 454–482.

Latour, B. (1987). *Science in action: How to follow scientists and engineers through society.* Cambridge, Massachusetts: Harvard University Press.

Latour, B. (1992). Where are the missing masses? A sociology of a few mundane artifacts. In W. E. Bijker & J. Law (Eds), *Shaping technology/building society: Studies in sociotechnical change.* Cambridge, Massachusetts: MIT Press.

Latour, B. (1994). On technical mediation: Philosophy, sociology, genealogy. *Common Knowledge, 3*(2), 29–64.

Latour, B. (1996). On interobjectivity. *Mind, Culture and Activity, 3*(4), 228–245.

Latour, B. (1999). *Pandora's hope: Essays on the reality of science studies.* Cambridge, Massachusetts: Harvard University Press.

Lave, J., & Wenger, E. (1991). *Situated learning.* Cambridge: Cambridge University Press.

Law, J. (1992). Notes on the theory of actor network: Ordering, strategy and heterogeneity. *Systems Practice, 5*(4), 379–93.

Law, J. (1994). *Organising modernity.* Oxford: Blackwell.

Law, J. (2002). *Aircraft stories: Decentering the object in technoscience.* Durham, North Carolina: Duke University Press.

Law, J., & Hassard, J. (Eds) (1999). *Actor-Network Theory and after.* Oxford: Blackwell.

Law, J., & Mol, A. (Eds) (2002). *Complexities: Social studies of knowledge practices.* Durham, North Carolina: Duke University Press.

Lawlor, L. (2003). *The challenge of Bergsonism: Phenomenology, ontology, ethics.* London: Continuum.

Leont'ev, A. N. (1981). *Problems of the development of the mind.* Moscow: Progress Publishers.

Linnel, P. (1998). *Approaching dialogue: Talk, interaction and contexts in dialogical perspectives.* Amsterdam: John Benjamins Publishing Company.

Locke, A., & Edwards, D. (2003). Bill and Monica: Memory, emotion and normativity in Clinton's Grand Jury testimony. *British Journal of Social Psychology, 42*(2), 239–256.

Locke, J. (transcribed and edited by P. H. Niddtch) (1690/1975). *Essay concerning human understanding.* Oxford: Oxford University Press.

Loftus, E. F. (1979). *Eyewitness testimony.* Cambridge, Massachusetts: Harvard University Press.

Loftus, E. F. (1994). Tricked by memory. In Jaclyn Jeffrey and Glenace Edwall (Eds), *Memory and history: Essays on recalling and interpreting experience* (pp. 17–32). Boston: University Press of America.

Loftus, E. F., & Ketchum, K. (1994). *The myth of repressed memory.* New York: St Martin's Press.

Luria, A. R. (edited by Michael & Sheila Cole) (1979). *The making of mind: A personal account of Soviet psychology.* Cambridge, Massachusetts: Harvard University Press.

Lury, C. (1997). *Prosthetic culture: Photography, memory and identity.* London: Routledge.

Lynch, M., & Bogen, D. (1996). *The spectacle of history: Speech, text, and memory at the Iran-Contra hearings.* Durham, North Carolina: Duke University Press.

Lyra, M. C. D. P. (1999). An excursion into the dynamics of dialogue: Elaborations upon the dialogical self. *Culture and Psychology, 5*(4), 477–489.

MacMillan, K., & Edwards, D. (1999). Who killed the princess? Description and blame in the British press. *Discourse Studies, 1*(2), 151–174.

Matsuda, M. K. (1996). *The memory of the modern.* New York: Oxford University Press.

Mayer, R. E. (1983). *Thinking, problem solving, cognition.* New York: W. H. Freeman & Co.

Mercer, N. (2000). *Words and minds: How we use language to think together*. London: Routledge.

Middleton, D. (1997a). The social organisation of conversational remembering: Experience as individual and collective concerns. *Mind, Culture and Activity*, *4*(2), 71–85.

Middleton, D. (1997b). Conversational remembering and uncertainty: interdependencies of experience as individual and collective concerns in team work. *Journal of Language and Social Psychology*, *16*(4), 389–410.

Middleton, D. (2002). Succession and change in the sociocultural use of memory: Building in the past in communicative action. *Culture & Psychology*, *8*(1), 79–95.

Middleton, D., & Curnock, D. (1995). Talk of uncertainty: Doubt as an organisational resource in neonatal intensive care. In *Risk in organisational settings* (pp. 1–23). London: ESRC.

Middleton, D., & Edwards, D. (1990a). *Collective remembering*. London: Sage.

Middleton, D., & Edwards, D. (1990b). Conversational remembering: A social psychological approach. In D. Middleton & D. Edwards (Eds), *Collective remembering* (pp. 23–46). London: Sage.

Middleton, D., Brown, S. D., & Curnock, D. (2000). Networks at work: Continuity and change in the social organisation of reason in remembering, to the 3rd Conference for sociocultural research, New conditions for the production of knowledge: Globalization and social practice, São Paulo, Brazil, 16–20 July.

Miller, P. J., Potts, R., Fung, H., Hoogstra, L., and Mintz, J. (1990). Narrative practices and the social construction of self in childhood. *American Ethnologist*, *17*(2), 292–311.

Misztal, B. A. (2003). *Theories of social remembering*. Buckingham: Open University Press.

Miyazaki, H. (2003). The temporalities of the market. *American Anthropology*, *105*(2), 255–265.

Moore, F. C. T. (1996). *Bergson: Thinking backwards*. Cambridge: Cambridge University Press.

Moscovici, S. (edited by Gerard Duveen) (2000). *Social representations: Studies in social psychology*. Oxford: Polity.

Mullarkey, J. (1999a). *Bergson and philosophy*. Edinburgh: Edinburgh University Press.

Mullarkey, J. (1999b). La philosophie nouvelle, or change in philosophy. In J. Mullarkey (Ed.), *The new Bergson*. Manchester: Manchester University Press.

Munro, R. (1998). Disposal of the gap: The production and consumption of accounting research and practical accounting systems. *Advances in Public Interest Accounting*, *7*, 139–159.

Murakami, K. (2001a). Revisiting the past: Social organisation of remembering and reconciliation. PhD thesis, Loughborough University, UK.

Murakami, K. (2001b). Talk about rice: A discourse analytical approach to studying culture. *Forum for Qualitative Social Research* (online journal), *2*(3) (at: www.qualitative-research.net/fqs/fqs-eng.htm)

Neisser, U. (1967). *Cognitive psychology*. New York: Appleton-Century-Crofts.

Neisser, U. (1976). *Cognition and reality: Principles and implications of cognitive psychology*. San Francisco: W. H. Freeman and Company.

Neisser, U. (1982). *Memory observed: Remembering in natural contexts*. San Francisco: W. H. Freeman and Company.

Neisser, U., & Winograd, E. (1988). *Remembering reconsidered: Ecological and traditional approaches to the study of memory*. Cambridge: Cambridge University Press.

Neisser, U., & Fivush, R. (Eds) (1996). *The remembered self: Construction and accuracy in self-narrative*. Cambridge: Cambridge University Press.

Norrick, N. R. (2000). *Conversational Narrative: Story telling in everyday conversation.* Amsterdam: John Benjamins Publishing Company.

Norrick, N. R. (2003). Remembering and forgetfulness in conversational narrative. *Discourse Processes, 36*(1), 47–76.

Nora, P. (1989). Between memory and history: Les lieux de mémoire. *Representations, 26* (Spring), 7–25.

Olick, J. K., & Robbins, J. (1998). Social memory studies: From 'collective memory' to the historical sociology of mnemonic practices. *Annual Review of Sociology, 24*, 105–140.

Orr, J. E. (1990). Sharing knowledge, celebrating identity: Community memory in a service culture. In D. Middleton & D. Edwards (Eds), *Collective remembering* (pp. 167–189). London: Sage.

Parsons, K., Long, R., & Sofka, M. D. (Eds) (2003). *The science wars: Debating scientific knowledge and technology.* London: Prometheus.

Pezdek, K., & Banks, W. P. (Eds) (1996). *The recovered memory/false memory debate.* London: Academic Press.

Potter, J. A., & Wetherell, M. (1987). *Discourse and social psychology: Beyond attitudes and behaviour.* London: Sage.

Proust, M. (translated by C. K. Scott-Moncrieff, T. Kilmartin & D. J. Enright) (1913/1981). In *Remembrance of things past*, Vol. 1. Harmandsworth: Penguin.

Proust, M. (translated by C. K. Scott-Moncrieff, T. Kilmartin & D. J. Enright) (1922/1992). *Remembrance of things past*, Vol. 3. London: Chatto & Windus.

Radley, A. (1990). Artefacts, memory and a sense of the past. In D. Middleton & D. Edwards (Eds), *Collective remembering* (pp. 46–59). London: Sage.

Rasmussen, S. (2002). The uses of memory. *Culture & Psychology, 8*(1), 113–129.

Rosa, A. (1996). Bartlett's psycho-anthropological project. *Culture & Psychology, 2*(2), 355–378.

Rosaldo, M. Z. (1984). Towards an anthropology of self and feeling. In Richard A. Shweder and Robert A. LeVine (Eds), *Culture theory: Essays on mind, self, and emotion* (pp. 137–157). Cambridge: Cambridge University Press.

Rose, N. (1989). *Governing the soul: The shaping of the private self.* London: Routledge.

Rose, N. (1996). *Inventing our selves: Psychology, power and personhood.* Cambridge: Cambridge University Press.

Rumelhart, D. E. (1975). Notes on a schema for stories. In D. G. Brobrow and A. M. Collins (Eds), *Representation and understanding: Studies in cognitive science.* New York: Academic Press.

Sacks, H. (1992a). Lecture 4: Storyteller as 'witness'. Entitlement to experience. In G. Jefferson (Ed.) (edited by Gail Jefferson, Introduction by Emanuel A. Schegloff), *Lectures on conversation*, Vol. 2 (pp. 242–248). Oxford: Blackwell.

Scarry, E. (1985). *The body in pain: The making and unmaking of the world.* Oxford: Oxford University Press.

Schacter, D. L. (1996). *Searching for memory: The brain, the mind, and the past.* New York: Basic Books.

Schank, R. C. (1982). *Dynamic memory: A theory of reminding and learning in computers and people.* Cambridge: Cambridge University Press.

Schmidt, K., & Bannon, L. (1992). Taking CSCW seriously: Supporting articulation work. *Computer Supported Cooperative Work, 1*(1–2), 7–40. (pdf at: www.itu.dk/people/schmidt/papers/cscw_seriously.pdf)

Schrager, S. (1983). What is social in oral history? *International Journal of Oral History, 4*(June), 76–98.

Schudson, M. (1990). Ronald Reagan misremembered. In D. Middleton & D. Edwards (Eds), *Collective remembering* (pp. 108–119). London: Sage.

Schudson, M. (1992). *Watergate in American memory: How we remember, forget and reconstruct the past*. New York: Basic Books.

Schwartz, B. (1986). The recovery of Masada: A study in collective memory. *The Sociological Quarterly*, *27*(2), 147–164.

Schwartz, B. (1999). Memory and the practices of commitment. In B. Glassner & R. Hertz (Eds), *Qualitative sociology as everyday life* (pp. 135–146). Thousand Oaks, California: Sage.

Schwartz, B. (2000). *Abraham Lincoln and the forge of national memory*. Chicago: University of Chicago Press.

Scribner, S. (1985). Vygotsky's use of history. In James V. Wertsch (Ed.), *Culture, Communication and Cognition*. Cambridge: Cambridge University Press.

Semon, R. (1923). *Mnemic psychology*. London: George Allen & Unwin.

Serres, M. (edited by J. V. Harari & D. F. Bell) (1982a). *Hermes: Literature, science, philosophy*. Baltimore, Maryland: Johns Hopkins University Press.

Serres, M. (translated by Lawrence R. Scheher) (1982b). *The parasite*. Baltimore, Maryland: Johns Hopkins.

Serres, M. (1991). *Rome: The book of foundations*. Stanford, California: Stanford University Press.

Serres, M. (translated by G. James & J. Nielson) (1995). *Genesis*. Ann Arbor: The University of Michigan Press.

Serres, M., with Latour, B. (translated by Roxanne Lapidus) (1995). *Conversations on science, culture and time*. Ann Arbor: The University of Michigan Press.

Shils, Edward, A. (1981). *Tradition*. Chicago: University of Chicago Press.

Shotter, J. (1990). The social construction of remembering and forgetting. In D. Middleton and D. Edwards (Eds), *Collective remembering* (pp. 120–138). London: Sage.

Shotter, J. (1993). *Conversational realities: constructing life through language*. London: Sage.

Simmel, G. (edited by D. Frisby & M. Featherstone) (1908/1997). The stranger. In *Simmel on culture*. London: Sage.

Sokal, A., & Bricmont, J. (1999). *Intellectual impostures*. London: Verso.

Sproull, L., & Kiesler, S. (1991). *Connections: New ways of working in the networked organization*. Cambridge, Massachusetts: MIT Press.

Star, S. L., & Strauss, A. (1999). Layers of silence, arenas of voice: The ecology of visible and invisible work. *Computer Supported Cooperative Work: The Journal of Collaborative Computing*, *8*, 9–30.

Stephenson, G. M., Kniveton, B. H., & Wagner, W. (1991). Social influences on remembering: Intellectual, interpersonal and intergroup components. *European Journal of Social Psychology*, *21*(6), 463–475.

Strathern, M. (1996). Cutting the network. *Journal of the Royal Anthropological Institute*, NS., *2*, 517–535.

Suchman, L. (1993). Technologies of accountability: Of lizards and aeroplanes. In G. Button (Ed.), *Technology in working order*. London: Routledge.

Thorburn, G. (2002). *Men and sheds*. London: New Holland.

Tschuggnall, K., & Welzer, H. (2002). Rewriting memories: Family recollections of national socialist past in Germany. *Culture & Psychology*, *8*(1), 130–145.

Tulving, E. (1983). *Elements in episodic memory*. Oxford: Clarendon Press.

Valsiner, J. (1994). Irreversibility of time and the construction of historical developmental psychology. *Mind, Culture and Activity*, *1*(1&2), 25–42.

van der Veer, R., & Valsiner, J. (1991). *Understanding Vygotsky: A quest for synthesis*. Oxford: Blackwell.

Vygotsky, L. S. (edited by Michael Cole, Vera John-Steiner, Sylvia Cole & Ellen Souberman) (1978). *Mind in action: The development of higher psychological processes*. Cambridge, Massachusetts: Harvard University Press.

Vygotsky, L. S. (1987). *Thought and language*. Cambridge, Massachusetts: MIT Press.

Walker (1997). *Of rice and men: The only true war story with a happy ending*. Stockport: Arthur Lane Books.

Wegner, D. (1986). Transactive memory. In B. Mullen & G. Goethals (Eds), *Theories of group behaviour*. New York: Springer-Verlag.

Weldon, M. S., & Bellinger, K. D. (1997). Collective memory: Collaborative and individual processes in remembering. *Journal of Experimental Psychology: Learning, Memory & Cognition, 23*, 1160–1175.

Weldon, M. S. (2001). Remembering as a social process. In D. L. Medin (Ed.), *The psychology of learning and motivation* (pp. 67–120). San Diego: Academic Press.

Wertsch, J. V. (1985). *Vygotsky and the social formation of mind*. Cambridge, Massachusetts: Harvard University Press.

Wertsch, J. V. (1998). *Mind as action*. New York; Oxford: Oxford University Press.

Wertsch, J. V. (2002). *Voices of collective remembering*. Cambridge: Cambridge University Press

Wittgenstein, L. (1953). *Philosophical investigations*. Oxford: Basil Blackwell.

Whitehead A. N. (1933). *Adventures of ideas*. Harmondsworth: Penguin.

Wooffitt, R. (1992). *Telling tales of the unexpected: The organization of factual discourse*. Hemel Hempstead: Harvester.

Worms, F. (1999). Matter and memory on mind and body: Final statements and new perspectives. In J. Mullarkey (Ed.), *The new Bergson*. Manchester: Manchester University Press.

Yates, F. A. (1966). *The art of memory*. Chicago: University of Chicago Press.

Young, J. E. (1993). *Texture of memory: Holocaust memorials and meaning*. New Haven, Connecticut: Yale University Press.

Zangwill, O. L. (1972). Remembering revisited. *Quarterly Journal of Experimental Psychology, 24*, 123–138.

Zelizer, B. (1992). *Covering the body: The Kennedy assasination, the media, and the shaping of collective memory*. Chicago: University of Chicago Press.

Zelizer, B. (1995). Reading the past against the grain: The shape of memory studies. *Critical Studies in Mass Communication, 12*, 214–239.

Zerubavel, E. (1996). Social memories: Steps to a sociology of the past. *Qualitative Sociology, 19*(3), 283–299.

Zerubavel, E. (1997). *Social mindscapes: An invitation to cognitive sociology*. Cambridge, Massachusetts: Harvard University Press.

Index

Compiled by INDEXING SPECIALISTS
(UK) LTD, Regent House, Hove Street,
Hove, East Sussex BN3 2DW. Tel: 01273
738299. E-mail: richardr@indexing.co.uk
Website: www.indexing.co.uk